# *Native American Traditions*

**The Religious Life of Man Series**
FREDERICK J. STRENG, SERIES EDITOR

**Texts**

*Understanding Religious Life*, Second Edition
Frederick J. Streng

*The House of Islam*, Second Edition
Kenneth Cragg

*Japanese Religion: Unity and Diversity*, Third Edition
H. Byron Earhart

*Chinese Religion: An Introduction*, Third Edition
Laurence G. Thompson

*The Christian Religious Tradition,*
Stephen Reynolds

*The Buddhist Religion: A Historical Introduction*, Third Edition
Richard H. Robinson and Willard L. Johnson

*The Way of Torah: An Introduction to Judaism*, Third Edition
Jacob Neusner

*The Hindu Religious Tradition*
Thomas J. Hopkins

*Native American Religions: An Introduction*
Sam D. Gill

**Anthologies**

*The Chinese Way in Religion*
Laurence G. Thompson

*Religion in the Japanese Experience: Sources and Interpretations*
H. Byron Earhart

*The Buddhist Experience: Sources and Interpretations*
Stephan Beyer

*The Life of Torah: Readings in the Jewish Religious Experience*
Jacob Neusner

*Islam from Within: Anthology of a Religion*
Kenneth Cragg and R. Marston Speight

*Native American Traditions: Sources and Interpretations*
Sam D. Gill

# Native American Traditions

## *Sources and Interpretations*

Sam D. Gill

*Arizona State University*

*Wadsworth Publishing Company*

*Belmont, California*

*A Division of Wadsworth, Inc.*

Religion Editor: Sheryl Fullerton
Production Editor: Hal Humphrey
Designer: Adriane Bosworth
Copy Editor: Susan Caney-Peterson



Printed in the United States of America

1 2 3 4 5 6 7 8 9 10—87 86 85 84 83

ISBN 0-534-01374-0

**Library of Congress Cataloging in Publication Data**

Gill, Sam D., 1943–
Native American traditions.

(The Religious life of man series)
Includes index.
1. Indians of North America—Religion and mythology—Addresses, essays, lectures. I. Title. II. Series: Religious life of man (Belmont, Calif.)
E98.R3G49 1983 299′.793 82–20096
ISBN 0–534–01374–0

In Memory of

George Washington Gill 1871–1958
Mattie Delphine Fulton Gill 1870–1967
Susan Alice Avey 1877–1971
Margaret Elizabeth Avey Tallman 1878–1971
Florence Dell Avey Tannehill 1882–1971
Samuel Earl Avey 1895–1962

# *Contents*

# *Preface*

NEVER IN THE HISTORY of human cultures have the religious practices, stories, structures, and objects been so carefully and extensively recorded as they have for the tribal cultures of North America, especially during the last century. Native American religions are commonly recognized as at the heart of Native American cultures. Yet, even with this general perception and with such abundant materials, in the history of the academic study of religion the religions of few cultures have been so ignored as those of Native Americans. Claude Levi-Strauss has noted that the accomplishments of the Bureau of American Ethnology, as evidenced in their series of bulletins and annual reports, are "so impressive that despite the use they have been put to for nearly a century, it is safe to say that only the surface has been scratched."[1] He expressed concern over the neglect into which these materials have fallen, noting by comparison that the sources available for the study of ancient Greek and Roman cultures are far less rich.

The thorny issue of neglect is one of American history and the history of the academe, and—in its full measure—is not our concern here. Nonetheless, the issue suggests that there remains a gap between the existence of rich and abundant resources on Native American religions and the use of these resources for the study of Native American religions and cultures. It is my view that at least some dimensions of this gap may be explained rather simply. The extent of the relevant materials is of such an order that it tends to discourage their use. Besides the formidable tomes produced by the Bureau of American Ethnology, there are dozens of long-established series containing abundant materials relevant to the study of Native American religions. In short, the difficulties of finding, evaluating, and organizing the materials on Native American religions is itself a formidable task.

While no selection of materials for an anthology is wholly adequate, I nonetheless feel that the selection and presentation of a sampling of these materials is of considerable value for it makes them more available to be read and enjoyed, studied, and evaluated. Preparing this anthology has been a frustrating task, not because it has been so difficult to find suitable materials, but because it has been so difficult to choose among those that exist. I deeply regret the exclusion of so many fine examples.

Wherever possible I have selected materials that I judge to be as close as possible to primary sources. These are statements written or spoken by Native Americans—descriptions, comments, statements, stories, songs, and prayers. Until quite recently, writings by Native Americans were very rare because of the nonliterate character of Native American languages. I have tried to avoid accounts by non-Native Americans unless they provide direct and clear descriptions of ritual, dance, or other nonverbal acts of religious culture. Some few, especially in Chapter One, are chosen to illustrate European-American images of Native Americans. Since the significance and range of meanings of Native American religious acts and events are not self-evident to outsiders, interpretation is essential; yet good and valid interpretation is difficult and rare. I have selected a few examples of interpretive essays, by both Native Americans and non-Native Americans, representing a variety of points of view and some exemplary studies.

The organization of the selections in an anthology is always a difficulty. So many of the selections are so rich that they speak to many issues and defy simple categorization. Thus, to place a selection in any category tends to emphasize one aspect or issue to the exclusion of others. Partially because of this, I have avoided as a general organizational scheme such categories as mythology (oral traditions), folklore, rites, ceremonials, and the like. I have also avoided a geographic schema; yet the selections are drawn primarily from North America. As an alternative, I have organized the selections of this anthology to parallel the chapters in *Native American Religions* (Wadsworth, 1982). I have taken care not to duplicate here any of the examples described for discussion in that book. Used with *Native American Religions*, this anthology will provide supplementary primary texts and interpretive essays for the major topics presented in that text. Yet I have provided brief introductory comments for each selection to place the material ethnographically or in the frame of the topic being considered. With these introductions I hope *Native American Traditions* will also be suitable for a wide range of uses apart from *Native American Religions.*

## *NOTE*

1. Claude Levi-Strauss, "The Disappearance of Man," *New York Review of Books* 7/1 (July 28, 1966), p. 6.

# *Acknowledgments*

THE SUPPORT FOR THE preparation of this anthology has been extensive and I wish to acknowledge those most involved. The Departments of Religious Studies at Arizona State University and at the University of Colorado, Boulder, have provided greatly appreciated secretarial and graduate student support. Professor Robert Michaelson, University of California, Santa Barbara, helped me trace some sources I had lost. Professors Joseph Epes Brown, University of Montana; Thomas Overholt, University of Wisconsin, Stevens Point; Henry Bowden, Douglass College; Amanda Porterfield, Syracuse University; James Thayer, Oklahoma State University, Stillwater; and Robert K. Gustafson, Pembroke State University, read the manuscript and offered important evaluations and suggestions. I want to sincerely thank them. Most of all I would like to thank Professor Frederick J. Streng, Southern Methodist University, for continually encouraging me to do this anthology and for spending many hours on the original manuscript, which was at least twice as long as its published version, carefully weighing and evaluating the selections to offer greatly appreciated cutting and editing suggestions at a stage in the process I found to be most painful.

# CHAPTER 1

# *Imagining Native American Religions*

## INTRODUCTION

Increasingly during the last decade we have come to recognize that statements made throughout American history about Native Americans by Americans with European ancestry probably reflect a great deal more about the world views and perspectives of the authors than about Native Americans.[1] As Roy Harvey Pearce and others have shown, "the Indian" has occupied a series of imagined symbolic roles throughout American history, and by reviewing this history one may come to understand much about the European settlement of America, indeed, about the very idea of America itself.

Radically stated, it appears from this perspective that the idea of "the Indian," as it occurs in the many documents of American history, is to a great extent the creation of the expectations and views of European-Americans. That is, "the Indian" is the result of a process of imagination set in motion by peoples native to America within the context of the American experience. Thus, these imaginings have a peculiar—tenacious, almost incidental, and often questionable—relationship with the reality of Native American peoples, a reality that includes hundreds of distinct peoples, often widely diverse in terms of culture, language, and religion.

Since any effort to understand Native Americans historically depends on these documents, and since the knowledge that we currently hold of Native Americans is largely derived from this heritage of imagining, we must understand with the greatest clarity this process of imagining in order to evaluate the documents available to us, as well as to reexamine the knowledge we hold without question. Both are influenced and shaped by this history of imagining we have inherited.

Religion is a major subject upon which the images of "the Indian" have focused. The American experience has often been described as a religious experience and thus images of Native American religions have been formed in terms of the religious consciousness of European-Americans. The effect has been great for, throughout American history, even the existence of religion, which is so essential and vital to Native American cultures, has commonly been ignored, unseen, rejected, unknown, or denied. Only in 1978 did the United States Congress guarantee religious freedom to Native American peoples. Only now are Native American religions beginning to be recognized as subjects of interest to the humanities for the sake of their current and future vitality. Only recently has there been even a suggestion that Native American religious cultures are not survivals or remnants to be either recorded before they disappear or to be denied and discouraged because they hamper the Christianization and civilization of America. The end of these views has not yet arrived, but perhaps the beginning of the end is taking place.

Certainly in any current attempt to understand Native American religions in more their own terms, we must comprehend as much as possible the history that has shaped the images we so commonly hold as self-evident. Even then we will not be able to wholly free ourselves from them, but that is the nature of any human effort to understand others. In this respect, it is absolutely essential not to simply turn the process of stereotyping and imagining on its head as is presently popular, by presenting an endless recitation of the evils that European-Americans and western world views have perpetrated upon "the Indians" throughout American history, and holding as an alternative the glory and rightness of "the Indian way." I see this as simply another chapter in European-Americans' imagining without the experience of really seeing Native Americans. While at the surface it is a more flattering image, it still is in that long-standing tradition of the noble savage that has been used for centuries. This image is not aimed at understanding Native Americans so much as providing criticism of European-American ways. Thus, it is a more subtle form of racism, but, because of its effect on Native Americans, it may be more destructive. Native Americans have not protested this image so much as they have tried to conform to it; the effect is to remake Native Americans in the image others have of them.

Another dimension of the story that must be told is that the imagining and stereotyping process goes both ways. While we are used to some aspects of the story of how "the white man" sees "the Indian," we have not yet accounted sufficiently for how "the Indian" has seen "the white man." Clearly our historical documents are not as rich here because an extensive and lasting record of these views has not been made, but there is enough evidence to show that such views have existed from the time of Columbus. It has even become a genre of oral tradition and art in many Native American cultures.

The extent of the record on this subject is so enormous that it is possible in this chapter to present only a small sampling of the views Native Americans and Europeans have had of each other organized around predominant eras, views, and issues. The selections focus on the area of religion and have been selected to demonstrate both the variety and history of, what we might term, this *nonencounter*.

## FIRST IMPRESSIONS: COLUMBUS AND VESPUCCI

Columbus's understanding of religion and the religious character of his mission are evident in the surviving record of his encounters with "los Indios" in 1492.[2] The conclusion of his entry reads:

> They should be good servants and very intelligent, for I have observed that they soon repeat anything that is said to them, and I believe that they would easily be made Christians, for they appear to me to have no religion. God willing, when I make my departure I will bring half a dozen of them back to their Majesties, so that they can learn to speak. I saw no animals of any kind on this island except parrots.[3]

Just five days later as Columbus wrote of his observations of the island he named Fernandina, immediately following his detailed description of the trees, and preceding his note that the fish were very different, he wrote:

> They have no religion and I think that they would be very quickly Christianized, for they have a very ready understanding.[4]

Columbus's criteria for calling something religion was clearly determined by his understanding of Christianity or certain perversions of it. He did not observe them engaged in Christian actions nor in idolotrous acts expected of non-Christians, so he could, even in such a brief encounter, state without apparent equivocation that they had no religion.

In the account of his second voyage, while steadily maintaining that the people whom he visited in Hispaniola had no religious belief nor did they practice idolatry, Columbus described several cultural activities that we cannot avoid considering as religious. His description of them in the same paragraphs in which he stated that they have no religion suggests that Columbus made this association himself. This account was prepared by Fernando, the son of Christopher, who claims to "copy the Admiral's own words."

> I have not been able to discover any idolatry or other religious belief among them. However, each of the many kings in Hispaniola and the other islands and on the mainland has his special house apart from the village. This house contains only wooden images carved in relief, and called by them *cemies*. Here there is no other activity except the service of the *cemies* and the Indians perform certain prayers and ceremonies here as we do in church. In these houses are highly carved tables, round in shape like a chopping table, on which lies a special powder which they place on the heads of their *cemies* with certain rites. They then sniff up this powder through a double-branched cane, which they place in their nostrils. This powder intoxicates them and they babble like drunkards, but none of our men understand the words they use.
>
> Each of these images has a name, and I think that some represent the father, others the grandfather and others both. Some houses contain more than one and some more than ten, commemorating, as I have said, various ancestors. I have noticed that they do not value all of them alike but pay more devotion and respect to some than to others, as we do on the occasion of religious processions. Each *cacique* and his people take pride in having better *cemies* than their neighbours.

They conceal their visits to the *cemi* from the Christians and do not let them enter the image house. If they think that a Christian is coming they pick up the *cemies* and conceal them in the woods, fearing that the Christians will take them from them, since they have the ridiculous custom of stealing one another's *cemies*.

It once happened when they were most suspicious of us that some Christians entered an image house with them. A *cemi* emitted a shout in words of their language, and this revealed the fact that it was hollow. A hole had been cut in the lower part, into which a trumpet or speaking tube had been fitted, which communicated with a dark corner of the house obscured by branches. Behind these branches stood a servant who spoke whatever words the *cacique* wished, as we do through a speaking tube. Our men suspected this, kicked the *cemi* over and discovered the contrivance we have described. When the *cacique* saw that we had discovered the trick, he most insistently begged our men not to reveal it to his subjects or anyone else, since by this device he kept everyone obedient to him. We can therefore say there is some tinge of idolatry, at least in those who do not suspect the tricks and devices of their *caciques*, since they believe that it is the *cemi* that speaks and the deception is fairly general. The *cacique* alone knows and preserves their superstitious belief, by which he exacts all the tribute he desires from his people.

Most of the *caciques* have also three stones, to which they and their people pay great devotion. They say that one of them is beneficial to the plants and grains they sow, another brings painless childbirth, and the third rain and sun when they are needed. I have sent your Highnesses three of these stones by Antonio de Torres, and I will bring another three myself.

Their funeral rites are of various kinds. They prepare their *caciques* for the tomb by cutting open the body and drying it over a fire so as to preserve it entire. Of some common people they preserve only the head; others they bury in a grave, placing above the head bread and a gourd of water; and yet others they burn in the houses where they die. When they see a man on the point of death, they strangle him, and this is their practice with *caciques*. Others they carry out of the house, and yet others they place on hammocks or string beds, laying bread and water beside their heads. They then leave them and do not come back to see them again. When some men are gravely sick, they take them to the *cacique*, who decides whether they should be strangled or not, and they do as he says.

I have made strenuous efforts to discover what they know and believe about the place to which they go at death. I inquired particularly of Caonabo, the chief king of Hispaniola, a man of mature years, great knowledge and very lively intelligence. He and others answered that they go to a certain valley which each principal *cacique* imagines to lie in his own country. They state that here the dead meet their fathers and ancestors, eat, have wives and take their pleasure and consolation with them.[5]

There are many other records of the early travelers. Amerigo Vespucci, the Italian whose name was adapted to provide a name for the world which Columbus died believing was Asia, made observations on the religiousness of the peoples he encountered. Curiously, he, as did many, seemed to have been interested in the state of clothedness of the peoples (with clearly more interest in the females), their sexuality, and their religiousness, or rather what he saw as the lack thereof. Often, he described them seemingly all in the same stream of thought, a stream in which the lack of dress suggests sexuality, which suggests morality, which suggests religion. For example, in a letter written to Piero Soderini, Gonfaloniere, in 1504, Vespucci described people he encountered during his 1497 voyage:

They are women of pleasing person, very well proportioned, so that one does not see on their bodies any ill-formed feature or limb. And although they go about utterly naked, they are fleshy women, and that part of their privies which he who has not seen them would think to see is invisible; for they cover all with their thighs, save that part (for) which nature made no provision, and which is modestly speaking, the *mons veneris*. In short they are no more ashamed (of their shameful parts) than we are in displaying the nose and mouth. Only exceptionally will you see a woman with drooping breasts, or with belly shrunken through frequent parturition, or with other wrinkles, for all look as though they had never given birth. They show themselves very desirous of copulating with us Christians. While among these people we did not learn that they had any religion. They can be termed neither Moors nor Jews; and they are worse than heathen; because we did not see that they offered any sacrifice, nor yet did they have [any] house of prayer. . . .[6]

## THE FORMATION OF EARLY IMAGES OF "INDIANS"

Rather early the images of "the Indians" began to polarize. On the one side nothing bad could be said of these peoples, save perhaps their lack of Christianity, and nothing good could be said of the European treatment of "the Indians" in their conquest of America. The other side was, of course, just the opposite. Indians were hated. They were considered barely human, totally disgusting and repugnant. In this view, any manner of treatment was unquestionably justified in light of the great European mission in America.

The Spanish Dominican Bartolomé de las Casas (1474–1566) was a major figure associated with the sixteenth century Spanish conquest of the New World. He served much of his life as a missionary in the Indies and wrote prolifically and debated vigorously in defense of the peoples among whom he served. The following is a selection of an essay in which las Casas severely criticized the Spanish conquest and its bloody ways, while defending and lauding the native peoples. Spanish historians have been highly critical of the work, accusing las Casas of gross exaggeration, yet none deny that the Spanish massacre of native peoples was huge. Criticism has also been directed at the propagandistic use to which this document has been put against Spain. It was republished in English to coincide with the English seizure of Jamaica from the Spanish in 1656 and republished in an American edition during the Spanish-American War. Clearly las Casas was an early proponent of what would come to be known as the image of the noble savage, an image he develops seemingly as much to criticize his own country and its actions as to present the true character and ways of the native peoples he described.

### *THE TEARS OF THE INDIANS by Bartolomé de las Casas*[7]

In the year 1492, the *West-Indies* were discovered, in the following year they were inhabited by the *Spaniards*: a great company of the *Spaniards* going about 49 years agoe. The first place they came to, was *Hispaniola*, being a most fertile Island, and for the bignesse of it very famous, it being no less than six hundred miles in compass. Round about it lie an innumerable company of Islands, so throng'd with

Inhabitants, that there is not to be found a greater multitude of people in any part of the world. The Continent is distant from this about Two hundred miles, stretching it self out in length upon the sea side for above Ten thousand miles in length. This is already found out, and more is daily discovered. These Countreys are inhabited by such a number of people, as if God had assembled and called together to this place, the greatest part of Mankinde.

This infinite multitude of people was so created by God, as that they were without fraud, without subtilty or malice, to their natural Governours most faithful and obedient. Toward the *Spaniards* whom they serve, patient, meek and peaceful, and who laying all contentious and tumultuous thoughts aside, live without any hatred or desire of revenge; the people are most delicate and tender, enjoying such a feeble constitution of body as does not permit them to endure labour, so that the Children of Princes and great persons here, are not more nice and delicate then the Children of the meanest Countrey-man in that place. The Nation is very poor and indigent, possessing little, and by reason that they gape not after temporal goods, neither proud nor ambitious. Their diet is such that the most holy Hermite cannot feed more sparingly in the wildernesse. They go naked, only hiding the undecencies of nature, and a poor shag mantle about ell or two long is their greatest and their warmest covering. They lie upon mats, only those who have larger fortunes, lye upon a kinde of net which is tied at the four corners, and so fasten'd to the roof, which the *Indians* in their natural language call *Hameeks*. They are a very apprehensive and docible wit, and capable of all good learning, and very apt to receive our Religion, which when they have but once tasted, they are carryed on with a very ardent and zealous desire to make a further progress in it; so that I have heard divers *Spaniards* confesse that they had nothing else to hinder them from enjoying heaven, but their ignorance of the true God.

To these quiet Lambs, endued with such blessed qualities, came the *Spaniards* like most c[r]uel Tygres, Wolves and Lions, enrag'd with a sharp and tedious hunger; for these forty years past, minding nothing else but the slaughter of these unfortunate wretches, whom with divers kinds of torments neither seen nor heard of before, they have so cruelly and inhumanely butchered, that of three millions of people which *Hispaniola* it self did contain, there are left remaining alive scarce three hundred persons. And for the Island of *Cuba*, which contains as much ground in length, as from *Valladolid* to *Rome*; it lies wholly desert, until'd and ruin'd. The Islands of *St. John* and *Jamaica* lie waste and desolate. The *Lucayan* Islands neighbouring toward the North upon *Cuba* and *Hispaniola*, being above Sixty or thereabouts with those Islands that are vulgarly called the Islands of the Gyants, of which that which is least fertile is more fruitful then the King of *Spains* Garden at *Sevil*, being situated in a pure and temperate air, are now totally unpeopled and destroyed; the inhabitants thereof amounting to above 5000000. souls, partly killed, and partly forced away to work in other places: so that there going a ship to visit those parts and to glean the remainder of those distressed wretches, there could be found no more than eleven men. Other Islands there were near the Island of *St. John* more then thirty in number, which were totally made desert. All which Islands, though they amount to such a number containing in length of ground the space of above Two thousand miles, lie now altogether solitary without any people or Inhabitant.

Now to come to the Continent, we are confident, and dare to affirm upon our own knowledge, that there were ten Kingdomes of as large an extent as the Kingdome of *Spain*, joyning to it both *Arragon*, and *Portugal*, containing above a thousand miles every one of them in compass, which the unhumane and abominable villanies of the *Spaniards* have made a wilderness of, being now as it were stript of all their people, and made bare of all their inhabitants, though it were a place formerly possessed by vast and infinite numbers of men; And we dare confidently aver, that for those Forty years, wherein the *Spaniards* exercised their abominable cruelties, and detestable tyrannies in those parts, that there have innocently perish'd above Twelve millions of souls, women and children being numbered in this sad and fatall list; moreover I do verily believe that I should speak within compass, should I say that above Fifty millions were consumed in this Massacre.

An enemy of las Casas was Gonzalo Fernández de Oviedo (1478–1577). Las Casas's debate with another of his enemies, Juan Gines de Sepúlveda, is recounted in *Native American Religions*. Oviedo, who went first to the Caribbean in 1514 to oversee mining operations, eventually settled in Columbia. In his *Natural hystoria de las Indias*, published at Toledo in 1526, he gave extensive accounts of the flora, fauna, and geography of the area and of the customs of the natives of the Caribbean area. These reports were later used by Sepúlveda in support of his argument that "the Indians" were slaves by nature, a view strongly opposed by las Casas. Wherein las Casas held in high regard the intelligence and ability of "the Indians" and considered them easy to convert to Christianity if approached peaceably, Oviedo saw them in a markedly contrasting image—as worshippers of the devil who had gained complete control of them. This view has been commonly held throughout American history, as some of the following selections will reveal. Notably, even Oviedo, finds an element in "the Indian" situation to turn into a severe criticism of some of the Christians living among Native Americans. On their service to the devil, Oviedo wrote the following about "the Indians."

### *WORSHIPPERS OF THE DEVIL by Gonzalo Fernández de Oviedo*[8]

The devil, being so ancient an astronomer, knoweth the times of things and seeth how they are naturally directed and inclined. And maketh them believe that they come so to pass by his ordinance, as though he were the lord and mover of all that is and shall be. And that he giveth the day-light and rain; causeth tempest and ruleth the stations of times, giving life or taking away life at his pleasure. By reason whereof, the Indians being deceived of him, and seeing also such effects to come certainly to pass as he hath told them before, believe him in all other things and honour him in many places with sacrifices of the blood and lives of men, and odiferous spices. And when God disposeth the contrary to that which the devil hath spoken in oracle whereby he is proved a liar, he causeth the *Tequinas* [priests] to persuade the people that he hath changed his mind and sentence for some of their sins, or deviseth some against so mighty and crafty an adversary. And as they call the devil *Tuyra*, so do they in many places call the Christians by the same name, thinking that they greatly honour them thereby, as indeed it is a name very sweet and agreeable to many of them, having laid apart all honesty and virtue, living more like dragons than men among these simple people.

From very early in the sixteenth century, the process by which Native Americans were imagined into existence by Europeans, polarized into distinct and clearly contrasting images. Notably, both simply collapse variations among cultures and within given cultures and communities. Each presents a singular unified "image" of these "other peoples." Neither accurately reflects more than certain incidental and surface features of the peoples or their religious beliefs. The religions of Native Americans can be dealt with only in the Christian terms familiar to the Europeans, although there were contrasting ways in which these terms could be applied. This process of imagining characterizes European-American views of Native American religions throughout most of American history.

## COLONIZATION AND CHRISTIANIZATION

In 1607 with the settlement of Jamestown, the English colonial era began, and, notably, with it American religious history as it has commonly been told by American religious historians.[9] The English settlements found that they not only had to deal with "the Indians," but that they felt their ways and beliefs stood in sharp contrast to the Spanish Catholics who had preceded them to the New World. This is reflected in the colonial documents that describe how "the Indians" should be Christianized. Perhaps the seal of the Massachusetts Bay Colony picturing an Indian saying "Come Over and Help Us" suggests not only that "the Indians" needed help in overcoming their own ignorance, but also help from the forceful ways of Christianizing that the Protestant English colonists attributed to the Spanish Catholics.

Roger Williams (1603?–1683), founder of the Rhode Island Colony, was a Baptist leader. His first published book, *A Key Into the Language of America* (1643), portrays "Indian" life with sympathy while casting criticism upon European civilization, especially as it appears in New England. The following passage with biblical base reflects the tenor and irony of Williams' perspective.

### *THE GENERALL OBSERVATION FROM THE PARTS OF THE BODIE by Roger Williams*[10]

Nature knowes no difference between *Europe* and *Americans* in blood, birth, bodies, &c. God having of one blood made all mankind, *Acts* 17. and all by nature being children of wrath, *Ephes*. 2.

More particularly:

1. *Boast not proud* English, *of thy birth & blood,*
*Thy brother* Indian *is by birth as Good.*
*Of one blood God made Him, and Thee & All,*
*As wise, as faire, as strong, as personall.*

2. *By nature wrath's his portion, thine no more*
*Till Grace* his *soule and* thine *in Christ restore,*
*Make sure thy second birth, else thou shalt see,*
*Heaven ope to* Indians *wild, but shut to thee.*

The Quakers in America maintained a fairly tolerant attitude toward Native Americans, for in their religious belief, ritual and ceremony was not of importance. What counted was human action through which a God demonstrates his presence in all human beings. William Penn (1644–1718), who received the tract of land now known as Pennsylvania from Charles II as payment for a debt owed his father, was a forceful figure in America.

The following selection is from a pamphlet published in London in 1683 in which Penn attempted to describe the "natives or aborigines" as he had observed them (he speaks of them in general, but his experience was mainly with the Delaware) and to persuade others to correct the unjust ways in which they had been treated. He encouraged others to listen to the will of God in their dealings with the Indians: "do not abuse them, but let them have justice, and you win them."

It is notable that despite Penn's seeking for just treatment of Native Americans, he wished to win them and their lands over, and he found their religion sorely lacking. He expressed an opinion as to their origins and by comparison on religious matters considered them Jews.

## *ON INDIAN RELIGION by William Penn*[11]

These poor people are under a dark night in things relating to religion, to be sure, the tradition of it. Yet they believe [in] a God and immortality without the help of metaphysics. For they say there is a great king that made them, who dwells in a glorious country to the southward of them, and that the souls of the good shall go thither where they shall live again. Their worship consists of two parts, sacrifice and *cantico*. Their sacrifice is their first fruits: the first and fattest buck they kill goeth to the fire, where he is all burnt with a mournful ditty of him that performeth the ceremony, but with such marvelous fervency and labor of body that he will even sweat to a foam. The other part is their *cantico*, performed by round dances, sometimes words, sometimes songs, then shouts, two being in the middle that begin and, by singing and drumming on a board, direct the chorus. Their postures in the dance are very antic and differing, but all keep measure. This is done with equal earnestness and labor, but great appearance of joy. In the fall, when the corn cometh in, they begin to feast one another. There have been two great festivals already, to which all come that will. I was at one myself: their entertainment was a green seat by a spring under some shady trees and twenty bucks with hot cakes of new corn, both wheat and beans, which they make up in a square form in the leaves of the stem and bake them in the ashes. And after that they fell to dance, but they that go must carry a small present in their money, it may be sixpence, which is made of the bone of a fish; the black is with them as gold, the white, silver; they call it all wampum. . . .

Don't abuse them, but let them have justice and you win them. The worst is that they are the worse for the Christians, who have propagated their vices and yielded them tradition for ill and not for good things. But as low an ebb as they are at and as glorious as their condition looks, the Christians have not outlived their sight with all their pretensions to a higher manifestation. What good then might not a good people graft where there is so distinct a knowledge left between good and evil? I beseech God to incline the hearts of all that come into these parts to outlive the knowledge of the natives by a fixed obedience to their greater knowledge of the will of God, for it were miserable indeed for us to fall under the unjust censure of the poor Indians' conscience while we make profession of things so far transcending.

For their original, I am ready to believe them of the Jewish race, I mean of the stock of the Ten Tribes, and that for the following reasons: first, they were to go to a land not planted or known which, to be sure, Asia and Africa were, if not

Europe; and He that intended that extraordinary judgment upon them might make the passage not uneasy to them, as it is not impossible in itself, from the easternmost parts of Asia to the westernmost of America. In the next place, I find them of like countenance and their children of so lively resemblance that a man would think himself in Duke's Place or Berry Street in London when he seeth them. But this is not all: they agree in rites, they reckon by moons, they offer their first fruits, they have a kind of feast of tabernacles, they are said to lay their altar upon twelve stones, their mourning a year, customs of women, with many things that do not now occur.

Cotton Mather (1663–1728) was a powerful and influential Puritan who expressed his views in prolific and stylistic writings. In his *Magnalia Christi Americana,* published in 1702, he wrote a history of the wars of the early settlers including a series of biographies of Puritan leaders, and it later incorporated a series of captivity narratives.[12] John Eliot, missionary to the Indians, was the subject of one of Mather's biographies. It serves well to reveal something of Mather's views on the religions of Native Americans. He found these servants of the devil so despised that, in Mather's view, it heightened Eliot's missionary task almost beyond the possible. Doubtless, Mather found it difficult to believe that one would wish to attempt to better the conditions among the natives. The despised state in which "the Indians" were considered to be, raised for Eliot the question of their origins. Notably, Eliot engaged in a task of comparing religious beliefs and practices to resolve this matter. This led him to conclude that "the Indians" were "dispersed and rejected Israelites."

While Mather's views are presented in very strong language, it is likely that they reflect common opinion of his time.

## *JOHN ELIOT, MISSIONARY TO THE INDIANS by Cotton Mather*[13]

The natives of the country now possessed by the New-Englanders had been forlorn and wretched heathen ever since their first herding here; and though we know not when or how those Indians first became inhabitants of this mighty continent, yet we may guess that probably the devil decoyed those miserable savages hither, in hopes that the gospel of the Lord Jesus Christ would never come here to destroy or disturb his absolute empire over them. But our Eliot was in such ill terms with the devil, as to alarm him with sounding the silver trumpets of Heaven in his territories, and make some noble and zealous attempts towards ousting him of ancient possessions here. There were, I think, twenty several nations (if I may call them so) of Indians upon that spot of ground which fell under the influence of our Three United Colonies; and our Eliot was willing to rescue as many of them as he could from that old usurping landlord of America, who is, "by the wrath of God, the prince of this world."

I cannot find that any besides the Holy Spirit of God first moved him to the blessed work of evangelizing these perishing Indians; it was that Holy Spirit which laid before his mind the idea of that which was on the seal of the Massachuset colony: a poor Indian having a label going from his mouth, with a *come over and help us.* It was the spirit of our Lord Jesus Christ, which enkindled in him a pity for the dark souls of these natives, whom the "god of this world had blinded," through all the bypast ages. He was none of those that make "the salvation of the heathen" an article of their creed; but (setting aside the unrevealed and extraordinary steps which the "Holy One of Israel" may take out of his usual paths) he thought men to be lost if our gospel be hidden from them. . . .

All the religion they have amounts unto thus much: they believe that there are many gods, who made and own the several nations of the world; of which a certain great God in the south-west regions of heaven bears the greatest figure. They believe that every remarkable creature has a peculiar god within it or about it: there is with them a Sun God, a Moon God, and the like; and they cannot conceive but that the fire must be a kind of a god, inasmuch as a spark of it will soon produce very strange effects. They believe that when any good or ill happens to them, there is the favor or the anger of a god expressed in it; and hence, as in a time of calamity, they keep a dance, or a day of extravagant ridiculous devotions to their god; so in a time of prosperity they likewise have a feast, wherein they also make presents one unto another. Finally, they believe that their chief god (Kautantowit) made a man and a woman of a stone; which, upon dislike, he broke to pieces, and made another man and woman of a tree, which were the fountains of mankind; and that we all have in us immortal souls, which, if we were godly, shall go to a splendid entertainment with Kautantowit, but otherwise must wander about in restless horror forever. But if you say to them anything of a resurrection, they will reply upon you, "I shall never believe it!" And when they have any weighty undertaking before them, it is a usual thing for them to have their assemblies, wherein, after the usage of some diabolical rites, a devil appears unto them, to inform them and advise them about their circumstances; and sometimes there are odd events of their making these applications to the devil. For instance, it is particularly affirmed that the Indians, in their wars with us, finding a sore inconvenience by our dogs, which would make a sad yelling if in the night they scented the approaches of them, they sacrificed a dog to the devil; after which no English dog would bark at an Indian for divers months ensuing. This was the miserable people which our Eliot propounded unto himself to teach and save! And he had a double work incumbent on him; he was to make men of them, ere he could hope to see them saints; they must be civilized ere they could be Christianized; he could not, as Gregory once of our nation, see anything angelical to bespeak his labors for their eternal welfare: all among them was diabolical. To think on raising a number of these hideous creatures unto the elevations of our holy religion, must argue more than common or little sentiments in the undertaker; but the faith of an Eliot could encounter it!

## EXPLORATIONS AND EARLY SCIENTIFIC RECORDS

The nineteenth century brought an extensive expansion to the American lands, opening territories to the west. The great burst of expansion during this century led to the virtual end of many tribes and thus the violent exchanges that characterized the encounter during much of this century began to subside. As the end of "the Indians" was anticipated, and as they were stripped of their capacities to do harm to settlers, an interest arose in securing a record of what were believed to be the last remnants of vanishing peoples. Early in the nineteenth century, Lewis and Clark traveled among many tribes recording what they observed.[14] With Christian objectives not being dominant, their reports and images of the religious practices were somewhat less ruled by preconceived ideas.

This more open and scientific stance appeared with increasing frequency throughout this century, emerging fully with the founding of the Bureau of

Ethnology (known later as the Bureau of American Ethnology) in 1879. The BAE has produced an enormous and important series of monographs, many of which document tribal religions. Beginning late in the nineteenth century and extending into the first two decades of the twentieth century, Edward S. Curtis, best known for his remarkable photographs of Native Americans, compiled an unprecedented record of Native Americans published in his twenty-volume work, *The North American Indians,* which contains oral traditions, ritual descriptions, and other pertinent data.[15]

Certainly the rise of this more scientific effort to record Native American cultures is not without a complex set of biases and expectations, not the least of which is that the motivation for the work was the belief that Native American cultures were vanishing, but certainly there is a marked change in the manner and stance in which took place the imagination of "Indians."

George Catlin traveled widely among Native American peoples, especially in what is now the central United States and Florida. He is widely known for his paintings of Native Americans, paintings that often serve as ethnographic documents. He also recorded his encounters and observations with Native Americans. In the following passage from his book, *The North American Indians,* in an encounter which took place between 1832 and 1839, we may see reflected this detached stance with regard to Native Americans and their religions.

## *GEORGE CATLIN AND A SIOUX CHIEF*[16]

On an occasion when I had interrogated a Sioux chief, on the Upper Missouri, about their government—their punishments and tortures of prisoners, for which I had freely condemned them for the cruelty of the practice, he took occasion when I had got through, to ask me some questions relative to modes in the civilised world, which, with his comments upon them, were nearly as follow; and struck me, as I think they must every one, with great force.

*"Among white people, nobody ever take your wife—take your children—take your mother—cut off nose—cut eyes out—burn to death?" No! "Then you no cut off nose—you no cut out eyes—you no burn to death—very good."*

He also told me he had often heard that white people hung their criminals by the neck and choked them to death like dogs, and those their own people; to which I answered, "yes." He then told me he had learned that they shut each other up in prisons, where they keep them a great part of their lives because they can't pay money! I replied in the affirmative to this, which occasioned great surprise and excessive laughter, even amongst the women. He told me that he had been to our Fort, at Council Bluffs, where we had a great many warriors and braves, and he saw three of them taken out on the prairies and tied to a post and whipped almost to death, and he had been told that they submit to all this to get a little money. "Yes."

He said he had been told, that when all the white people were born, their white medicine-men had to stand by and look on—that in the Indian country the women would not allow that—they would be ashamed—that he had been along the Frontier, and a good deal amongst the white people, and he had seen them whip their little children—a thing that was very cruel—he had heard also, from several white medicine-men, that the Great Spirit of the white people was the child of a white woman and that he was at last put to death by the white people! This seemed to be a thing that he had not been able to comprehend, and he concluded by saying, "The Indians' Great Spirit got no mother—the Indians no kill him, he never die." He put me a chapter of other questions, as to the trespasses of the white people on their lands—their continual corruption of the morals of their women—and digging open the Indian's graves to get their bones, etc. To all of which I was compelled to reply in the affirmative, and quite glad to close my note-book, and quietly to escape from the throng that had collected around me, and saying (though to myself and silently), that these and a hundred other vices belong to the civilised world, and are practised upon (but certainly, in no instance, reciprocated by) the "cruel and relentless savage." . . .

To each other I have found these people kind and honourable, and endowed with every feeling of parental, of filial, and conjugal affection, that is met in more enlightened communities. I have found them moral and religious; and I am bound to give them great credit for their zeal, which is often exhibited in their modes of worship, however insufficient they may seem to us, or may be in the estimation of the Great Spirit.

I have heard it said by some very good men, and some who have been preaching the Christian religion amongst them, that they have no religion—that all their zeal in their worship of the Great Spirit was but the foolish excess of ignorant superstition—that their humble devotions and supplications to the Sun and the Moon, where many of them suppose that the Great Spirit resides, were but the absurd rantings of idolatry. To such opinions as these I never yet gave answer, nor drew other instant inferences from them, than, that from the bottom of my heart, I pitied the persons who gave them.

I fearlessly assert to the world (and I defy contradiction), that the North American Indian is everywhere, in his native state, a highly moral and religious being, endowed by his Maker with an intuitive knowledge of some great Author of his being, and the Universe; in dread of whose displeasure he constantly lives, with the apprehension before him, of a future state, where he expects to be rewarded or punished according to the merits he has gained or forfeited in this world. . .

Morality and virtue, I venture to say, the civilised world need not undertake to teach them, . . .

Of their extraordinary modes and sincerity of worship, I speak with equal confidence; and although I am compelled to pity them for their ignorance, I am bound to say that I never saw any other people of any colour, who spend so much of their lives in humbling themselves before, and worshipping the Great Spirit, as some of these tribes do, nor any whom I would not as soon suspect of insincerity and hypocrisy.

Self-denial, which is comparatively a word of no meaning in the enlightened world; and self-torture and almost self-immolation, are continual modes of appealing to the Great Spirit for his countenance and forgiveness; and these, not in studious figures of rhetoric, re-sounding in halls and synagogues, to fill and astonish the ears of the multitude; but humbly cried forth from starved stomachs and parched throats, from some lone and favourite haunts, where the poor penitents crawl and lie with their faces in the dirt from day to day, and day to day sobbing forth their humble confessions of their sins, and their earnest implorations for Divine forgiveness and mercy.

The publication of Lewis Henry Morgan's *League of the Ho-De-No Sau-Nee, or Iroquois* in 1851 was considered by many the first scientific treatise on "the Indians." Certainly Morgan must be considered a forerunner of modern ethnography. His recognition of the high development of the Iroquois is in marked contrast with the popular views of tribal cultures of his day. He believed that the Iroquois "achieved for themselves a more remarkable civil organization, and acquired a higher degree of influence than any other race of Indian lineage, except those of Mexico and Peru."[17] Even though Morgan observed Iroquois agriculture, he considered them a hunting culture and attributed their savagery to this—and their need for communal hunting lands as the cause for their failure to accumulate private property and to develop the idea of progress. This very idea of the need to transform "the Indians" from a hunting stage of cultural development to one of agriculture shaped the U.S. government's approach to resolving "the Indian problem" throughout the last half of the nineteenth century. Certainly the Dawes Act (1887), which allotted land to individuals, was the major expression of this view. It divided native lands among individual Native Americans in order to make them farmers and thus to instill in them the notion of progress and civilization.

Morgan believed that to understand any Native American culture it was essential to understand their religion. Even earlier in the century, Father Geronimo Boscana, a Franciscan missionary in southern California, held the same view, yet his desire to understand the religion of the natives was to better and more effectively Christianize them.[18] Morgan framed his considerations of Iroquois religion in a more universal domain, using his knowledge of the religious inquiries of Western antiquity to both interpret and to validate what he observed among the Iroquois. This enterprise of comparing the Greeks and "the Indians" has a considerable history. Doubtless, its most ardent practitioner has been Hartley Burr Alexander.[19]

## LEGISLATION OF NATIVE AMERICAN RELIGIONS

From at least colonial times, Native Americans' practice of religion was a matter to be legislated by European-Americans. For example, the following orders of the General Court of the Colony of the Massachusetts Bay require, by law, that "these natives should come to the good knowledge of God."

### *MASSACHUSETTS BAY COLONY INDIAN ORDINANCES*[20]

#### *10 June 1644*

It is ordered, that noe Indian shall come att any towne or howse of the English (without leave) uppon the Lords day, except to attend the publike meeteings; neither shall they come att any English howse uppon any other day in the weeke, but first shall knocke att the dore, and after leave given, to come in, (and not otherwise;) and if any (hereafter) offend contrary to this order, the constable, uppon notice given him, shall bringe him or them Indians, soe offendinge, to a magestrate to bee punisht according to his offence.

Whereas it is the earnest desire of this Courte, that these natives (amongst whome wee live, and whoe have submitted themselves to this governmente) should come to the good knowledge of God, and bee brought on to subject to the scepter of the Lord Jesus, it is therefore ordred, that all such of the Indians as have subjected themselves to our governmente bee henceforward enjoyned (and that they fayle not) to meete att such severall places of appoyntmente as shalbee most convenient on the Lords day, where they may attend such instruction as shalbee given them by those whose harts God shall stirr upp to that worke; and it is hereby further declared (as the desire of this Courte) that those townes that lye most convenient to such places of meetinge of the Indians would make choyce of some of theire brethren (whom God hath best quallified for that worke) to goe to them, (beeinge soe mett,) and instruct them, (by the best interpriter they can gett,) that if possible God may have the glory of the conversion (at least) of some of them in the use of such meanes God gives us to afoard them.

### *4 November 1646*

Albeit faith be not wrought by the sword, but by the word, and therefore such pagan Indians as have submitted themselves to our government, though wee would not neglect any dew helpes to bring them on to grace, and to the meanes of it, yett wee compell them not to the Christian faith, nor to the profession of it, either by force of armes or by poenall lawes, neverthelesse, seing the blaspheming of the true God cannot be excused by any ignorance or infirmity of humane nature, the aetaernall power and Godhead being knowne by the light of nature and the creation of the world, and common reason requireth every state and society of men to be more careful of preventing the dishonnor and contempt of the Most High God (in whom wee all consist) then of any mortall princes and magistrates, itt is therefore ordered and decreed by this Courte, for the honnour of the aetaernall God, whome only wee worshipp and serve, that no person within this jurisdiction, whether Christian or pagan, shall wittingly and willingly presume to blaspheme his holy name, either by wilfull or obstinate denying the true God, or reproach the holy religion of God, as if it were but a pollititicke devise to keepe ignorant men in awe, or deny his creation or government of the world, or shall curse God, or shall utter any other eminent kind of blasphemy of the like nature and degree; if any person or persons whatsoever, within our jurisdiction, shall breake this lawe, they shallbe putt to death.

From the early 1880s up to the time John Collier became Commissioner of Indian Affairs in 1933, there was a persistent governmental effort, made through directives to Indian agents, to discourage, in fact to outlaw, the practice of tribal religious traditions. Feasts, dances, and giveaways were discouraged and the Sun Dance and what were termed "scalp dances and war dances" drew special attention in being specifically prohibited.

Even though Native Americans gained United States citizenship in 1924, their religious freedom was not officially guaranteed until August 1978, when President Jimmy Carter signed into law the Joint Resolution, "American Indian Religious Freedom."

## *AMERICAN INDIAN RELIGIOUS FREEDOM, 1978*[21]

Whereas the freedom of religion for all people is an inherent right, fundamental to the democratic structure of the United States and is guaranteed by the First Amendment of the United States Constitution;

Whereas the United States has traditionally rejected the concept of a government denying individuals the right to practice their religion and as a result, has benefited from a rich variety of religious heritages in this country;

Whereas the religious practices of the American Indian (as well as Native Alaskan and Hawaiian) are an integral part of their culture, tradition and heritage, such practices forming the basis of Indian identity and value systems;

Whereas the traditional American Indian religions, as an integral part of Indian life, are indispensable and irreplaceable;

Whereas the lack of a clear, comprehensive, and consistent Federal policy has often resulted in the abridgment of religious freedom for traditional American Indians;

Whereas such religious infringements result from the lack of knowledge or the insensitive and inflexible enforcement of Federal policies and regulations premised on a variety of laws;

Whereas such laws were designed for such worthwhile purposes as conservation and preservation of natural species and resources but were never intended to relate to Indian religious practices and, therefore, were passed without consideration of their effect on traditional American Indian religions;

Whereas such laws and policies often deny American Indian access to sacred sites required in their religions, including cemeteries;

Whereas such laws at times prohibit the use and possession of sacred objects necessary to the exercise of religious rites and ceremonies;

Whereas traditional American Indian ceremonies have been intruded upon, interfered with, and in a few instances banned: Now, therefore, be it

*Resolved by the Senate and House of Representatives of the United States of America in Congress assembled,* That henceforth it shall be the policy of the United States to protect and preserve for American Indians their inherent right of freedom to believe, express, and exercise the traditional religions of the American Indian, Eskimo, Aleut, and Native Hawaiians, including but not limited to access to sites, use and possession of sacred objects, and the freedom to worship through ceremonials and traditional rites.

## NOTES

1. See, for example, Robert F. Berkhofer, Jr., *The White Man's Indian: Images of the American Indian from Columbus to the Present* (New York: Knopf, 1978); Fredi Chiappelli, ed., *First Images of America: The Impact of the New World on the Old*, two volumes (Berkeley: University of California Press, 1976); W. Richard Comstock, "On Seeing with the Eye of the Native European," in *Seeing With a Native Eye*, ed. Walter H. Capps (New York: Harper & Row, 1976); Richard Drinnon, *Facing West: The Metaphysics of Indian-Hating and Empire Building* (Minneapolis: University of Minnesota Press, 1980); Lewis Hanke, *Aristotle and the American Indians: A Study in Race Prejudice in the Modern World* (Bloomington: University of Indiana Press, 1971); Edmundo O'Gorman, *The Invention of America: An Inquiry into the Historical Nature of the New World and the Meaning of its History* (Bloomington: Indiana University Press, 1961); Roy H. Pearce, *The Savages of America: A Study of the Indian and the Idea of Civilization* (Baltimore: The Johns Hopkins Press, 1953, rev. ed., 1965); H. C. Porter, *The Inconstant Savage: England and the North American Indian* 1500–1660 (London: Duckworth, 1979); and Ronald Sanders, *Lost Tribes and Promised Lands: The Origins of American Racism* (Boston: Little, Brown and Company, 1978).
2. The actual log book was given to Ferdinand and Isabella and did not

survive. Our knowledge of it is a digest made of it by Bartolomé de las Casas from a copy of the original log.

3. Christopher Columbus, *The Four Voyages of Christopher Columbus*, translated by J. M. Cohen (New York: Penguin Classics, Harmondsworth, 1969), p. 56. Quotations reprinted by permission of J. M. Cohen.
4. Ibid., p. 64.
5. Ibid., pp. 192–194.
6. Amerigo Vespucci, *Amerigo Vespucci: Letter to Piero Soderini, Gonfaloniere*, trans. & ed., George T. Northup (Princeton: Princeton University Press, 1916), pp. 7–8.
7. Bartolomé de las Casas, *Brief Relation of the Destruction of the Indies* (Seville, 1552). Present quotation from English edition *The Tears of the Indians: Being An Historical and true Account of the Cruel Massacres and Slaughters of above Twenty Millions of innocent People* (John Phillips, trans., 1656).
8. Gonzalo Fernández de Oviedo, *Natural hystoria de las Indias*, 1526, trans. and ed. Sterling A. Stoudemire, *Natural History of the West Indies* (Chapel Hill, N.C.: University of North Carolina Press, 1959), pp. 33–34. Copyright 1959 The University of North Carolina Press. Reprinted by permission of The North Carolina Press.
9. It is notable that American religious history reflects a Protestant bias in generally ignoring the pre-Puritan era in American religious history, that period from 1520 to 1607. Notably Sante Fe, the present capital city of New Mexico, was a capital city of New Spain, years before the Mayflower sailed
10. Roger Williams, *A Key into the Language of America*, edited with a critical introduction, notes, and commentary by John J. Teunissen and Evelyn J. Hinz (Detroit: Wayne State University Press, 1973), p. 133. First published 1643.
11. *A Letter from William Penn, Proprietary and Governour of Pennsylvania in America, to the Committee of the Free Society of Traders. . . .* (London, 1683), reprint by J. Coleman (London, 1881). Notes omitted.
12. Captivity narratives were an important form of literature. See Roy H. Pearce, "The Significances of the Captivity Narrative," *American Literature*, XIX (1947): 1–20.
13. Cotton Mather, *Magnalia Christi Americana*, vol. I (Hartford, 1852), pp. 556–62.
14. R. G. Thwaites, ed., *Original Journals of the Lewis and Clark Expedition 1804–1806*, vols. I–VII (New York, 1904–5). See also V. R. Ray and N. O. Lurie, "The Contributions of Lewis and Clark to Ethnography," *Journal of the Washington Academy of Sciences* XLIV (1954).
15. Edward S. Curtis, *The North American Indian*, 20 vols. (New York: Pierpont Morgan Library, 1906–30).
16. George Catlin, *The North American Indians* (Philadelphia: Leary, Stuart & Co., 1923, first ed., 1841), vol. II, pp. 272–76.
17. Lewis Henry Morgan, *League of the Ho-De-No Sau-Nee, or Iroquois* (New Haven: Human Relations Area Files, 1954, originally published Rochester, 1851), p. 3. For a biographical and critical study of Morgan, see Bernhard Stern, *Lewis Henry Morgan, Social Evolutionist* (Chicago, 1931).
18. Father Geronimo wrote, "I am of the persuasion that if we are ignorant

of the belief held by the Indians, of their usages and customs, it is very difficult to take them out of the error in which they live and to give them to understand the true religion, and to teach them the true way to their salvation." (See John P. Harrington, *A New Original Version of Boscana's Historical Account of the San Juan Capistrano Indians of Southern California* (Washington, D.C.: Smithsonian Miscellaneous Collections, vol. 92, no. 4, 1934). The above quotation is from p. 5.

19. See particularly Hartley Burr Alexander, *The World's Rim: Great Mysteries of the North American Indians* (Lincoln: University of Nebraska Press, 1953).
20. Nathaniel B. Shustleff (ed.), *Records of the Governor and Company of the Massachusetts Bay in New England* (Boston: 1854), vol. III, pp. 6–7, 98.
21. Public Law 95–341, August 11, 1978.

# CHAPTER 2

# *Religious World View: A Matter of Place*

## INTRODUCTION

The immediate problem we face in the study of Native American religions has to do with approach. What do we view of Native American cultures to understand their religions? Do we simply ask them: "What is your religion?" or "What do you believe?" or "What are the names of your gods?" There are many approaches we might take and each is necessarily limiting and incomplete. Whatever we look at and whatever we ask, we focus on one dimension of religious culture and ignore certain other dimensions. In this chapter and in each of the following ones, we will take successive points of view. In each one we will look at a certain slice of Native American cultures to perceive something of the character of Native American religions. In later chapters we will focus on nonliteracy and the mode of communication as it shapes and reflects religion, on sacred objects and actions, on the life cycle, on sustenance activities, and on the history of intercultural encounters and the resulting religious movements. In this chapter we will consider some of the broadest and most fundamental categories of Native American cultures, those broad categories of world view that frame and give orientation to all else.

Here our concern is how to discern those most grand and global understandings. World view, the way one views the world, is experienced and expressed at one level at least in very concrete, although very symbolic, terms. World view is formulated in terms of the physical landscape, architecture, and even in the forbidden and discouraged forms of action and relationships.

In the examples in this chapter, one should look for the general categories that underlie all behavior and thought in a culture. One should look for principles of order and the threat of chaos. One should consider the complex interrelationships of these principles and categories.

## PLACE AS A LANGUAGE OF VALUE AND RELIGION

One way of approaching world view is to recognize that human beings express and transmit their religious world views by making physical distinctions, by specifying the character of the place where they live. That is, we view the world in terms of fundamental distinctions that are projected upon the physical world—houses, ceremonial and ritual structures, villages, fields, hunting grounds, mountains, monoliths, rivers, deserts, cardinal directions, earth, sky, and underworld. Place distinctions are often extended into the imaginative world through oral traditions, ritual drama, and art. These distinctions support a system of values and ideas stated in terms of the relationships among respective places and the characterization of being in or out of place. The value and status of social, cultural, and moral actions are stated in these terms, so that actions that are acceptable and encouraged are distinguished from those that are taboo, discouraged, or unthinkable. Such place distinctions, then, are usually equivalent to ideological distinctions, so to consider categories of place and how they are characterized is one way of beginning the process of understanding and interpreting the religion of a particular culture or the significance of a particular religious event.[1]

In this chapter we will present examples to illustrate this approach to discerning religious world view. We will include examples that span many dimensions of culture, and more specifically, examples of oral and ritual forms of action. It is important to recognize that religious actions can portray both a sense of order and disorder, and that when placed in the perspective and service of a religious world view, even shocking acts which seemingly portray disorder or chaos, are potentially of positive religious value.

Some existing studies of Native American religions and cultures have focused on this symbolic language of place as the principal basis for interpretation and understanding, and therefore stand as exemplary of the approach I am illustrating. Alfonso Ortiz's book, *The Tewa World: Time, Space, Being, and Becoming in a Pueblo Society*, is a full-scale study of a very complex culture based on this approach.[2] Barbara Myerhoff's book, *Peyote Hunt: The Sacred Journey of the Huichol Indians*, and the classic description of Ojibwa culture by A. Irving Hallowell are notable among other examples.[3]

The following selection on Beaver culture of southwestern Canada is a concise yet illuminating study exemplary of this general approach. Notice how such simple distinctions as house arrangements and sleeping orientations speak of religious views of the world. This selection, which introduces this approach in a general sense, will be followed by a variety of examples to illustrate the importance of the symbolic language of place in the areas of oral traditions, ritual and formal actions, and in physical distinctions made in landscape and architecture.

### *BEAVER DREAMING AND SINGING by Robin Ridington*[4]

Human infants live in a world of experience unmediated by symbols, and Beaver infancy is not sufficiently discriminative from our own (and no more easily fathomable) to warrant discussion on my part. I shall begin at the stage of life where experience begins to encounter symbol. A Beaver child generally sleeps with his

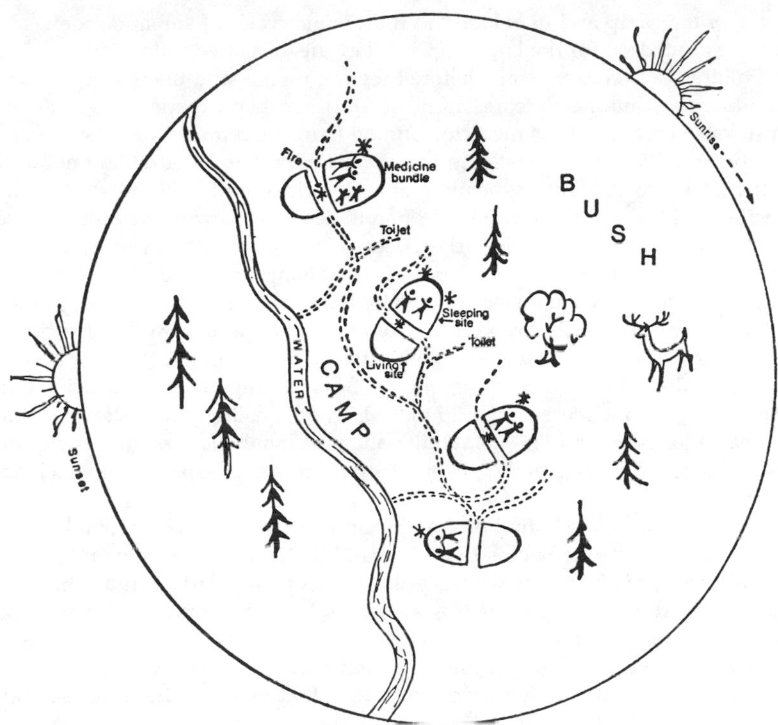


*FIGURE 1. Beaver Camp*

mother and father until he is weaned, on the birth of a new baby. Later he may sleep with an older brother, uncle or grandfather until he moves into a camp that some unmarried boys have set up. His sleeping is as important to him, in its own way, as his daytime activity. Every night and day of his life impresses upon him, gently and unselfconsciously, the unquestionable and almost unspoken realities of existence. Night comes when the sun sets (*sa na'a*, literally "daytime sun goes under"), each sunrise and sunset moving "one chicken step" toward its winter or summer time turning point, and each day increasing or decreasing in length according to season. While night lasts, the night time sun, *hatlege sa* or moon, is seen as it follows its own revolutions. It is the shadow of the sun just as "ghosts", about which a child hears much talk, are the shadows of men. The people always sleep toward the sunrise place in anticipation of its return. The experience of sleeping in that way is so much a part of the background and fabric of life that a child can hardly be consciously aware of it, yet as he will discover at some point in his life it is as important to him, and as unobtrusive, as his breathing.

A typical Beaver nomadic camp is shown in Figure 1. The houses are a sort of double lean-to with a fire in between the two halves. At times during the winter people may live in circular log tipis, more recently in log cabins. Now they rather confusingly find themselves in prefabricated government designed pastel plywood boxes set in rows. The double lean-tos are still in use by some of the people some of the time, and I have lived in and around camps like the one shown here. Children do not seem to know that they sleep facing the sunrise place because, I think, they do not yet know what it means. Yet it is obvious to a child as he observes countless camps set up and struck on the family's yearly rounds that the orientation (an appropriate symbol from our own culture that you may have used without knowing what it meant) of a camp is part of the way things are. The living space of the camp and its relation to the cosmic cycles of sun and moon, form a constant backdrop for the large and small events of a child's life.

Children can recognize men before they can understand them, for their understanding must ultimately come from within their own experience. A man is unmistakable because of his medicine bundle hanging behind where he sleeps and testifying to his existence even in his physical absence. Children are not told directly about the content or meaning of a medicine bundle, but many people my own age told me that as a child they had fooled around with the bundle of some relative and received a terrible fright because there were things in it that moved; they were alive. The medicine bundle usually hangs from one of the poles of the lean-to above where a man sleeps, and he leaves it there during the day when he is away from camp. Children know, from the very special way it is handled and referred to, that it is somehow connected with the deepest powers of an adult's understanding. In my own experience of Beaver camp life, the medicine bundle seemed a constant presence, and I picked up the quality of respect with which it is treated long before I knew anything about its symbolic meaning. A child feels its power as he might feel the power of a gun from the respect with which adults treat it.

Sometimes a child will find himself precipitated into the powers of the medicine bundle long before he begins to understand it. Nearly every Beaver child has at some time in his life been seriously ill, and in this uncertain and otherworldly state of mind has been touched by someone's medicine bundle. When this happens, the familiar yet mysterious medicine bundle leaps out at him from its place in the background of his everyday experience and touches him with the force of life and death. It is a reminder of the power that exists in the universe and the understanding that he will seek as his experience grows.

Children learn from experience that the space behind where a man sleeps, behind his medicine bundle, is somehow different from the space in front of a camp. When families camp together no-one puts his house between another's house and the sunrise place. There are no trails behind the houses. As a child learns the spaces within which people order their lives he is also learning the spaces within which experience becomes symbol.

I am told that traditionally men and women, boys and girls used different places for leaving and entering a house; men to the north and women to the south. The most important difference I observed between men and women in their use of space had to do with a distinction between bush and camp. On the camp side of a house there are trails connecting the houses of a camp together, and leading from each to wood, water and toilet. Everyone is free to walk these trails and it seems natural to follow them rather than strike out across unbroken terrain. On the other side of the house there are no regular trails. Men and children may walk there but women, particularly women who might be menstruating, may not cross behind where a man sleeps, behind his medicine bundle. This means that for every camp there is a camp area where cooking, hide-working and other domestic activities take place, and a bush area that is exclusive to the hunters. The camp is associated with women and family life and the bush with men and the animals they mysteriously go out to hunt and miraculously bring back to be transformed into food by the women.

From an early age children hear stories of giant animals that existed long ago and hunted men. They are told that these animals are still sometimes seen in the bush, that the culture hero, Usakindji, both divided and dispersed them in their present form and drove them to a place beneath the ground. The bush is a place that both surrounds and sustains every camp through the actions of men, and also the place where the creatures of the stories actually exist. It is an ultimate reality testified to by the past and surrounding the present; a place of living symbol, a mythic dimension. Ghosts are also found in the bush but they can only go around to the places where people used to camp along the trails of their own past lives. They pass through the bush but are not of it and seek the camps that are no longer there.

As children learn the physical layout of the world in which they play they also begin to observe its immaterial terrain. Certain spaces belong to the activities of women and others to the activities of men. The medicine bundle links a man to the bush realm and the sunrise place, the world where giant animals may still be found and from which the actual animals he eats every day have come. Hardly a day passes without some mention of a dream and its possible relation to past, present or future events. Nearly every time a hunter brings meat into camp he connects the event to his dreaming and his dreaming is related to the bush through his medicine bundle. The North and East are associated with men, the South and West with women. This symbolic terrain is laid out in a variety of ways in the stories a child hears.

Singing and dreaming and eating, sunrise and sunset, birth and death, winter and summer, bush and camp, myth and experience, build into a totality as a child grows. Dreaming, medicine bundles and songs are a mystery to children but not an exclusive one. They know them in their way and as they grow older they grow into knowledge appropriate to their new experiences. Even children under five often find themselves away from the trails of camp and into the bush realm, a symbolically charged transformation even if they are barely out of earshot of their people. When it is discovered that a child has wandered into the bush, the parents think and dream about what animal might be calling him. As children grow older and begin to learn the stories, they are prepared, told to fast and abstain from drinking water, and sent out early in the morning to spend time alone in the bush. By the time a child is eight or ten he is ready to receive experiences that will change the character of his later life.

I cannot tell you what "really happens" to children in the bush, just as they cannot tell other people their experience directly. I was told that if a child has the right thoughts, if his head is in the right place, a medicine animal will come to him. There is a moment of meeting and transformation when he is "just like drunk" or in vocabulary more familiar to us, "stoned," or in a dream-like state. In this experience he can understand the animal's speech, and the animal speaks to him. It may seem to him that he stays with the animal for days or even weeks. The animal usually tells him when to leave, and when he starts to re-enter everyday reality he lurks in the bush outside the people's camp, afraid of the smell of smoke and unable to understand human speech. Eventually the people spot him, bring him in and give him food and water. An older man puts his medicine coat around him and he sleeps. When he wakes he has returned to the world of men. He can talk to them again but cannot reveal anything, because he has not fully understood what happened in the bush.

What actually happens in the bush? I believe that children do live with animals and learn to speak their language. If ethologists can do this, surely Indians whose way of life brings them onto intimate terms with animals can attain the same rapport. So much for the physical events that may happen. A more complex question is, What does it mean? I can only begin to answer that question just as a Beaver child newly returned from the experience can only begin to learn the answers over the rest of his life. However it is clear that the experience goes far deeper than learning the habits of animals and attaining a rapport useful for hunting in later life. Although it is all these things, it is also and more fundamentally the beginning of a path of seeking to understand his own humanity. They do not find animals in themselves, but rather begin to find themselves in the natures of animals. Each species has its unique and distinctive nature, and people can see in themselves qualities that are most like the qualities of a particular animal species. Animals, besides being themselves, are symbols for men of the varieties of human nature and a man can learn his combination of qualities through getting close to the qualities of animals. The experience with a medicine animal in the bush is the culmination of childhood and the beginning of adulthood. Children do not find their medicines then but they do find the path that will lead them to this discovery later on. It is a path of dreaming and singing.

Children no longer seek to live with animals after puberty. For girls puberty is marked by an important ceremony on her first menstruation, and for boys the first kill of every major species of game is the occasion for a giveaway and dance. Their vision quest experiences are not exactly forgotten but are pushed to the background of an exciting busy adolescence. When a boy-man becomes one of the core adults of a band and has his own children (sometimes not until he is around thirty since he is likely to marry an older widow first), the experience of his pre-adolescent vision quest and post-adolescent maturity come together in a powerful symbolic synthesis. He dreams. Of course he has always dreamed and known that dreams are crystalizations of reality, but these first dreams of maturity are special because they show him his medicines with the clarity of wisdom that adds a new direction to the innocence of childhood and to the illumination of the vision itself. This clarity and wisdom can only come when he has entered responsibly into the lives of others and learned to see himself in them. He has always in a sense known his medicines, but now he knows what they mean. The path his life has taken from the moment of his birth has come full circle, and he is ready to begin other paths to the completion of other circles. In the dreams he sees himself as a child living in the bush and knows that the stories he has both taken for granted, and taken literally, are about *him*. When he entered the world of animals as a child he also entered into the stories. The animals he knows and *is*, are the animals of the creation.

The knowledge that comes through dreaming is absolute because it comes from a level of symbolic association that is deeper than consciousness. Throughout Beaver life, this link through dreaming to a level of absolute certainty is given the importance it deserves. Dreams reveal the often hidden significance of events, and the immediacy of their imagery is accepted as an important gift. In this respect dreams for the Beavers are linked with songs since songs are experiences that convey the imagery of a dream into the conscious realm and allow this kind of experience to be communicated. Both songs and dreams are paths that take one into the realm where symbol and experience merge. The most important dreams a Beaver can have are those in which he follows a song, for the thread of a Beaver's song is the path his mind can take into the deepest realms of his subjectivity and out to reach the subjectivities of others. It is frustrating to have to use words to describe what must essentially be heard and experienced, but the reader must use his imagination and perhaps some experience with Indian music to see how songs become the medium of this inner journey. As you follow the turns of the song and learn them you are learning the inner paths of the mind. The Beavers translate *songs* into English as prayer because they reach simultaneously inward and outward.

The Beaver word for medicine is *mayine*, his or its song, and the central symbol of a man's medicine dream is a song given to him by his medicine animal. The songs are those sung by the giant animals when they hunted men, and the medicine dream reveals that the childhood experience with the animals was also the mind's journey into its song. The dreams also reveal to a man how to assemble a medicine bundle of objects symbolizing the powers of the mythic animals and instruct him to avoid certain foods or situations. By these signs other men know that he "knows something."

A man's medicine bundle hanging above where he sleeps toward the rising sun is a focus for his dreaming, a point at which the paths of thought and song begin and end. Through dreams he can receive and assimilate the flow of events into a significant order. Let me try to explain my understanding of what is, after all, the innermost subjectivity of people in a culture very different from mine. Hunters nearly always say that a successful hunt has been preceeded by a dream. Elsewhere I interpreted this as an *ex post facto* claim for having caused the outcome. Now I believe it would be more in line with what I know of their dreaming to say the dream grasps the essence of a particular moment rather than causing it in our objective sense of cause and effect. Perhaps it would be better to say that the dream brings an event into being from the multitudinous events of possibility. There are many more possible occurrences than can actually be realized and in hunting, as in gambling, one seeks to know the dimensions of possibility and to know something of the odds with regard to various classes of possible events. There are many animals in the bush, and any one could be willing to give himself to the people. When man and animal do meet it is a moment of transformation, like the moment of meeting in the vision quest when the child enters the animal's world of experience and is devoured by another realm of consciousness. In hunting, the animal enters the man's experience and his meat is eaten by the people. Through their meeting the man can be instrumental in bringing into actuality a transformation that existed before only as a possibility, just as through the meeting of child and animal in the vision quest the child is given a path to the realization of his humanity. The vision quest symbolically transforms the child's meat into spirit, and the hunt transforms the animal's spirit into meat. But the moment of killing is also a moment of creation for it brings potential into actuality, the manifesting into the manifested. The hunter's dreams come from the sunrise, the place where the new day is created, and come to him through his medicine bundle, the symbols of his entry into the world of animals and myth.

The Beavers symbolize the creative mystery of this transformation by saying that the shadows of animals killed in hunting return to the sky to be born again in the meat of another body. This completes and begins the circle of creation, for the animal's spirit continues its journeys through the peoples' respectful acceptance of its meat. That is why the Beavers place such a great emphasis on proper care of meat and respect to the remains left at the kill site. The hunter's dream is as much of a shadow waiting to be born as it is of an animal preparing to die. The dream does not cause the meeting between man and animal, but it puts them into the proper sense of understanding that can make the meeting possible and meaningful. The dream emanates from an unconscious repository of the man's whole lifetime of experience and reaches out to touch a possible moment of creation. At every stage of his life his culture has provided symbols that help him organize and understand his experience, and these symbols are almost literally compacted and bundled together in a little pouch that hangs above his head as he sleeps in anticipation of the sun's return to the earth and an animal's return to the sky. The songs of his medicine are always in his inner ear for they tell him what it is to be a man.

I have only once heard a Beaver medicine song, *ma yine* ("his-its" song), for they stem from the deepest reaches of a person's subjectivity. They are the songs of the medicine animals within the man, and they well up and reach out only when he, or one close to him, is in some way close to death, either in a fight or grave illness or great need to succeed in hunting. The only time I heard them was when an old man was preparing to die. But although the medicine songs are seldom sung in public, they are always in a person's mind and in his dreams.

*Ma yine* medicine songs carry a person's mind up and down the abysses of his subjectivity, but there are other gentler songs that reach out horizontally to touch the subjectivities of others through a sharing of common experience. These are the songs a man sings in his camp when he is not out hunting and the songs that bring people together to dance. They are called *ahata yine*, God songs or *nachene yine*, dreamers' songs, because they are brought back from heaven by a man who

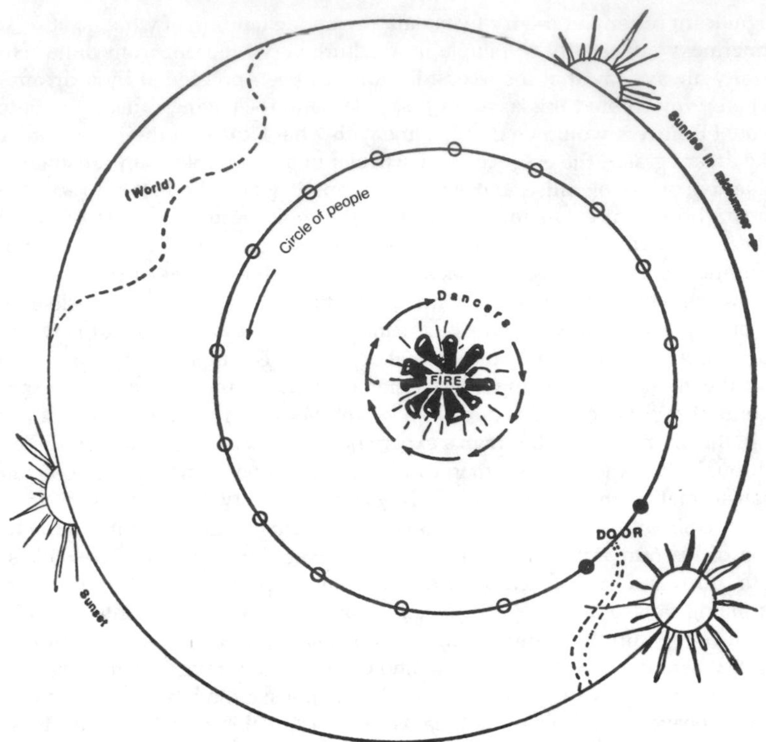


*FIGURE 2.* *Dance Lodge*

has died, a dreamer or shaman. The dreamer (*naachi*) can bridge the gap between subjectivities, because he has followed the vertical dimension of mind to its polar extremities and discovered that they form a circle into another dimension that links his mind to those of The People. He follows the inner path, led on by a song he hears in his dreams to the point of death, the ultimate in subjective isolation but also the point of transformation, to find that beyond is a realm where all subjectivities merge into one. This is heaven (*yage*) from which six dreamers, six grandfathers (actual men who are remembered by their descendents), have sent down a *nachene yine* whose turns are the path of heaven. If he can follow the song's path, "grab hold of it with his mind," in what we would call a state of trance or deep meditation, and they call dreaming, he will become the seventh of the grandfathers and return to the ordinary world as a dreamer carrying a new song for the people. The dreamer is actually seven men and his earthly person becomes the seventh shaman. Dreamers are the only men who sleep toward the sunset. The ultimate source of dreamers' songs is in the animal world for they are the prayers that animals sing when they have hard times. The dreamers in heaven have heard the animals dancing and singing and sent the songs down into the dreams of the seventh shaman, who then gives them to the people. Every song that the Beavers sing is both an animal's song and the song of a particular dreamer. The songs bring people together to dance in prayer, and every man knows that when he dies he will follow the path of a dreamer's song to heaven.

There is much more I could say about the penetration of dreaming and singing into every aspect of Beaver life, but in the short space remaining I would like to leave you with a picture of a Beaver ceremonial, shown in Figure 2. The Beavers dance, usually in a large tipi, clockwise or as they say, "following the sun" around a fire. The fire is the centre of the circle and its column of smoke joins heaven and earth, the axis of subjective experience. Extending horizontally out from the fire is a circle of people. The singers and drummers are mainly young adults, the hunters. They sit in the direction of the sunrise, just as they sleep in their own camps toward the sunrise. Older men sit toward the north, and the very old, as well as the dreamer if he is present, sit toward the sunset. Women and their children sit along the southern circumference of the circle and the door is generally the dividing line between men and women. The singing and dancing goes on for three or four nights, and during the day the dreamer may dream for the people or talk to them about his dreaming. A comparison of Figures 1 and 2 will reveal that the dance lodge is a ceremonial extension of the domestic camp whose metaphor is extended to include all the people who have come together to dance. The singers sit to the east and sing, but instead of medicine bundles that bring medicine songs to their minds, they have drums that carry heaven songs out to the people. The dance is a hopping shuffle around the fire. They say it is walking to heaven. The rhythm is a steady, powerful beat, evocative of walking, and the melodic line with its intricate turns is the path that the animals, the dreamer and ultimately you yourself will follow. . . .

Among the Beaver, personal medicines and public shamanism are parts of a single philosophy whose reality is grounded in common understandings about the meaning of dreams and songs. The hunter's personal medicine and the dreamer's public medicine are both songs that have been given in dreams. The hunter has learned through his vision quest to enter the cycle of death and creation that brings meat into camp to feed the people, while the dreamer through his own death has been given the gift of guiding men through the experience of their anticipated death and creation.

In Beaver culture, house, village, bush, and ceremonial lodge constitute a symbolic language of religious world views. We find such a symbolic language of place in Navajo culture particularly evident in the common house, or hogan. The house structures of the Navajo are identified as male or female depending on what form they take. The conical structure is male and the dome-shaped or cribbed-roof style is female. The Navajo hogan is a microcosmic structure serving as both ordinary dwelling and as sacred ceremonial chamber. Its form came about at the beginning of creation, for the acts that gave origin to the Navajo world were performed within a ceremonial hogan or creation hogan. That first structure became the model for present day Navajo hogans. The distinction of areas within and around the hogan is itself something of a map of the Navajo religious world view. The basic distinctions of the world are found in the songs sung at the dedication and sanctification of the hogan. Many religious beliefs are associated with the hogan. It is a domain of the living and not of the dead. If a person dies in a hogan, the body is removed through a hole knocked in the north side of the structure and the house is abandoned and from thenceforth carefully avoided as a place of the dead.

The following selections reflect something of the sacred character of the Navajo hogan. The first selection is an example of one set of the many hogan songs. This is followed by the statement of a Navajo singer, Frank Mitchell, in which he describes the hogan as a place to make plans. Planning is an act essential to Navajo conceptions of creation.

## *NAVAJO HOGAN SONGS*[5]

### *House Song to the East*

Far in the east far below there a house was made;
Delightful house.
God of Dawn there his house was made;
Delightful house.
The Dawn there his house was made;
Delightful house.
White corn there its house was made;
Delightful house.
Soft possessions for them a house was made;
Delightful house.
Water in plenty surrounding for it a house was made;
Delightful house.
Corn pollen for it a house was made;
Delightful house.
The ancients make their presence delightful;
Delightful house.

Before me may it be delightful;
Behind me may it be delightful;
Around me may it be delightful;
Below me may it be delightful;
Above me may it be delightful;
All (universally) may it be delightful.

### *House Song to the West*

Far in the west far below there a house was made;
Delightful house.
God of Twilight there his house was made;
Delightful house.
Yellow light of evening there his house was made;
Delightful house.
Yellow corn there its house was made;
Delightful house.
Hard possessions there their house was made;
Delightful house.
Young rain there its house was made;
Delightful house.
Corn pollen there its house was made;
Delightful house.
The ancients make their presence delightful;
Delightful house.

Before me may it be delightful;
Behind me may it be delightful;
Around me may it be delightful;
Below me may it be delightful;
Above me may it be delightful;
All (universally) may it be delightful.

The song to the east is repeated, addressed now to the south, followed by the song to the west, addressed now to the north. These two songs are repeated alternately until sung three times to each cardinal direction. The Navajo word (*hózhó*) which is rendered here as "delightful" is most commonly rendered by the English word "beautiful."

### *NAVAJO HOGAN—THE PLACE TO MAKE PLANS by Frank Mitchell*[6]

The Chief Hogan songs started even before the first hogan was built. After the songs about building the hogan, step by step, then that home is complete, and the People move in there. They built that hogan to install leaders who were to instruct and to lead the People. All of those things were made holy in the first hogan. That is the start of the human race on earth. Even today we have good examples to show that without a hogan you cannot plan. You can't just go out and plan other things for your future; you have to build a hogan first. Within that, you sit down and begin to plan. It is similar to the way it was in the beginning. When the first people appeared on earth here, they did not have anything. They did not have any hogans, they had no dwelling places where they could gather together and plan. So they had to build a hogan where they could meet and discuss things for the future. That is the reason *naat'á* means to plan ahead and *naat'áani* means the planner, the one who plans for the future. In English, you say king, president, dictator; we say planner. I guess the word "dictator" would be closest, since that is a person whose orders people must obey. A *naat'áani* is similar to that.

## PLACE SYMBOLS IN ORAL TRADITIONS

When events in a story are set "in the beginning," that temporal setting is a symbolic designation of place indicating not first in a sequence of history but rather that which is basic and fundamental, that which is without precedent or prior authority. The perspective is that of the present view of the world. The very placement of stories in a primal setting is one of the basic ways a culture has at its disposal for making fundamental and primary statements about reality. Thus stories of origin, stories of the ancestors and heroic figures and mythic characters who lived in the primal era, are a basic religious use of the symbolic language of place, simply because of their symbolic temporal setting. Of course, the language of place goes far beyond the temporal setting in these stories, for the subject of the stories is the putting of things in order, the distinction and valuation of the physical, social, and moral world in which the people live. Such story traditions are often crucial to the transmission of values and ideology, which are expressed in terms of commonplace distinctions.

Expectations regarding creation fostered by familiarity with Western religious traditions are of a powerful creator figure who decides how things should be and mightily brings his or her wishes into effect. This is not very common in native North America. There are as many as eight different general types of origin stories found among tribes in North America.[7] These range from the familiar earth-diver type story to stories of emergence. Creator figures, when they exist, are of a wide variety—from one who thinks the world into existence to twin brothers who create the world through their struggles with one another. Creation and origin traditions are generally well developed among North American tribes.

Stories of heroes and heroines of an enormous variety can be found in the oral traditions of tribes all over North America. Often their heroism is linked with their courage and powers to cross established boundaries, to disobey the restrictions most human beings must accept, to venture beyond defined places, and, in the process, often through their suffering, they establish the conditions for human life or they reveal more fully the value of human life and the nature of reality.

There are many versions of the heroic theft of light. In this story the world is in darkness because the sun or fire has either never been released or, more commonly, has been stolen by some malevolent agent. The hero accepts the challenge of this "out of place" situation. He departs from the human world to enter the home of the keeper of light and through trick or by strength wins the release of light, thus establishing its rightful place so that human beings gain the proper conditions for life. The following is a Tsimshian story.

## *THE THEFT OF LIGHT (Tsimshian)*[8]

Giant flew inland (toward the east). He went on for a long time, and finally he was very tired, so he dropped down on the sea the little round stone which his father had given to him. It became a large rock way out at sea. Giant rested on it and refreshed himself, and took off the raven skin.

At that time there was always darkness. There was no daylight then. Again Giant put on the raven skin and flew toward the east. Now, Giant reached the mainland and arrived at the mouth of Skeena River. There he stopped and scattered the salmon roe and trout roe. He said while he was scattering them, "Let every river and creek have all kinds of fish!" Then he took the dried sea lion bladder and scattered the fruits all over the land, saying, "Let every mountain, hill, valley, plain, the whole land, be full of fruits!"

The whole world was still covered with darkness. When the sky was clear, the people would have a little light from the stars; and when clouds were in the sky, it was very dark all over the land. The people were distressed by this. Then Giant thought that it would be hard for him to obtain his food if it were always dark. He remembered that there was light in heaven, whence he had come. Then he made up his mind to bring down the light to our world. On the following day Giant put on his raven skin, which his father the chief had given to him, and flew upward. Finally he found the hole in the sky, and he flew through it. Giant reached the inside of the sky. He took off the raven skin and put it down near the hole of the sky. He went on, and came to a spring near the house of the chief of heaven. There he sat down and waited.

Then the chief's daughter came out, carrying a small bucket in which she was about to fetch water. She went down to the big spring in front of her father's house. When Giant saw her coming along, he transformed himself into the leaf of a cedar and floated on the water. The chief's daughter dipped it up in her bucket and drank it. Then she returned to her father's house and entered.

After a short time she was with child, and not long after she gave birth to a boy. Then the chief and the chieftainess were very glad. They washed the boy regularly. He began to grow up. Now he was beginning to creep about. They washed him often, and the chief smoothed and cleaned the floor of the house. Now the child was strong and crept about every day. He began to cry, "Hama, hama!" He was crying all the time, and the great chief was troubled, and called in some of his slaves to carry about the boy. The slaves did so, but he would not sleep for several nights. He kept on crying, "Hama, hama!" Therefore the chief invited all his wise men, and said to them that he did not know what the boy wanted and why he was crying. He wanted the box that was hanging in the chief's house.

This box, in which the daylight was kept, was hanging in one corner of the house. Its name was Mā. Giant had known it before he descended to our world. The child cried for it. The chief was annoyed, and the wise men listened to what the chief told them. When the wise men heard the child crying aloud, they did not know what he was saying. He was crying all the time, "Hama, hama, hama!"

One of the wise men, who understood him, said to the chief, "He is crying for the mā." Therefore the chief ordered it to be taken down. The man put it down. They put it down near the fire, and the boy sat down near it and ceased crying. He stopped crying, for he was glad. Then he rolled the mā about inside the house. He did so for four days. Sometimes he would carry it to the door. Now the great chief did not think of it. He had quite forgotten it. Then the boy really took up the mā, put it on his shoulders, and ran out with it. While he was running, some one said, "Giant is running away with the mā!" He ran away, and the hosts of heaven pursued him. They shouted that Giant was running away with the mā. He came to the hole of the sky, put on the skin of the raven, and flew down, carrying the mā. Then the hosts of heaven returned to their houses, and he flew down with it to our world.

At that time the world was still dark. He arrived farther up the river, and went down river. Giant had come down near the mouth of Nass River. He went to the mouth of Nass River. It was always dark, and he carried the mā about with him. He went on, and went up the river in the dark. A little farther up he heard the noise of the people, who were catching olachen in bag nets in their canoes. There was much noise out on the river, because they were working hard. Giant, who was sitting on the shore, said, "Throw ashore one of the things that you are catching, my dear people!" After a while, Giant said again, "Throw ashore one of the things you are catching!" Then those on the water scolded him. "Where did you come from, great liar, whom they call Txä'msem?" The (animal) people knew that it was Giant. Therefore they made fun of him. Then Giant said again, "Throw ashore one of the things that you are catching, or I shall break the mā!" and all those who were on the water answered, "Where did you get what you are talking about, you liar?" Giant said once more, "Throw ashore one of the things that you are catching, my dear people, or I shall break the mā for you!" One person replied, scolding him.

Giant had repeated his request four times, but those on the water refused what he had asked for. Therefore Giant broke the mā. It broke, and it was daylight. The north wind began to blow hard; and all the fisherman, the Frogs, were driven away by the north wind. All the Frogs who had made fun of Giant were driven away down river until they arrived at one of the large mountainous islands. Here the Frogs tried to climb up the rock; but they stuck to the rock, being frozen by the north wind, and became stone. They are still on the rock. The fishing frogs named him Txä'msem, and all the world had the daylight.

Wherein heroic figures transcend or defy time and space, rules and orders, with the result of helping establish a more perfect and meaningfully ordered world, the many trickster figures in North America often personify disorder and chaos, a backdrop against which to see the value of living by the established and sanctioned rules. Here we see the tension between the necessity of establishing boundaries, rules, and order against the urges for a utopian existence in which any desire, any fancy, any fantasy, can be carried out. Trickster figures typically follow their base desires for good, freedom, and sexuality, ignoring any confinement and constrictions that might be placed upon them. The consequences suffered reveal the foolishness of this way. The considerable power and religious significance of the trickster stems from his folly, from his being out of place. The stories that follow reflect some of his many escapades.

## *THE TRICKSTER AND HIS DAUGHTER (Shoshone)*[9]

Cünā'waʙ[1] wanted to go hunt rabbits with his mother-in-law where they were going to camp for a long while. They went. After a while he said, "Let us camp here in the cave." They lay down for the night and he cohabited with her all night till she was dead. He left her there, and returned. He had cut himself and said to his wife, "Look at what someone has done to me, nearly killing me. That old woman there is dead and I think I am going to die. Don't bury me when I die, but burn me." He had a son and a daughter. When he died, they piled up brush. Before this he had said, "Don't look backward when you burn me, but run home." So they kindled a fire and ran home.

Cünā'waʙ[1] wanted to marry his daughter. He rolled off the pile. One member of his family almost caught him in the act. He went up the country, returned about ten days later, and transformed himself. He also spoke in a different way and told them about the other tribe's customs. At night he slept with his own daughter, for they did not recognize him. The following morning he wanted to hunt rats. He said to his son, "Show me the rats, so we can hunt and eat them." He got from twenty to forty rats. At last they reached a rock. He went to one end, and his son to the other. His son looked through and recognized him. He went home while Cünā'waʙ[1] continued talking to him. At last he noticed that no one was there and said, "He must have recognized me." He felt badly about it and followed his son to camp. There was no one there, they had all gone up into the air. At last the boy thought to himself, "I wish he would look up." Then he looked up and said, "You are good for nothing, I call you 'Seven Stars' (*sonī'au*[uu])." He was alone now.

## *COYOTE'S CARELESSNESS (Wasco-Warm Springs)*[10]

Coyote was going along, and he came to a river where five pretty sisters were bathing and washing clothes some distance from each other. "What pretty girls," said Coyote to himself, "I wonder how I can enjoy them all." He thought a little, and then turned himself into a baby laced up in a papoose-board, and set himself adrift on the river.

Pretty soon he drifted down to the oldest sister. "Oh, what a beautiful baby!" she said and pulled it ashore and picked it up. Well, that Coyote turned back into himself before she knew what was happening, and he had his way with her; then he became a baby again and drifted down to the second oldest sister. "Oh, my, what a cute baby!" she said, "I must save it!"—but when she picked it up it was that Coyote! And so he fooled two more sisters in the same way, until he got down to to the last one, the youngest.

When she saw the baby drifting down she said, "There's something funny about this; let me see—" and she held the baby in the water with one hand and quickly unlaced it with the other. Sure enough, it was that Coyote! When he turned himself into a baby, he just forgot to change his penis too, and when the youngest sister saw he was no baby, she threw him far out into the river. He was careless, but she was careful.

### *THE COYOTE AND THE EAGLE (Hopi)*[11]

Alíksai! North of Shupaúlavi is the Kateína House (Kateínki). West of this is a bluff, and on top of this bluff used to live an Eagle. One time the Coyote came along. "What are you wandering around for?" the Eagle asked. "Yes," the Coyote said. The Eagle was standing on one foot, having the other foot hidden in his feathers. The Coyote was wondering, and asked: "Why are you standing on one foot?" "Yes," the Eagle said, "I cut one leg off, and so I am standing on one foot." "Is that so?" the Coyote said, and was thinking. "I am envious at you," he said to the Eagle; "I shall try to stand on one leg too; but how did you cut your leg off, how is that done?" "Why," the Eagle replied, "you just lay your leg across a stone and strike on it with a sharp stone and then it will be cut off. It does not hurt, and you need not be afraid."

So the Coyote hunted for a sharp stone and there was another sharp stone with a sharp edge. He laid his right hind leg across the latter, raised the small sharp stone and cut off his leg. Hereupon the Eagle lowered his second leg, stretched out his wings, and laughed at the Coyote and said: "I have two legs, see here." "Oh!" the Coyote said, "I, poor one, that I thoughtlessly cut off my leg." And while the Eagle flew away the Coyote was crying, and, limping away, probably perished somewhere.

## PLACE SYMBOLS IN RITUAL AND FORMAL ACTIONS

A pilgrimage, a dance, a festival, a rite of passage, a rite of curing—each is defined in the terms of how time and space are shaped by the acts performed. A pilgrimage, for example, is a transformative rite distinguished by points of departure and destination and the process of traversing the space in between. These symbols of place are inseparable from the effects and meanings rendered by the formal actions that distinguish pilgrimage. Since it is the character of ritual and formal actions to manipulate time and space in the creation of meaningful place categories, to focus upon the symbolic language of place is a way of attempting to understand the religious importance of these kinds of actions. The following selections will present a variety of Native American examples that we will consider from this point of view.

In a remarkable document written in Oglala, Thomas Tyon described some of the many complex actions associated with the Oglala Sun Dance. Through the creation of and use of powerful symbols of time and space, the Sun Dance creates for the participants the experience of being in the center of the world in communion with all life-giving powers.

## *THOMAS TYON ON THE OGLALA SUN DANCE*[12]

If a man's child is very sick, or his wife, or if enemies shoot at him in a fight and he fears very much, yet he survives and is not killed, in such case he may vow the Sun Dance. Hence an account of such vows, they seek a good man, one without offense who knows the complete ceremony. The man who is to dance the Sun Dance bears a pipe and at sunrise he goes and extends the pipe and prays for that which he desires. When he is finished, the man, from then on, proceeds very carefully. In the days to come, the one who is to dance the Sun Dance should always try to do what is proper. When he decides a thing is not proper, he is afraid of it, it is said. Something the Sun Dancers know is that in the Moon When the Sage Is Long, then it is time to go, it is said. Therefore the leader of the Sun Dancers, along with the people living about, fills a pipe and carries it in procession on foot. And they select a place for the camp circle so that all may come together properly in camp and do all things properly.

Now the leader of the Sun Dancers erects a tipi in the middle of the camp circle for them and inside the tipi he covers the floor well with sage. The man who will dance the Sun Dance now makes a sweat bath for himself in a formal way and cleanses himself (*Sapa sni igluhan*). Whoever is an attendant must do the same as the leader does. Now they do things in this manner. They strip themselves completely and over their shoulders they wear furred robes with the hair out. And now they will live in the tipi. Before the Sun Dance there are strict rules made for them. No one swims. They can only take the sweat bath.

Well now, the people all camp in a big formal camp circle, and then the Sun Dancers will properly observe the rules made for them. No one laughs in the tipi and they regard everything within as *wakan* [sacred, powerful, spiritual]. Also, outside, around the tipi, they spread a blanket of tree leaves. They make a good place inside. They place a buffalo bull head inside. They place a pipe there also. The pipe belongs to the leader. Well, these men dress themselves as follows. They fold blue blankets around themselves and they also use scarlet blankets for skirts. Then the men repeatedly paint themselves red. They wear twisted sage around their head; they have buffalo hair tied on both wrists and on both ankles. They also have the same made of rabbit skin. Also they make a hoop covered with otter skin and they wear an otter skin cape.

Well, having finished these things properly, now during the nights, they feast. An old man cries out for those men who are skillful singers to assemble there; women also go. They sit in the tipi and they make no fire and sing. There are many songs but they sing the first. When the men who will dance the Sun Dance are singing, then all the Sun Dancers wail. Well now, they feast each night for four nights and [in this way] four days pass and then those who are to seek the *wakan* tree get busy with their work.

Now the men who are leaders decide how to divide up the work agreeably. And now the beloved children are gathered together; they assemble them, and they command them to go to seek the *wakan* tree. Only the children who are relatives go. Well now, before they finish the search themselves, a good man selects the *wakan* tree and marks it, it is said. Well, when the seekers go, they all intermingle. They sing this song. They sing the second song. All who go are on horseback. They go here and there, round and round. All the people stand looking toward them and when the seeker returns they will again completely intermingle. Again they sing.

Now they finally arrive home so all the people bustle about (*skinciyapi*). They will now go and bring the *wakan* tree. But they do not go yet to bring the *wakan* tree. A good man goes on foot to where the *wakan* tree will be erected. They select a man who has done nothing bad and have him dig a hole in the ground, it is said. And while the hole is being dug they begin to erect leafy tree branches the height of a man. Now the entire people go to bring the *wakan* tree. Now they go there together. When they arrive at the *wakan* tree, a holy man again stands there and talks. Then he sings. During this time all the people stand very quietly. Then the men who are leaders gather the beloved children together again. Again the holy man talks there, and again he sings. And then he stands and looks toward the four winds and now he stands by the *wakan* tree holding an ax and in that place he talks again, and he pretends to strike the *wakan* tree three times and the fourth time he strikes it. Then he stops striking with the ax. Therefore the leaders now meditate. . . .

They dance the White Owners dance (*Ska yuha wacipi*). At this time, those who choose to give to them make many presents to the children one by one in a line, and when they have finished there, then they choose a good woman and she alone cuts down the *wakan* tree and completely separates the branches from it. And when they have completely finished this, they pick some very good men who have never done anything bad. And those will bear the *wakan* tree as they go, returning to camp.

Well those on horseback are there and again they are prepared to hurry about (*skanpi*). Those who bear the sacred pole return on foot and they will make three pauses and each time they will howl. The fourth time, the last, they howl like dogs. Now those on horseback will race vigorously to the place in the camp circle where the *wakan* tree is to be erected. They make their goal an enemy and he who first strikes that will really kill an enemy in the future. They wish for this and race vigorously.

Well now, all the people returning arrive on foot at the camp circle, and where the *wakan* tree will stand they bring yellow clay and the *wakan* tree. Then all the various societies sit in a circle and sing: White Owners and Kit Foxes and White Marked and Bare Lances and Pawnee and Omaha. Then they sit around while they cook food in kettles and sing while cooking. These societies set up their tipis.

Well now the place where the sacred pole is has been made *wakan*; no one goes near that place. Now again the holy man goes there and commands them to bring the offerings. The *wakan* tree is forked. The top of the tree is towards where the sun goes down. First are the stems of chokecherry bushes that have no leaves and then the fat of a ruminant's heart and then red clay and then the fat of a buffalo loin, and a wooden rod, the stem of a chokecherry bush completely peeled, thrust into the buffalo loin. They mix the red clay in one of a pair of parfleches. They paint red the entire green bark of the forks. They mix Pawnee and common tobacco and put it on, and a feather decorated with red-dyed porcupine quills down the middle. Then they wrap the chokecherry stems in a bundle. And now they put them in the forks of the *wakan* tree.

Now all the people stand respectfully and quietly. They make an image of a man of rawhide and paint it entirely red. They place a plume on the head completely reddened. And they also make an image of a buffalo and paint it entirely black. They tie on the pole two small thongs so they will hang down from it. Now they carefully push upright the *wakan* tree, the forked tree. Now they place it erect and the people all shout together excitedly. Then all the women sing. At the top of the tree they tie a red blanket and then they paint the *wakan* tree on the sides of the four winds. Then the women raise the tremolo (*ongna kical*).

Well now, the entire people move about very excitedly and they set up the Sun Dance lodge. When they finish the lodge, a man again proclaims in a loud voice. Now all the young men paint themselves red. Now they will have the ground-smoothing dance. So now all the young men come according to their band (*tiyospaye*) to the middle of the camp circle. Each band has thirty-five or forty. In this way they come.

Well now, when they come to the place of the Sun Dance they run excitedly around the lodge. And now they go within the lodge. Within the lodge they dance around firing guns. They shoot both the image of the man and the image of the buffalo. There is the song for the dance. Then there is a song for the *wasicunpi* [guardian spirits]. Now they come outside altogether, moving quietly. Now those who will dance the Sun Dance separate and the Sun Dancers go together into the tipi.

Now they have finished the lodge for the Sun Dance so they come around the lodge praying. Now they stand at the entrance of the lodge. They go to the *catku* [place of honor]. The leader of the Sun Dance goes first, formally bearing the buffalo head. Bearing it to the *catku,* he stands there. He feigns four times to lay it down and then lays it down. And again they feign laying their hands on it three times and the fourth time they really lay their hands on it formally and then take them away. They all sit at the *catku*. These men will sing but they will not use a drum. A dried buffalo hide is used for the singers. They use quite a long wooden rod with a ruminant's tail tied on the end to beat the dried buffalo hide. And again they sing a song. And then they dance all around the lodge. They sing a song. Well, from now on they dance throughout the night. And thus the day passes.

So now the leader of all the Sun Dancers prepares the ground. At first he stands facing the west. He talks. Then the people stand looking toward him and say, "We wish you life." And with an ax he feigns three times to strike the ground and the fourth time he strikes it. And then in the same manner he strikes towards the east. And then he strikes the middle of the ground. Well now, he digs the ground and pulverizes it. Now he replaces all the earth and makes a star at the center of it. And there he sprinkles Pawnee tobacco and red clay. And then he erects on this pulverized earth a pipe and a rod of chokecherry stem completely painted blue. This pipe is formally filled with tobacco. And then he places the pipe on a dried buffalo chip.

Well now, the sun is at the meridian, so they will now mark the Sun Dancers. So they first take two braided thongs and approach the *wakan* tree and then tie them to the *wakan* tree so that they will hang suspended from it. And now when the sun is at the meridian the holy man again sings. Men, for the sake of the people, give names to the children. As long as they are Sun Dancing, they run to give away presents.

The men drink no water while they dance and they do not eat. They will compose and sing songs on this day. While dancing in the circle they sing.

Well now, the ceremony is completed and the people disperse widely. All go to whatever place they wish. All the Sun Dancers sound a large whistle while dancing and look at the sun as it moves (*hinapa*). And the words of the songs for the dance are such as are appropriate. If they wish for many buffalo, they will sing of them; if victory, sing of it; and if they wish to bring good weather, they will sing of it.

Shamanic rites are generally not performed on such a grand public scale as is the Sun Dance, yet shamanic performances may still be understood in terms of place, for the shaman is one who may transcend by means of an ecstatic state of trance the ordinary human world to engage spiritual helpers and powers to bring effects to the human world. Commonly the shaman is called upon to cure someone ill whose suffering is thought to be due to the intrusion of some evil object placed in his or her body by a witch or other malevolent force. The following selection describes a Bear River female shaman performing a curative rite.

## *BEAR RIVER SHAMANIC CURE described by Gladys A. Nomland*[13]

This dance was made on Eel river near Fernbridge, Humbolt county, California, on April 24th, 1930, by a woman of about sixty-five years of age, called Nora Coonskin. She is a Bear River woman of the Northern California Athabascan group.

In early life she had been trained for a doctor or shaman by her mother, who was also a powerful shaman, at a place called Mess-e-ah on the lower Bear river, but she was thought to have too much power for her tender years and did not practice doctoring from the time that she was about thirteen years old until very recently. She told me that spirit voices had warned her lately that she would die soon unless she again practiced shamanism. She began to dance and sing for the sick when called upon and has now been given so much spiritual power that she is impelled to continue with her doctoring.

The dance was held in a vacant house where a heating stove had been installed and a bed for the sick boy, a tuberculosis patient about sixteen years old who was so emaciated and weak he had to be carried in from the automobile and put into the bed. Chairs and benches were arranged around the room and two lanterns hung on the walls at opposite corners. The floor had been swept and dampened. A special chair was placed for the shaman facing the east, with a mat of rush in front of it.

The doctoring ceremony began about 8:30 p.m. The shaman first removed shoes and stockings and put on a cotton wash dress, after which she smoked from an old sacred tubular pipe about six inches long, which had a ferrule about two inches wide of polished stone at the large end and a smooth wooden mouthpiece inset with diamond-shaped pieces of abalone shell. At each puff on the pipe she exhaled with a hissing sound and called out in a loud voice "Shah!" looking upward and all around the room. The spectators then kept silence. She smoked five or six puffs and then handed the pipe to an old woman assistant who sat on her right. The assistant held out the pipe in her right hand and began to recite, in a loud voice, a formula prayer calling upon the spirits to aid the shaman and give her power. Immediately after the prayer the shaman began to sing, very low, and the spectators sang a second part accompanying her. She sang louder and louder, her assistant singing her song, while the spectators sang the second part to the main song. As she sang louder and faster she reached behind her for her staff of hazelwood, which was about five feet long, and held it out from her with her right hand using the floor as a pivot for one end and shaking it in a circular motion as she sang. As soon as the spiritual power became strong enough, she got up and began dancing on the mat in front of her chair, holding out the staff in different directions with first her right and then her left hand, singing and stamping in time to the music. She stopped singing at times and let the assistant and the spectators carry on the song, breaking in at intervals and singing again. As she became more excited she handed the staff to a man sitting on her left and danced to different parts of the room, sometimes singing, always facing the east, holding up first one arm and then the other and sometimes both of them. At this point the assistant took out some live coals and put them on top of the stove and then burned angelica root on them until the smoke penetrated to all parts of the room. (Angelica root is sacred to the spirits and induces them to enter the house, and gives spiritual power to the shaman.) The shaman finally danced to one corner where some children were sleeping and got a little girl. She held the two hands of the child lifted above the head and danced with her to the patient's bed, and back and forth for a few times. She then discarded the child, who went back to bed, and danced to the side and in front of the patient's bed, holding out her hands towards him. By this time she was so excited and exhausted that she was panting audibly and two men stood behind her ready to catch her when she fell. Suddenly she threw herself backwards onto the floor, screaming piercingly. The men caught hold of her and eased her to a better position. The singing stopped abruptly. Her hands grasped her throat and her legs and body contorted as if in an epileptic fit. The men held her to prevent injury, and finally partly lifted and dragged her to her chair as the paroxysm lessened. She remained in her chair, half reclining, half resting, and moaning for some little time. She then began to hiccough, cough, retch and vomit, holding her two hands in her mouth, until she extracted the pain which had entered her, through her hands, from the patient's body. She stood up and held her two hands clasped together, with the pain between the palms. As soon as she had regained her breath, she opened her hands cautiously and examined the pain, laughed a little, and started to sing and dance again in order to dispose of the pain, which she sent away in the direction from which it came. The spectators sang with her until she sent the pain away, then everyone stopped singing, talked of everyday happenings, smoked cigarettes, and jested, while the shaman rested.

The second part of the ceremony began with the reciting of the prayer, by the assistant. The shaman sang a different song and danced as before, but this time instead of burning angelica root the assistant stood in front of her chair and danced with two eagle feathers in her right hand. She sat down as the shaman began panting and was about to extract the pain. The shaman got the pain from the patient so swiftly this second time, that she was knocked over flat on her back, the supporting men failing to catch her—a very hard fall—she became unconscious but revived after having a cup of water thrown in her face. She then began to moan and groan and contort with all the appearances of great suffering. The men dragged her to her chair, where she rested, moaning, and then coughed and vomited up the pain, as before, stood up and began dancing and singing again, accompanied by the spectators. After regaining her breath she opened her hands and looked at the pain, laughed again and got down on all fours, and walked like a dog. She danced, on all fours, to the door, which was opened for her, and took the pain "outside, where it belonged," sending it in the direction from which it came. She explained to me afterward that poison is made by cutting off the end of a dog's nose and boiling it and using the water to sprinkle on the ground where the victim steps on it or breathes the evaporating liquid, or by putting it on the end of a stick or string and dangling it in front of the sleeping victim's nose or open mouth. The person administering the poison puts on a dog's skin and goes out among people at night to find his victims. He is counted as a "devil" and when this kind of a pain is extracted the shaman is impelled to act like a dog in order to send the pain away in the direction from which it came. This conception of a devil is, however, intrusive from the Wiyot and was not used by the Bear River Indians in olden times.

The third pain was extracted by the same ceremony except that there was no burning of angelica nor dancing by the assistant with the two eagle feathers; instead, the shaman opened the stove as she danced, took out a handful of live coals, put them on top of the stove, and used them with bare hands to light her doctoring pipe, which she smoked for a time while dancing. She again took the little girl and danced with her, taking the pain out of the patient through the child's hands.

The next two pains were extracted by repeating the ceremony, again with some variation. The assistant shouted out the prayer, then the shaman sang a different song, danced but failed to finish taking out the pain. She went back to her chair, smoked the pipe and began all over again with the same song, this time carrying the ceremony through to the end.

After the fifth pain was extracted, the regular shaman's treatment for the patient was finished and she sat down and smoked cigarettes while the assistant gave the last dance.

The assistant smoked the doctoring pipe, and at each expulsion of smoke called out "Shah," and looked upward and around the room. She took out her two eagle feathers and held them in her right hand. With her left hand she threw a basket, about eight inches in diameter, on the floor in front of her feet. She began to sing, the spectators accompanying her, and finally got to her feet, picked up the basket, and began to dance, waving the feathers and making a scooping and brushing motion with them and the basket, all the while singing and ejaculating "Shah!" She danced all over the room—always facing east—into the corners, calling out "Shah!", and at last danced to the door, which was opened for her, where she waved, brushed and scooped with basket and feathers, and sang for some time crying "Shah!" "Shah!" Then the door was closed, everyone stopped singing, and she sat down. This dance was explained to me afterward by the shaman as being always the finish of the curative ceremony, and is made to drive out all evil spirits that may be hovering around the room or house.

Everyone talked and smoked as soon as the assistant finished dancing. The shaman got up and went to the river and swam, although it was 1:30 a.m. and raining. After the shaman returned from her swim, we all went to the patient's parents' house, where we had a big feast of boiled eels, fish, eggs, bread, coffee, etc. The assemblage broke up at 2:30 a.m. and everyone went home.

Witchcraft is another form of action that is indentifiable in terms of the characteristics of place. A witch is one who is out of place socially and spiritually, one who seeks to bring harm to others by willfully contradicting the established social and cosmic order. Witches are commonly associated with night, with the dead, with neglect of social responsibility, with malevolence toward all humans.

Clown performances are important formal and often religious occasions. These displays of "out of place" actions, when controlled by the occasion of sanctioned ritual performance, permit a community to participate vicariously in the forbidden or in the pursuit of human desires unreigned by cultural restrictions. This not only provides release from the tensions of social restrictions, it provides members of a community to see the foolishness and meaninglessness of such actions.

These clown acts can run a rather extensive gamut from backwards actions, exaggerations, and mild social criticism to the performance of acts which raise the very issue of the nature of being human. The actions of clowns may inspire gales of laughter or shock and disbelief. We see this full range in the following example of a clown performance at Zuni in the late nineteenth century as described by John G. Bourke who was a Captain in the U.S. Army. He was visiting Frank Hamilton Cushing who was an ethnologist living at Zuni.

### *THE URINE DANCE OF THE ZUNIS described by John G. Bourke*[14]

On the evening of November 17, 1881, during my stay in the village of Zuni, New Mexico, the *Nehue-Cue*, one of the secret orders of the Zunis, sent word to Mr. F.

Cushing (whose guest I was) that they would do us the unusual honor of coming to our house to give us one of their characteristic dances, which Cushing said, was unprecedented.

The squaws of the Governor's family put the long "living room" to rights, sweeping the floor and sprinkling it with water to lay the dust. Soon after dark the dancers entered; they were twelve in number, two being boys. The centre men were naked with the exception of black breech-clouts of archaic style. The hair was worn naturally with a bunch of wild turkey feathers tied in front, and one of corn-husks over each ear. White bands were painted across the face at eyes and mouth. Each wore a collar or neck-cloth of black woollen stuff. Broad white bands, one inch wide, were painted around the body at the navel, around the arms, the legs at mid-thighs and knees. Tortoise-shell rattles hung from the right knee. Blue woollen footless leggings were worn with low cut moccasons, and in the right hand, each waved a wand made of an ear of corn, trimmed with the plumage of the wild turkey and macaw. The others were arrayed in old cast-off American army clothing, and all wore white cotton night-caps, with cornhusks twisted into the hair at top of head and ears. Several wore, in addition to the tortoise-shell rattles, strings of brass sleigh-bells at knees. One was more grotesquely attired than the rest in a long, India-rubber gossamer "over all" and a pair of goggles, painted white, over his eyes. His general "get up" was a spirited take-off upon a Mexican priest. Another was a very good counterfeit of a young woman.

To the accompaniment of an oblong drum, and of the rattles and bells spoken of, they shuffled into the long room, crammed with spectators of both sexes, and of all sizes and ages. Their song was apparently a ludicrous reference to everything and everybody in sight, Cushing, Mendeleff and myself receiving special attention, to the uncontrolled merriment of the red-skinned listeners. I had taken my station at one side of the room, seated upon the banquette, and having in front of me a rude bench or table upon which was a small coal-oil lamp. I suppose that in the halo diffused by the feeble light and in my "stained-glass attitude," I must have borne some resemblance to the pictures of saints hanging upon the walls of old Mexican churches; to such a fancied resemblance, I at least attribute the performance which followed.

The dancers suddenly wheeled into line, threw themselves on their knees before my table, and with extravagant beatings of breast, began an outlandish but faithful mockery of a Mexican Catholic congregation at vespers. One bawled out a parody upon the Pater Noster, another mumbled along in the manner of an old man reciting the rosary, while the fellow with the India-rubber coat jumped up, and began a passionate exhortation or sermon, which for mimetic fidelity was inimitable. This kept the audience laughing with sore sides for some moments, until at a signal from the leader, the dancers suddenly countermarched out of the room, in single file, as they had entered.

An interlude followed of ten minutes, during which the dusty floor was sprinkled by men who spat water forcibly from their mouths. The *Nehue Cue* reentered; this time two of their number were stark naked. Their singing was very peculiar and sounded like a chorus of chimney-sweeps, and their dance became a stiff-legged jump, with heels kept twelve inches apart. After they had ambled around the room two or three times, Cushing announced in the Zuni language that a "feast" was ready for them, at which they loudly roared their approbation and advanced to strike hands with the munificent "Americanos," addressing us in a funny gibberish of broken Spanish, English, and Zuni. They then squatted upon the ground and consumed with zest, large "ollas" full of tea, and dishes of hard tack and sugar. As they were about finishing this, a squaw entered, carrying an "olla" of urine, of which the filthy brutes drank heartily.

I refused to believe the evidence of my senses, and asked Cushing if that were really human urine. "Why, certainly," replied he, "and here comes more of it."

This time it was a large tin pailful, not less than two gallons. I was standing by the squaw as she offered this strange and abominable refreshment. She made a motion with her hand to indicate to me that it was urine, and one of the old men repeated the Spanish word *mear* (to urinate), while my sense of smell demonstrated the truth of their statements.

The dancers swallowed great draughts, smacked their lips, and, amid the roaring merriment of the spectators, remarked that it was very, very good. The clowns were now upon their mettle, each trying to surpass his neighbors in feats of nastiness. One swallowed a fragment of corn-husk, saying he thought it very good and better than bread; his vis à vis attempted to chew and gulp down a piece of filthy rag. Another expressed regret that the dance had not been held out of doors, in one of the plazas; there they could show what they could do. There, they always made it a point of honor to eat the excrement of men and dogs.

For my own part I felt satisfied with the omission, particularly as the room, stuffed with one hundred Zunis, had become so foul and filthy as to be almost unbearable. The dance, as good luck would have it, did not last many minutes, and we soon had a chance to run into the refreshing night air.

To this outline description of a disgusting rite I have little to add. The Zunis, in explanation, stated that the *Nehue-Cue* were a Medicine Order which held these dances from time to time to inure the stomachs of members to any kind of food, no matter how revolting.

## NOTES

1. For further discussion of the symbolic language of place see Sam D. Gill, *Native American Religions*, ch. 1.
2. See also Alfonso Ortiz, "The Tewa World View," in *Teachings from the American Earth: Indian Religion and Philosophy*, ed. Dennis and Barbara Tedlock (New York: Liveright, 1975), pp. 179–189.
3. A. Irving Hallowell, "Ojibwa Ontology, Behavior, and World View," in *Culture in History: Essays in Honor of Paul Radin*, ed. Stanley Diamond (New York: Columbia University Press, 1960), pp. 19–52. See also Elaine Jahner, "The Spiritual Landscape," *Parabola* II (1977):32–48.
4. A selection from Robin Ridington, "Beaver Dreaming and Singing" in "Pilot Not Commander: Essays in Memory of Diamond Jenness," ed. Pat and Jim Lotz, *Anthropologica*, Special Issue, n.s. #1 and 2 (1971): 115–128. Reprinted by permission of Robin Ridington.
5. Cosmos Mindeleff, *Navaho Houses* (Washington, D.C.: Bureau of American Ethnology, Annual Report 17, Part 2, 1898), pp. 507–8.
6. Frank Mitchell, *Navajo Blessingway Singer*, from *The Autobiography of Frank Mitchell, 1881–1967*, ed. Charlotte J. Frisbie and David P. McAllester (Tuscon: University of Arizona Press, copyright 1978), pp. 244–45. Reprinted by permission of The University of Arizona Press.
7. For a survey of types of origin stories see Anna B. Rooth, "The Creation Myths of the North American Indians," *Anthropos* 52 (1957):497–508.
8. Franz Boas, *Tsimshian Mythology*, Bureau of American Ethnology, Annual Report # 31, Washington, D.C., 1916, p. 60. Notes omitted. Reprinted by permission of the Smithsonian Institution.

9. Robert H. Lowie, "Shoshonean Tales," *Journal of American Folklore* 37 (1924):172. Reprinted by permission of the American Folklore Society.
10. Jarold Ramsey, "Three Wasco-Warm Springs Stories," *Western Folklore* 31 (April 1972):119. Told by Mrs. Alice Florendo. Reprinted by permission of the California Folklore Society.
11. H. R. Voth, *The Traditions of the Hopi* (Chicago: Field Museum, Anthropology Series, vol. 8, 1905), p. 198.
12. James R. Walker, *Lakota Belief and Ritual*, ed. Raymond J. De Mallie and Elaine A. Jahner (Lincoln: University of Nebraska Press, 1980), pp. 176–180. Notes omitted. Copyright © 1980 by the University of Nebraska Press. Reprinted by permission of the University of Nebraska Press.
13. Gladys A. Nomland, "A Bear River Shaman's Curative Dance," *American Anthropologist* 33 (1931):38–41. Notes omitted. Reprinted by permission of the American Anthropological Association.
14. John G. Bourke, "The Urine Dance of the Zunis," Proceedings of the American Association for the Advancement of Science, 34th Meeting, August, 1885. (Salem, Mass.: The Salem Press, 1886), pp. 400–403.

# CHAPTER 3

# *Nonliteracy, Language, and Oral Traditions*

## INTRODUCTION

In Native American cultures there is a rich array of language acts that are central to religious life. Prayers, songs, and oral performances of stories are the core of many formal religious occasions. Even ordinary daily speech is colored by complex and sophisticated principles of construction and usage, which often reflect world view and religious belief. Unfortunately, the fact that Native American languages were not written has too commonly suggested that Native American languages are crude and undeveloped, a view which couldn't be further from accurate. We have not adequately come to appreciate the extent to which the mode of communication is important to the way one thinks and conceptualizes, as well as communicates.[1] The following are selections of a variety of genre of Native American language acts and essays that interpret and discuss them.

## LANGUAGE: A CONSTITUTIVE FORCE OF REALITY

Kiowa author N. Scott Momaday, addressing the First Convocation of American Indian Scholars in 1970, spoke on the notions of imagination and storytelling as central to the way Native Americans have commonly created their world and placed themselves meaningfully within it. He shows that Native American oral traditions are not meaningless stories of fanciful characters and places, but that they engage history and human culture in a vital manner. We need not subscribe totally to a theory of language-determinism to appreciate the obvious constitutive power of language in its various forms in Native American cultures.

## THE MAN MADE OF WORDS by N. Scott Momaday[2]

I want to try to put several different ideas together this morning. And in the process, I hope to indicate something about the nature of the relationship between language and experience. It seems to me that in a certain sense we are all made of words; that our most essential being consists in language. It is the element in which we think and dream and act, in which we live our daily lives. There is no way in which we can exist apart from the morality of a verbal dimension.

In one of the discussions yesterday the question "What is an American Indian?" was raised.

The answer of course is that an Indian is an idea which a given man has of himself. And it is a moral idea, for it accounts for the way in which he reacts to other men and to the world in general. And that idea, in order to be realized completely, has to be expressed.

I want to say some things then about this moral and verbal dimension in which we live. I want to say something about such things as ecology and storytelling and the imagination. Let me tell you a story:

One night a strange thing happened. I had written the greater part of *The Way to Rainy Mountain*—all of it, in fact, except the epilogue. I had set down the last of the old Kiowa tales, and I had composed both the historical and the autobiographical commentaries for it. I had the sense of being out of breath, of having said what it was in me to say on that subject. The manuscript lay before me in the bright light, small, to be sure, but complete; or nearly so. I had written the second of the two poems in which that book is framed. I had uttered the last word, as it were. And yet a whole, penultimate piece was missing. I began once again to write.

During the first hours after midnight on the morning of November 13, 1833, it seemed that the world was coming to an end. Suddenly the stillness of the night was broken; there were brilliant flashes of light in the sky, light of such intensity that people were awakened by it. With the speed and density of a driving rain, stars were falling in the universe. Some were brighter than Venus; one was said to be as large as the moon. I went on to say that that event, the falling of the stars on North America, that explosion of meteors which occurred 137 years ago, is among the earliest entries in the Kiowa calendars. So deeply impressed upon the imagination of the Kiowas is that old phenomenon that it is remembered still; it has become a part of the racial memory.

"The living memory," I wrote, "and the verbal tradition which transcends it, were brought together for me once and for all in the person of Ko-sahn." It seemed eminently right for me to deal, after all, with that old woman. Ko-sahn is among the most venerable people I have ever known. She spoke and sang to me one summer afternoon in Oklahoma. It was like a dream. When I was born she was already old: she was a grown woman when my grandparents came into the world. She sat perfectly still, folded over on herself. It did not seem possible that so many years—a century of years—could be so compacted and distilled. Her voice shuddered, but it did not fail. Her songs were sad. An old whimsy, a delight in language and in remembrance, shone in her one good eye. She conjured up the past, imagining perfectly the long continuity of her being. She imagined the lovely young girl, wild and vital, she had been. She imagined the Sun Dance:

There was an old, old woman. She had something on her back. The boys went out to see. The old woman had a bag full of earth on her back. It was a certain kind of sandy earth. That is what they must have in the lodge. The dancers must dance upon the sandy earth. The old woman held a digging tool in her hand. She turned towards the south and pointed with her lips. It was like a kiss, and she began to sing:

We have brought the earth.
Now it is time to play.

As old as I am, I still have the feeling of play. That was the beginning of the Sun Dance.

By this time I was back into the book, caught up completely in the act of writing. I had projected myself—imagined myself—out of the room and out of time. I was there with Ko-sahn in the Oklahoma July. We laughed easily together; I felt that I had known her all of my life—all of hers. I did not want to let her go. But I had come to the end. I set down, almost grudgingly, the last sentences:

It was—all of this and more—a quest, a going forth upon the way of Rainy Mountain. Probably Ko-sahn too is dead now. At times, in the quiet of evening, I think she must have wondered, dreaming, who she was. Was she become in her sleep that old purveyor of the sacred earth, perhaps, that ancient one who, old as she was, still had the feeling of play? And in her mind, at times, did she see the falling stars?

For some time I sat looking down at these words on the page, trying to deal with the emptiness that had come about inside of me. The words did not seem real. I could scarcely believe that they made sense, that they had anything whatsoever to do with meaning. In desperation almost, I went back over the final paragraphs, backwards and forwards, hurriedly. My eyes fell upon the name Ko-sahn. And all at once everything seemed suddenly to refer to that name. The name seemed to humanize the whole complexity of language. All at once, absolutely, I had the sense of the magic of words and of names. Ko-sahn, I said, and I said again KO-SAHN.

Then it was that that ancient, one-eyed woman Ko-sahn stepped out of the language and stood before me on the page. I was amazed. Yet it seemed to me entirely appropriate that this should happen.

"I was just now writing about you," I replied, stammering. "I thought—forgive me—I thought that perhaps you were . . . that you had . . . "

"No," she said. And she cackled, I thought. And she went on. "You have imagined me well, and so I am. You have imagined that I dream, and so I do. I have seen the falling stars."

"But all of this, this imagining," I protested, "this has taken place—is taking place in my mind. You are not actually here, not here in this room." It occurred to me that I was being extremely rude, but I could not help myself. She seemed to understand.

"Be careful of your pronouncements, grandson," she answered. "You imagine that I am here in this room, do you not? That is worth something. You see, I have existence, whole being, in your imagination. It is but one kind of being, to be sure, but it is perhaps the best of all kinds. If I am not here in this room, grandson, then surely neither are you."

"I think I see what you mean," I said meekly. I felt justly rebuked. "Tell me, grandmother, how old are you?"

"I do not know," she replied. "There are times when I think that I am the oldest woman on earth. You know, the Kiowas came into the world through a hollow log. In my mind's eye I have seen them emerge, one by one, from the mouth of the log. I have seen them so clearly, how they were dressed, how delighted they were to see the world around them. I must have been there. And I must have taken part in the old migration of the Kiowas from the Yellowstone to the Southern Plains, near the Big Horn River, and I have seen the red cliffs of Palo Duro Canyon. I was with those who were camped in the Wichita Mountains when the stars fell."

"You are indeed very old," I said, "and you have seen many things."

"Yes, I imagine that I have," she replied. Then she turned slowly around, nodding once, and receded into the language I had made. And then I imagined I was alone in the room.

Once in his life a man ought to concentrate his mind upon the remembered earth, I believe. He ought to give himself up to a particular landscape in his experience, to look at it from as many angles as he can, to wonder about it, to dwell upon it. He ought to imagine that he touches it with his hands at every season and listens to the sounds that are made upon it. He ought to imagine the creatures that are there and all the faintest motions in the wind. He ought to recollect the glare of noon and all the colors of the dawn and dusk.

The Wichita Mountains rise out of the Southern Plains in a long crooked line that runs from east to west. The mountains are made of red earth, and of rock that is neither red nor blue but some very rare admixture of the two like the feathers of certain birds. They are not so high and mighty as the mountains of the Far West, and they bear a different relationship to the land around them. One does not imagine that they are distinctive in themselves, or indeed that they exist apart from the plain in any sense. If you try to think of them in the abstract, they lose the look of mountains. They are preeminently an expression of the larger landscape, more perfectly organic than one can easily imagine. To behold these mountains from the plain is one thing; to see the plain from the mountains is something else. I have stood on the top of Mt. Scott and seen the earth below, bending out into the whole circle of the sky. The wind runs always close upon the slopes, and there are times when you can hear the rush of it like water in the ravines.

Here is the hub of an old commerce. A hundred years ago the Kiowas and Comanches journeyed outward from the Wichitas in every direction, seeking after mischief and medicine, horses and hostages. Sometimes they went away for years, but they always returned, for the land had got hold of them. It is a consecrated place, and even now there is something of the wilderness about it. There is a game preserve in the hills. Animals graze away in the open meadows or, closer by, keep to the shadows of the groves: antelope and deer, longhorn and buffalo. It was here, the Kiowas say, that the first buffalo came into the world.

The yellow grassy knoll that is called Rainy Mountain lies a short distance to the north and west. There, on the west side, is the ruin of an old school where my grandmother went as a wild young girl in blanket and braids to learn of numbers and of names in English. And there she is buried.

Most is your name the name of this dark stone.
Deranged in death, the mind to be inheres
Forever in the nominal unknown,
Who listens here and now to hear your name.
The early sun, red as a hunter's moon,
Runs in the plain. The mountain burns and shines;
And silence is the long approach of noon
Upon the shadow that your name defines—
And death this cold, black density of stone.

I am interested in the way that a man looks at a given landscape and takes possession of it in his blood and brain. For this happens, I am certain, in the ordinary motion of life. None of us lives apart from the land entirely; such an isolation is unimaginable. We have sooner or later to come to terms with the world around us—and I mean especially the physical world, not only as it is revealed to us immediately through our senses, but also as it is perceived more truly in the long turn of seasons and of years. And we must come to moral terms. There is no alternative, I believe, if we are to realize and maintain our humanity; for our humanity must consist in part in the ethical as well as the practical ideal of preservation. And particularly here and now is that true. We Americans need now more than ever before—and indeed more than we know—to imagine who and what we are with respect to the earth and sky. I am talking about an act of the imagination essentially, and the concept of an American land ethic.

It is no doubt more difficult to imagine in 1970 the landscape of America as it was in, say, 1900. Our whole experience as a nation in this century has been a repudiation of the pastoral ideal which informs so much of the art and literature of the nineteenth century. One effect of the Technological Revolution has been to uproot us from the soil. We have become disoriented, I believe; we have suffered a kind of psychic dislocation of ourselves in time and space. We may be perfectly sure of where we are in relation to the supermarket and the next coffee break, but I doubt that any of us knows where he is in relation to the stars and to the solstices. Our sense of the natural order has become dull and unreliable. Like the wilderness itself, our sphere of instinct has diminished in proportion as we have failed to imagine truly what it is. And yet I believe that it is possible to formulate an ethical idea of the land—a notion of what it is and must be in our daily lives—and I believe moreover that it is absolutely necessary to do so.

It would seem on the surface of things that a land ethic is something that is alien to, or at least dormant in, most Americans. Most of us in general have developed an attitude of indifference toward the land. In terms of my own experience, it is difficult to see how such an attitude could ever have come about.

Ko-sahn could remember where my grandmother was born. "It was just there," she said, pointing to a tree, and the tree was like a hundred others that grew up in the broad depression of the Washita River. I could see nothing to indicate that anyone had ever been there, spoken so much as a word, or touched the tips of his fingers to the tree. But in her memory Ko-sahn could see the child. I think she must have remembered my grandmother's voice, for she seemed for a long moment to listen and to hear. There was a still, heavy heat upon that place; I had the sense that ghosts were gathering there.

And in the racial memory, Ko-sahn had seen the falling stars. For her there was no distinction between the individual and the racial experience, even as there was none between the mythical and the historical. Both were realized for her in the one memory, and that was of the land. This landscape, in which she had lived for a hundred years, was the common denominator of everything that she knew and would ever know—and her knowledge was profound. Her roots ran deep into the earth, and from those depths she drew strength enough to hold still against all the forces of chance and disorder. And she drew strength enough to hold still against all the forces of change and disorder. And she drew therefrom the sustenance of meaning and of mystery as well. The falling stars were not for Ko-sahn an isolated or accidental phenomenon. She had a great personal investment in that awful commotion of light in the night sky. For it remained to be imagined. She must at last deal with it in words; she must appropriate it to her understanding of the whole universe. And, again, when she spoke of the Sun Dance, it was an essential expression of her relationship to the life of the earth and to the sun and moon.

In Ko-sahn and in her people we have always had the example of a deep, ethical regard for the land. We had better learn from it: Surely that ethic is merely latent in ourselves. It must now be activated, I believe. We Americans must come again to a moral comprehension of the earth and air. We must live according to the principle of a land ethic. The alternative is that we shall not live at all.

Ecology is perhaps the most important subject of our time. I can't think of an issue in which the Indian has more authority or a greater stake. If there is one thing which truly distinguishes him, it is surely his regard of and for the natural world.

But let me get back to the matter of storytelling.

I must have taken part in that old migration of the Kiowas from the Yellowstone to the Southern Plains, for I have seen antelope bounding in the tall grass near the Big Horn River, and I have seen the ghost forests in the Black Hills. Once I saw the red cliffs of Palo Duro Canyon. I was with those who were camped in the Wichita Mountains when the stars fell. "You are very old," I said, "and you have seen many things." "Yes, I imagine that I have," she replied. Then she turned slowly around, nodding once, and receded into the language I had made. And then I imagined that I was alone in the room.

Who is the storyteller? Of whom is the story told? What is there in the darkness to imagine into being? What is there to dream and to relate? What happens when I or anyone exerts the force of language upon the unknown?

These are the questions which interest me most.

If there is any absolute assumption in back of my thoughts tonight, it is this: We are what we imagine. Our very existence consists in our imagination of ourselves. Our best destiny is to imagine, at least, completely, who and what, and *that* we are. The greatest tragedy that can befall us is to go unimagined.

Writing is recorded speech. In order to consider seriously the meaning of language and of literature, we must consider first the meaning of the oral tradition.

By way of suggesting one or two definitions which may be useful to us, let me pose a few basic questions and tentative answers:

(1) What is the oral tradition?

The oral tradition is that process by which the myths, legends, tales, and lore of a people are formulated, communicated, and preserved in language by word of mouth, as opposed to writing. Or, it is a *collection* of such things.

(2) With reference to the matter of oral tradition, what is the relationship between art and reality?

In the context of these remarks, the matter of oral tradition suggests certain particularities of art and reality. Art, for example . . . involves an oral dimension which is based markedly upon such considerations as memorization, intonation, inflection, precision of statement, brevity, rhythm, pace, and dramatic effect. Moreover, myth, legend, and lore, according to our definitions of these terms, imply a separate and distinct order of reality. We are concerned here not so much with an accurate representation of actuality, but with the realization of the imaginative experience.

(3) How are we to conceive of language? What are words?

For our purposes, words are audible sounds, invented by man to communicate his thoughts and feelings. Each word has a conceptual content, however slight; and each word communicates associations of feeling. Language is the means by which words proceed to the formulation of meaning and emotional effect.

(4) What is the nature of storytelling? What are the purposes and possibilities of that act?

Storytelling is imaginative and creative in nature. It is an act by which man strives to realize his capacity for wonder, meaning and delight. It is also a process in which man invests and preserves himself in the context of ideas. Man tells stories in order to understand his experience, whatever it may be. The possibilities of storytelling are precisely those of understanding the human experience.

(5) What is the relationship between what a man is and what he says—or between what he is, and what he thinks he is?

This relationship is both tenuous and complicated. Generally speaking, man has consummate being in language, and there only. The state of human *being* is an idea, an idea which man has of himself. Only when he is embodied in an idea, and the idea is realized in language, can man take possession of himself. In our particular frame of reference, this is to say that man achieves the fullest realization of his humanity in such an art and product of the imagination as literature—and here I use the term "literature" in its broadest sense. This is admittedly a moral view of the question, but literature is itself a moral view, and it is a view of morality.

Now let us return to the falling stars. And let me apply a new angle of vision to that event—let me proceed this time from a slightly different point of view:

In this winter of 1833 the Kiowas were camped on Elm Fork, a branch of the Red River west of the Wichita Mountains. In the preceding summer they had suffered a massacre at the hands of the Osages, and Tai-me, the sacred Sun Dance Doll and most powerful medicine of the tribe, had been stolen. At no time in the history of their migration from the north, and in the evolution of their plains culture, had the Kiowas been more vulnerable to despair. The loss of Tai-me was a deep psychological wound. In the early cold of November 13 there occurred over North America an explosion of meteors. The Kiowas were awakened by the sterile light of falling stars, and they ran out into the false day and were terrified.

The year the stars fell is, as I have said, among the earliest entries in the Kiowa calendars, and it is permanent in the Kiowa mind. There was symbolic meaning in that November sky. With the coming of natural dawn there began a new and darker age for the Kiowa people; the last culture to evolve on this continent began to decline. Within four years of the falling stars the Kiowas signed their first treaty with the government: within twenty, four major epidemics of smallpox and Asiatic cholera destroyed more than half their number; and within scarcely more than a generation their horses were taken from them and the herds of buffalo were slaughtered and left to waste upon the plains.

Do you see what happens when the imagination is superimposed upon the historical event? It becomes a story. The whole piece becomes more deeply invested with meaning. The terrified Kiowas, when they had regained possession of themselves, did indeed imagine that the falling stars were symbolic of their being and their destiny. They accounted for themselves with reference to that awful memory. They appropriated it, recreated it, fashioned it into an image of themselves—imagined it.

Only by means of that act could they bear what happened to them thereafter. No defeat, no humiliation, no suffering was beyond their power to endure, for none of it was meaningless. They could say to themselves, "yes, it was all meant to be in its turn. The order of the world was broken, it was clear. Even the stars were shaken loose in the night sky." The imagination of meaning was not much, perhaps, but it was all they had, and it was enough to sustain them.

One of my very favorite writers, Isak Dinesen, said this: "All sorrows can be borne if you put them into a story or tell a story about them."

Some three or four years ago, I became interested in the matter of "oral tradition" as that term is used to designate a rich body of pre-literate storytelling in and among the indigenous cultures of North America. Specifically, I began to wonder about the way in which myths, legends, and lore evolve into that mature condition of expression which we call "literature." For indeed literature is, I believe, the end-product of an evolutionary process, and the so-called "oral tradition" is primarily a stage within that process, a stage that is indispensable and perhaps original as well.

I set out to find a traditional material that should be at once oral only, unified and broadly representative of cultural values. And in this undertaking, I had a certain advantage, because I am myself an American Indian, and I have lived many years of my life on the Indian reservations of the southwest. From the time I was first able to comprehend and express myself in language, I heard the stories of the Kiowas, those "coming out" people of the Southern plains from whom I am descended.

Three hundred years ago the Kiowa lived in the mountains of what is now western Montana, near the headwaters of the Yellowstone River. Near the end of the 17th century they began a long migration to the south and east. They passed along the present border between Montana and Wyoming to the Black Hills and proceeded southward along the eastern slopes of the Rockies to the Wichita Mountains in the Southern Plains (Southwestern Oklahoma).

I mention this old journey of the Kiowas because it is in a sense definitive of the tribal mind; it is essential to the way in which the Kiowas think of themselves as a people. The migration was carried on over a course of many generations and many hundreds of miles. When it began, the Kiowas were a desperate and divided people, given up wholly to a day-by-day struggle for survival. When it ended, they were a race of centaurs, a lordly society of warriors and buffalo hunters. Along the way they had acquired horses, a knowledge and possession of the open land, and a sense of destiny. In alliance with the Comanches, they ruled the southern plains for a hundred years.

That migration—and the new golden age to which it led—is closely reflected in Kiowa legend and lore. Several years ago I retraced the route of that migration, and when I came to the end, I interviewed a number of Kiowa elders and obtained from them a remarkable body of history and learning, fact and fiction—all of it in the oral tradition and all of it valuable in its own right and for its own sake.

I compiled a small number of translations from the Kiowa, arranged insofar as it was possible to indicate the chronological and geographical progression of the migration itself. This collection (and it was nothing more than a collection at first) was published under the title *"The Journey of Tai-me"* in a fine edition limited to 100 hand printed copies.

This original collection has just been re-issued, together with illustrations and a commentary, in a trade edition entitled *"The Way to Rainy Mountain."* The principle of narration which informs this latter work is in a sense elaborate and experimental, and I should like to say one or two things about it. Then, if I may, I should like to illustrate the way in which the principle works, by reading briefly from the text. And finally, I should like to comment in some detail upon one of the tales in particular.

There are three distinct narrative voices in *"The Way to Rainy Mountain"*—the mythical, the historical, and the immediate. Each of the translations is followed by two kinds of commentary; the first is documentary and the second is privately reminiscent. Together, they serve, hopefully, to validate the oral tradition to an extent that might not otherwise be possible. The commentaries are meant to provide a context in which the elements of oral tradition might transcend the categorical limits of prehistory, anonymity, and archaeology in the narrow sense.

All of this is to say that I believe there is a way (first) in which the elements of oral tradition can be shown, dramatically, to exist within the framework of a literary continuance, a deeper and more vital context of language and meaning than that which is generally taken into account; and (secondly) in which those elements can be located, with some precision on an evolutionary scale.

The device of the journey is pecularily appropriate to such a principle of narration as this. And *"The Way to Rainy Mountain"* is a whole journey, intricate with notion and meaning; and it is made with the whole memory, that experience of the mind which is legendary as well as historical, personal as well as cultural.

Without further qualification, let me turn to the text itself.

The Kiowa tales which are contained in *"The Way to Rainy Mountain"* constitute a kind of literary chronicle. In a sense they are the milestones of that old migration in which the Kiowas journeyed from the Yellowstone to the Washita. They recorded a transformation of the tribal mind, as it encounters for the first time the landscape of the Great Plains; they evoke the sense of search and discovery. Many of the tales are very old, and they have not until now been set down in writing. Among them there is one that stands out in my mind. When I was a child, my father told me the story of the arrowmaker, and he told it to me many times, for I fell in love with it. I have no memory that is older than that of hearing it. This is the way it goes:

If an arrow is well made, it will have tooth marks upon it. That is how you know. The Kiowas made fine arrows and straightened them in their teeth. Then they drew them to the bow to see that they were straight. Once there was a man and his wife. They were alone at night in their tipi. By the light of a fire the man was making arrows. After a while he caught sight of something. There was a small opening in the tipi where two hides had been sewn together. Someone was there on the outside, looking in. The man went on with his work, but he said to his wife, "Someone is standing outside. Do not be afraid. Let us talk easily, as of ordinary things." He took up an arrow and straightened it in his teeth: then, as it was right for him to do, he drew it to the bow and took aim, first in this direction and then in that. And all the while he was talking, as if to his wife. But this is how he spoke: "I know that you are there on the outside, for I can feel your eyes upon me. If you are a Kiowa, you will understand what I am saying, and you will speak your name." But there was no answer, and the man went on in the same way, pointing the arrow all around. At last his aim fell upon the place where his enemy stood, and he let go of the string. The arrow went straight to the enemy's heart.

Heretofore the story of the arrowmaker has been the private possession of a very few, a tenuous link in that most ancient chain of language which we call the oral tradition: tenuous because the tradition itself is so; for as many times as the story has been told, it was always but one generation removed from extinction. But it was held dear, too, on that same account. That is to say, it has been neither more nor less durable than the human voice, and neither more nor less concerned to express the meaning of the human condition. And this brings us to the heart of the matter at hand: The story of the arrowmaker is also a link between language and literature. It is a remarkable act of the mind, a realization of words and the world that is altogether simple and direct, yet nonetheless rare and profound, and it illustrates more clearly than anything else in my own experience, at least, something of the essential character of the imagination—and in particular of that personification which in this instance emerges from it: the man made of words.

It is a fine story, whole, intricately beautiful, precisely realized. It is worth thinking about, for it yields something of value; indeed, it is full of provocation, rich with suggestion and consequent meaning. There is often an inherent danger that we might impose too much of ourselves upon it. It is informed by an integrity that bears examination easily and well, and in the process it seems to appropriate our own reality and experience.

It is significant that the story of the arrowmaker returns in a special way upon itself. It is about language, after all, and it is therefore part and parcel of its own subject; virtually, there is no difference between the telling and that which is told. The point of the story lies, not so much in what the arrowmaker does, but in what he says—and indeed that he says it. The principal fact is that he speaks, and in so doing he places his very life in the balance. It is this aspect of the story which interests me most, for it is here that the language becomes most conscious of itself; we are close to the origin and object of literature, I believe: our sense of the verbal dimension is very keen, and we are aware of something in the nature of language that is at once perilous and compelling. "If you are a Kiowa, you will understand what I am saying, and you will speak your name." Everything is ventured in this simple declaration, which is also a question and a plea. The conditional element with which it begins is remarkably tentative and pathetic; precisely at this moment is the arrowmaker realized completely, and his reality consists in language, and it is poor and precarious. And all of this occurs to him as surely as it does to us. Implicit in that simple occurrence is all of his definition and his destiny, and all of ours. He ventures to speak because he must; language is the repository of his whole knowledge and experience, and it represents the only chance he has for survival. Instinctively, and with great care, he deals in the most honest and basic way with words. "Let us talk easily, as of ordinary things," he says. And of the ominous unknown he asks only the utterance of a name, only the most nominal sign that he is understood, that his words are returned to him on the sheer edge of meaning. But there is no answer, and the arrowmaker knows at once what he has not known before; that his enemy is, and that he has gained an advantage over him. This he knows certainly, and the certainty itself is his advantage, and it is crucial; he makes the most of it. The venture is complete and irrevocable, and it ends in success. The story is meaningful. It is so primarily because it is composed of language, and it is in the nature of language in turn that it proceeds to the formulation of meaning. Moreover, the story of the arrowmaker, as opposed to other stories in general, centers upon his procession of words toward meaning. It seems in fact to turn upon the very idea that language involves the elements of risk and responsibility; and in this it seeks to confirm itself. In a word, it seems to say, everything is a risk. That may be true, and it may also be that the whole of literature rests upon that truth.

The arrowmaker is preeminently the man made of words. He has consummate being in language; it is the world of his origin and of his posterity, and there is no other. But it is a world of definite reality and of infinite possibility. I have come to believe that there is a sense in which the arrowmaker has more nearly perfect being than have other men, by and large, as he imagines himself, whole and vital, going on into the unknown darkness and beyond. And this last aspect of his being is primordial and profound.

And yet the story has it that he is cautious and alone, and we are given to understand that his peril is great and immediate, and that he confronts it in the only way he can. I have no doubt that this is true, and I believe that there are implications which point directly to the determination of our literary experience and which must not be lost upon us. A final word, then, on an essential irony which marks this story and gives peculiar substance to the man made of words. The storyteller is nameless and unlettered. From one point of view we know very little about him, except that he is somehow translated for us in the person of an arrowmaker. But, from another, that is all we need to know. He tells us of his life in language, and of the awful risk involved. It must occur to us that he is one with the arrowmaker and that he has survived, by word of mouth, beyond other men. We said a moment ago that, for the arrowmaker, language represented the only chance of survival. It is worth considering that he survives in our own time, and that he has survived over a period of untold generations.

Certainly the formal language acts of song, prayer and stories testify to the nature and capabilities of Native American languages and religions. We will see ample evidence of this below and in other chapters. Ordinary speech through its grammatical forms, vocabulary, and rules of use, reflects the way in which reality is conceived. It serves members of culture as a means by which to interact with the world, in which they, as members of a particular language community, live. Studies such as A. Irving Hallowell's on the Ojibway and Dorothy Lee's on the Wintu of California, illustrate these factors.[3]

## SONG

Song is often the central and most ubiquitous form of Native American religious expression. The Beaver word for medicine, as we have already noted, is *mayine* which means "his or its song" and, as is widely understood in native North America, songs are given to a person by his or her medicine animal or guardian spirit in dreams or visions. Ruth Underhill's book *Singing for Power* (1938) demonstrates the religious powers of song in the practices of the Papago of southern Arizona. She describes the Papago ritual planting of corn and other crops and the role of song in this process. Through song, the Papago join in beautiful and life-giving chorus with the corn, the insects, the birds, and the entire fertile environment.

### *SINGING UP THE CORN (Papago) described by Ruth Underhill*[4]

It is late July, the moon of rain. The desert riots with purple vetch and yellow rabbit brush, with the huge moons of white poppies and the flamepoints of pink starflowers. Now planting can begin.

Every man has his field at the mouth of a wash where the water comes down after the rains in a swirling red torrent. It floods the land for half a day till the desert sun has sucked it up and the dead dry soil has sucked it down. Then the ground is soft enough for the Papago to thrust into it a sharp-pointed stick which was once his only spade. He stands at the edge of the field, holding his digging stick and a buckskin pouch of corn kernels. Kneeling, he makes his hole and speaks to the seed, in the Papago manner of explaining all acts to Nature lest there be misunderstanding: "Now I place you in the ground. You will grow tall. Then they shall eat, my children and my friends who come from afar."

Carefully he makes the holes, one at each stride, and drops in four corn kernels, and behind him his woman covers the holes with her bare toes. Now the corn will come up "like a feather headdress" and the beans will come "singing together." But not without help. Night after night, the planter walks around his field "singing up the corn." There is a song for corn as high as his knee, for corn waist high, and for corn with the tassel forming. Sometimes, all the men of a village meet together and sing all night, not only for the corn but also for the beans, the squash, and the wild things. They make effigies contrived cunningly out of wood and leaves, for the Papago had few possessions except those supplied by Nature. Sitting in a circle before their rude imitations of the fruits of the earth, the men sang.

Evening is falling.
Pleasantly sounding
Will reverberate
Our songs.

The corn comes up;
It comes up green;
Here upon our fields
White tassels unfold.

The corn comes up;
It comes up green;

Here upon our fields
Green leaves blow in the breeze.

Blue evening falls,
Blue evening falls;
Near by, in every direction,
It sets the corn tassels trembling.

The wind smooths well the ground.
Yonder the wind runs
Upon our fields.
The corn leaves tremble.

On Tecolote fields
The corn is growing green.
I came there, saw the tassels waving in the breeze,
And I whistled softly for joy.

Blowing in the wind,
Singing,
Am I crazy corn?

Blowing in the wind,
Singing,
Am I laughing corn?

[Corn with kernels of two colors is called "crazy corn"; when there are three colors, it is "laughing corn."]

The night moves, singing.
Not sleepy, I.
A stick I cut to represent the corn.
Where I find the yellow bees
There will be much corn.

A little yellow cricket
At the roots of the corn
Is hopping about and singing.

A little yellow cricket
At the roots of the squash
Is hopping about and singing.

[*Corn speaks*:]
The little striped woodpecker
Descends right down into my heart.

[*Man speaks*:]
This my bow
Twangs in the cornfield.

It moves in different directions,
It moves in different directions,
And then it alights
From the south,
On the blue water—
The dragonfly.

It moves in different directions,
It moves in different directions,
And then it stands still

From the south,
On the yellow water—
The dragonfly.

All together, all together they sing—
The red beans.
All together, all together they sing—
The white beans.

Am I not the magic tobacco?
Here I come forth and grow tall.
Am I not the magic tobacco?
The blue hummingbird finds my flowers.
Above them softly he is humming.

At last they sing the harvest song, as the corn of different colors speaks from the harvester's arms.

Truly most comfortably you embrace me:
I am the blue corn.
Truly most comfortably you embrace me:
I am the red corn.

## PRAYER

Despite the widespread importance of prayer among Native Americans, few tribes have prayers as extensive and complex as the Navajo. Anthologies of Native American poetry often present segments of Native American prayers and the poetic quality of these prayers is evident. But what is not adequately appreciated is that prayers are understood as having power and are uttered in order that some effect might be achieved. Such is the case in the Navajo prayer below. It is recited in the midst of a complex ceremonial commonly lasting nine consecutive nights and the intervening eight days in which as many as five hundred songs are sung in a given sequence and many hundreds of complex ritual actions are performed, all without the aid of written texts. The ceremonial is performed to cure a Navajo person of an illness suffered and the prayers recited in the ceremonial are understood by Navajos as essential to the power of the ceremonial to cure. Navajo prayers are not atypical among Native American prayers in this respect. We must begin to better understand that while Native American oral traditions occur in many forms and appear often highly poetic, even to those unfamiliar with their place in culture or their intended use, their poetic quality is often secondary to or directed toward the participation in effective action in the world.

### *Navajo Nightway Prayer*[5]

*Tse'gehi*

House made of dawn.
House made of the dark cloud.
House made of male rain.
House made of dark mist.

House made of female rain.
House made of pollen.
House made of grasshoppers.
Dark cloud is at the door.
The trail out of it is dark cloud.
The zigzag lightning stands high up on it.
Male deity!
Your offering I made.
I have prepared a smoke for you.
Restore my feet for me.
Restore my legs for me.
Restore my body for me.
Restore my mind for me.
Restore my voice for me.
This very day take out your spell for me.
Your spell remove for me.
You have taken it away for me.
Far off it has gone.
Happily I recover.
Happily my interior becomes cool.
Happily I go forth.
My interior feeling cold, may I walk.
No longer sore, may I walk.
Impervious to pain, may I walk.
With lively feelings may I walk.
As it used to be long ago, may I walk.
Happily may I walk.
Happily with abundant dark clouds, may I walk.
Happily with abundant showers, may I walk.
Happily with abundant plants, may I walk.
Happily on a trail of pollen, may I walk.
Happily may I walk.
Being as it used to be long ago, may I walk.
May it be happy (or beautiful) before me.
May it be beautiful behind me.
May it be beautiful below me.
May it be beautiful above me.
May it be beautiful all around me.
In beauty it is finished.
In beauty it is finished.

This prayer is one of a pair recited together. The second is the same as the first except that it uses complementary features such as "dark mist" in place of "dark cloud" and "male rain" in place of "female rain." There is some alteration of line sequences and the final line is repeated four times.

## CHARMS, SPELLS, AND EVIL THOUGHTS

As we begin to appreciate the power that speech and thought may acquire in Native American cultures and recognize that even such a figure as Coyote has access to this power, we may begin to wonder if speech and thought are not at times used for self-serving or malevolent purposes. Such is certainly the case. Common are formulas and charms used to harm one's enemies or to attract the affections and stimulate the sexual desires of one of the opposite sex.

Many Native American peoples warn about harboring bad thoughts of others lest they bring harm to them. The power of thought and speech are usually among the powers held by witches and sorcerers. The malevolent power of thought is demonstrated in the following account by a Nez Perce on the subject of sorcery. According to Deward E. Walker, Jr., who has extensively studied Nez Perce language and culture, the term for sorcerer, *qetwí·ye?we·t*, is literally "the one who wishes the accident."[6]

### *THE POWER OF THOUGHT IN NEZ PERCE SORCERY recorded by Deward E. Walker, Jr.*[7]

*Qetí·wit* (to sorcerize) is when you have had bad thoughts about a person. It's when your thought will hurt him. You will think that, "Huh! from now on you will be unlucky." It's kind of like condemning him. *Qetí·wit* is kind of like sinning. . . . The man is *qetwí·ye?we·t*. . . Poor Coyote (sorcerer's name) used to live here at *ciwí·kte* (Coyote Gulch on the western edge of the present reservation). He was powerful, but he messed with the wrong man one time. There was this young Flathead man over here. He had gotten some horses at Umatilla and stopped here on the way home, and while he was here one of his horses happened to bump into Poor Coyote. When he did, it made Poor Coyote mad, and he shot *(qetí·wit)* at him. That boy went home, but the further he went, the sicker he got. When he got home they called in the doctor (M.D.), but he couldn't do anything. The longer he was there the sicker he got. They decided to call in the *tiwé·t* (shaman). He called other *tiwé·t*, and they began working on him. One wasn't strong enough to get Poor Coyote. They had a hell of a time getting him out. You could see how he was fighting by the way they moved their hands around. He didn't want to die. They were fighting him all over the place, but they finally got him. Then they heard him speaking Nez Perce. None of them could understand it but one *tiwé·t* (came there) who could, and he told them that was what he was talking. When they told the boy about bumping into the old man, the boy remembered it. He hadn't meant to do it. Those *tiwé·t* told the people they weren't killers, they were healers. You know if you start killing people you'll lose your power. They asked the people what they wanted to do with Poor Coyote, and they said to kill him. They cut him in two. Poor Coyote was going out to his barn to feed his horse, but he never made it. He fell flat, dead.

Many Native American tribes have a range of songs and formulas which are used to attract a lover, or to serve some other aspect of love. Sometimes these are used with malevolent intent as in attracting someone away from his or her chosen mate, or driving one sexually crazy, but there are other situations in which they serve in the courting process to make one attractive to the opposite sex.

Frances Densmore collected a number of these charm-songs during her study of Chippewa music. Such songs are often associated with a simple, but often very expressive, drawing by which the song may be recognized by others. The following song was recorded by Densmore at both White Earth and Red Lake, Wisconsin, from Chippewa women. One of them drew the accompanying picture which includes the singer's heart and her body surrounded by roses.

## CHIPPEWA LOVE-CHARM SONG AND PICTURE[8]

## *NOTES*

1. For discussion of aspects of this issue related to Native American cultures, see Sam D. Gill, *Native American Religions*, ch. 3.
2. N. Scott Momaday, "The Man Made of Words," in *Indian Voices: The First Convocation of American Indian Scholars* (San Francisco: The Indian Historian Press, 1970), pp. 49–62. Reprinted by permission of N. Scott Momaday and the American Indian Historical Society.
3. A. Irving Hallowell, "Ojibwa Ontology, Behavior and World View," in *Culture in History: Essays in Honor of Paul Radin*, ed. Stanley Diamond (New York: Columbia University Press, 1960), pp. 19–52, and Dorothy Lee, *International Journal of American Linguistics* 10 (1944):181–187, and *Freedom and Culture* (Englewood Cliffs, N.J.: Prentice-Hall, 1959), pp. 121–130.
4. Ruth Underhill, *Singing for Power: The Song Magic of the Papago Indians of Southern Arizona* (Berkeley: University of California Press, 1938), pp. 43–47. Reprinted by permission of the University of California Press.

5. Washington Matthews, "Navaho Myths, Prayers, and Songs with Texts and Translations," *University of California Publications in American Archaeology and Ethnology*, vol. 5, no. 2 (1907):54–55.
6. Deward E. Walker, Jr., "Nez Perce Sorcery," *Ethnology* 6:1 (1967):67. Quotations reprinted by permission of *Ethnology*.
7. Ibid., pp. 74–75.
8. Frances Densmore, *Chippewa Music*, Bureau of American Ethnology, Bulletin 45 (Washington, 1910), p. 89. See also Densmore, *Chippewa Music II*, Bureau of American Ethnology, Bulletin 53 (Washington, 1913). Reprinted by permission of the Smithsonian Institution.

# CHAPTER 4

# *Sacred Objects and Actions*

## INTRODUCTION

Native American religions are accessible primarily through their performance. Statements, especially in writing, of doctrine, formal theologies or philosophies are virtually nonexistent. Consequently, we are faced with a rich array of highly symbolic objects, actions, and orientations. Our approach to these sacred objects and actions has been largely confined to the way in which they appeal to our own understanding of the world. Therefore, the objects that appear of aesthetic value to us have been considered primarily as objects of art and have been viewed in terms of a history of art. Museums and film makers have captured certain elements of religious performance, yet most often they are presented to us without adequate interpretation in terms of their religious world views. Thus, we have a good deal of reorientation to do in attempting to understand the objects and actions of Native American religions as they present and represent religious thought and ideas.

In this chapter we will present a number of essays dealing with aspects of this topic. We will not offer an array of photographs of the objects and actions being considered. This is a conscious decision based on the belief that a greatly reduced single photographic image of an object severed from its cultural context supports erroneous perspectives toward which we are already inclined.

## ART, DESIGN, AND RELIGIOUS WORLD VIEW

In the following essay, Edmund Carpenter's discussion of Eskimo carving makes an eloquent and clear statement of the inseparability of art and design from Eskimo life and the living of it. While we cannot consider this view of Eskimo art as generally representative of all North American art, we can at least gain considerable sensitivity from Carpenter's insights and observations. While Carpenter may overdraw somewhat the contrast between Eskimo and Western art and may assume too great a unity for both cultural perspectives, he nonetheless demonstrates keen skills of observation and considerable insight as he discusses how language, plastic art forms, and poetry stem from common and fundamental principles of Eskimo reality and world view. His attention to the Eskimo orientation within space adds to our appreciation of space as one of the fundamental dimensions by which human beings express and create their realities.

## *IMAGE MAKING IN ARCTIC ART by Edmund Carpenter*[1]

In the mid-winter of 1772, in the desolate Canadian tundra, Samuel Hearne and his native companions saw the track of a strange snowshoe. They followed it to a little hut where they discovered a young woman sitting alone. She told of her capture by a hostile band, the murder of her parents, husband, and infant, and of her escape nearly seven months ago. Living alone, without seeing a human face, she supported herself by snaring small game.

"It is scarcely possible to conceive," observed Hearne, "that a person in her forlorn situation could be so composed as to contrive, or execute, anything not absolutely essential to her existence. Nevertheless, all her clothing, besides being calculated for real service, showed great taste, and no little variety of ornament. The materials, though rude, were very curiously wrought, and so judiciously placed as to make the whole of her garb have a very pleasing, though rather romantic appearance."

From northern Scandinavia, across the tundra and taiga of Siberia, Alaska, and Canada, to the ice-bound coast of East Greenland, men have lived for thousands of years. It is a hard land. The earth never thaws. It is snow-covered most of the year. Nothing grows. The mystery is not that men should be tossed by chance into this desolate waste; it is, rather, that within this prison of ice and wind they are able to draw from themselves images powerful enough to deny their nothingness.

Nowhere is life more difficult than in the Arctic, yet when life there is reduced to its barest essentials, art and poetry turn out to be among those essentials. Art to the Eskimo is far more than an object: it is an act of seeing and expressing life's values; it is a ritual of exploration by which patterns of nature, and of human nature, are revealed by man.

As the carver holds the unworked ivory lightly in his hand, turning it this way and that, he whispers, "Who are you? Who hides there?" And then: "Ah, Seal!" He rarely sets out to carve, say, a seal, but picks up the ivory, examines it to find its hidden form and, if that is not immediately apparent, carves aimlessly until he sees it, humming or chanting as he works. Then he brings it out: seal, hidden, emerges. It was always there: He did not create it. He released it: he helped it step forth.

I watched one white man, seeking souvenirs, commission a carving of a seal but receive instead a carving of a walrus. Another, who wanted a chess set, though his explicit instructions were clearly understood, received a set in which each pawn was different. *Ahmi*, "it cannot be known in advance" what lies in the ivory.

Eskimos have no real equivalents to our words "create" or "make," which presuppose imposition of the self on matter. The closest Eskimo term means "to work on," which also involves an act of will, but one which is restrained. The carver never attempts to force the ivory into uncharacteristic forms, but responds to the material as it tries to be itself, and thus the carving is continually modified as the ivory has its say.

This is the Eskimo attitude toward not only ivory, but toward all things, especially people: parent toward child, husband toward wife. Where we think of art as possession, and possession to us means control, means to do with as we like, art to them is a way of revealing.

In the Eskimo language, little distinction is made between nouns and verbs, but rather all words are forms of the verb "to be," which is itself lacking in Eskimo. That is, all words proclaim in themselves their own existence. Eskimo is not a nominal language; it does not simply name things which already exist, but rather brings both things and actions (nouns and verbs) into being as it goes along. This idea is reflected in the practice of naming a child at birth: when the mother is in labor, an old woman stands around and says as many different eligible names as she can think of. The child comes out of the womb when its own name is called. Thus the naming and the giving birth to the new thing are inextricably bound together.

The environment encourages the Eskimo to think in this fashion. To Western minds, the "monotony" of snow, ice, and darkness can often be depressing, even frightening. Nothing in particular stands out; there is no scenery in the sense in which we use the term. But the Eskimos do not see it this way. They are not interested in scenery, but in action, existence. This is true to some extent of many people, but it is almost of necessity true for the Eskimos, for nothing in their world easily defines itself or is separable from the general background. What exists, the Eskimos themselves must struggle to bring into existence. Theirs is a world which has to be conquered with each act and statement, each carving and song. The secret of conquering a world greater than himself is not known to the Eskimo. But his role is not passive. Man is the force that reveals form. He is the force which ultimately cancels nothingness.

Language is the principal tool with which the Eskimos make the natural world a human world. They use many "words" for snow which permit fine distinctions, not simply because they are much concerned with snow, but because snow takes its form from the actions in which it participates: sledding, falling, igloo-building, blowing. These distinctions are possible only when experienced in a meaningful context. Different kinds of snow are brought into existence by the Eskimos as they experience their environment and speak; the words do not label something already there. Words, for the Eskimo, are like the knife of the carver: they free the idea, the thing, from the general formlessness of the outside. As a man speaks, not only is his language *in statu nascendi*, but also the very thing about which he is talking. The carver, like the poet, releases form from the bonds of formlessness: he brings it forth into consciousness. He must reveal form in order to protest against a universe that is formless, and the form he reveals should be beautiful.

Since that form participates in a real situation, the carving is generally utilitarian. One very characteristic Eskimo expression means "What is that for?" It is most frequently used by an Eskimo when he finds some object and stands looking down at it. It does not mean "What can I use that for?" but rather something closer to "What is it intended to be used for?" That portion of the antler, the shape of which so perfectly fits the hand and gives a natural strength as well, becomes, with slight modification, a chisel handle. Form and function, revealed together, are inseparable. Add a few lines of dots or tiny rings or just incisions, rhythmically arranged to bring out the form, and it is finished.

Here, then, is a world of chaos and chance, a meaningless whirl of cold and white. Man alone can give meaning to this—its form does not come ready-made.

When spring comes and igloos melt, the old habitation sites are littered with waste, including beautifully designed tools and tiny ivory carvings, not deliberately thrown away, but, with even greater indifference, just lost. Eskimos are interested in the artistic act, not in the product of that activity.

A carving, like a song, is not a thing; it is an action. When you feel a song within you, you sing it; when you sense a form emerging from the ivory, you release it. The Eskimo word "to make poetry" is the word "to breathe"; both are derivatives of *anerca*, the soul, that which is eternal, the breath of life. A poem is words infused with breath or spirit: "Let me breathe of it," says the poem-maker and then begins: "One has put his poem in order on the threshold of his tongue."

There is no separation of prose and poetry; all Eskimo speech has a musical quality and for heightened emotional expressions the speaker moves easily into song. Eskimos often talk and sing to themselves. To them, thinking and speaking are one: there is no purely inner experience. Members of our culture who are indifferent to literacy also do this: the lone child talking to his toys, the drunk, the angry man who walks away mumbling, the senile, the insane. Momentarily or permanently, all have reverted to an earlier, perhaps more basic philosophy, in which individualism plays little part and thought is conceived of as an external experience.

To the Eskimo, all thought is "outside." "If thoughts were *in* a mind, how could they *do* anything?" Ohnainewk asked. Thought, Eskimos believe, is everything outside of man, especially natural forces. But thought cannot exist without man. It makes itself known to man: it speaks first and man in turn gives it shape and expression.

The old question, "What is the silent igloo-sitter thinking?", misses the point. Early ethnologists believed he was in a self-induced trance; Freudians said he was suppressing his anxieties. Both assumed there was an inner dialogue. But inner dialogue, far from being universal, is largely the product of literacy. It belongs to literate man whose mind is a never ending clock which his will cannot stop, sleep cannot still, madness only makes go faster, and death alone silences. I do not believe the silent Eskimo with his impassive, tribal face is thinking anything. He is just not "with it" and "it" in this case is generally hunting, which he loves above all else.

I have seen silent, gentle, slow-moving Eskimos, suddenly caught up in the hunt, accomplish astonishing feats of skill and daring. Yet there was consistency here. They were the same. They simply allowed the world to act towards them with complete freedom. They were not passive: they freed this experience from its formless state and gave it expression and beauty. When you feel a song welling up within you, you sing it; when Eskimos feel themselves possessed by the hunt, they commit themselves fully to it.

This sort of electrifying performance always reminded me of slouching new method actors who coast along and then suddenly "get with it," erupting with startling jets of power. The comparison may be legitimate, for postliterate method actors who regard all life as empty dialogue, save those moments when one is fully committed to an external experience, share much with preliterate hunters.

The Eskimo language contains no first-person pronoun, which in English is so important we make "I" upper case, an honor otherwise restricted to gods and kings. Eskimo does provide a suffix to indicate participation of self in experience, but generally Eskimos avoid even this, and use an impersonal pronoun: "One has driven his spear into a walrus." Yet, despite the absence of individualism in our sense, there is often spectacular achievement, and though there is no "I," there is great dignity.

Carvers make no effort to develop personal styles and take no care to be remembered as individuals, but simply disappear, as it were, behind their works. Their goal is not to develop unique art styles, not to present personal views, nor even to bring to fruition biases peculiar to them personally; rather, it is to express to perfection a timeless tradition, breathing into it "the breath of life" so that each form is fresh, though the grammar is never violated.

I recently traveled across Siberia, studying Arctic art. The contrast was remarkable: here was the most completely nonliterate art tradition known, seen against a setting of total literacy. For Soviet Russia is the final, most sterile expression of literacy, with all the worst of the Renaissance and none of the freedom and hope and release of that incredible experiment. Everything is segmental and replaceable—especially people: Napoleon's citizen army at last! Everything visual requires a single point of view—a review position, like Stalin reviewing troops; all painting is in three-dimensional perspective; every plaza is to be viewed from X. One cannot enter into an experience, complete it, modify it, interpret it. All communications: high-definition, exact, with the same meaning for everyone. Dictionaries are popular. Lectures involve learning the correct, single meaning: copy it, memorize it. Da Vinci, yes; Miro, no.

Literacy creates a "middle distance"; it separates observer from observed, actor from action; it leads to single perspective, fixed observation, singleness of tone, and introduces into poetry and music the counterpart of three-dimensional perspective in art, all, of course, artistic expressions of the Western notion of individualism, every element being now related to the unique point of view of the individual at a given moment.

The phonetic alphabet and all its derivatives stress a one-thing-at-a-time analytic awareness in perception. This intensity of analysis is achieved at the price of forcing all else in the field of perception into the subliminal. For twenty-five hundred years literate man lived in what Joyce called "ABCED-mindedness." As a result of this fragmenting of the field of perception and the breaking of movement into static bits, man won a power of applied knowledge and technology unrivaled in human history. The price he paid was existing personally and socially in a state of almost total subliminal awareness.

The Eskimo artist emphasizes all-at-onceness. For him there is no subliminal factor in experience; his mythic forms of explanation explicate all levels of any situation at the same time. Freud makes no sense when applied to him. The carver leaves nothing hidden, suppresses nothing. He employs X-ray techniques, carving an animal with its rib cage open and an inner being exposed, or with ribs and vertebrae etched on its surface; he delights in visual puns that show the many dimensions of a being; he uses multiple perspective, observing an experience with the eyes of many. At the same time, he never expresses thoughts openly, but rather drops slight hints, not to censor or suppress, but rather to force his audience to participate, to join in the creation, to complete. There is freedom in all this; nothing is presented ready-made.

A distinctive mark of Eskimo art is that many of the ivory carvings, generally of sea mammals, will not stand up, but roll clumsily about. Each lacks a single, favored point of view and hence a base. They were never intended to be set in place and viewed, but rather to be worn and handled, turned this way and that. I knew a trader with a fine, showpiece collection of such carvings who solved this problem by lightly filing each piece "on the bottom" to make it stand up, but alas he also made them stationary, something the carver never intended.

The carving lives in the hand as it is moved, spoken to and about. Charm, toggle, ornament move on the clothing of the wearer. Some, especially ones of the Dorset Culture dating from as early as 800 B.C., are so detailed and so accurate we can identify species, even subspecies: a red-throated loon from a common loon. Yet one carving of a ptarmigan is scarcely larger than the head of a match; an ivory bear—running, with claws—is less than three-eighths of an inch high; a carving of a glaucous gull weighs less than one-sixtieth of an ounce. I photographically magnified, 1000–1200 times, a number of these pieces. All shared a quality of sizelessness: each, when blown up to monumental size, suffered no qualitative change of effect, for the artists had reduced each form to its basic essentials. All were produced, of course, without the aid of lenses or steel. Though incredibly minute, they lack the charming fragility of miniatures, and give instead the impression of mature power. Each seems independent, self-contained.

Eskimo tales share this quality. Generally the narrator speaks only of things you can touch and see. He constantly chooses the concrete word, in phrase after phrase, forcing you to touch and see. No speaker so insistently teaches the general through the particular. He has mastery over the definite, detailed, particular, visualized image.

The Eskimo language, being polysynthetic, favors such construction. Phrases are not composed of little words chronologically ordered, but of great, tight conglomerates, like twisted knots, within which concepts are juxtaposed and inseparably fused. Such conglomerates are not verbs or nouns or even words; each "is a linguistic expression for an impression forming a unit to the speaker. Thus, the house is red" in Eskimo is phrased "the-house, looking-like-flowing-blood-it-is"; the sequence may indicate a kind of subordination, but "red" is felt and treated as a substantive. Such parts of speech, though they follow one another, are remarkably independent, with the result that Eskimo is jerky; it does not flow. What we call action, Eskimos see and describe as a pattern of succeeding impressions.

I ran an experiment with a number of Eskimos. I sketched on paper some twenty figures, each oriented in a different direction. Then I asked each individual to point to the seal, the walrus, the bear. Without hesitation, all located the correct figures. But though I had myself made the drawings I found it necessary to turn the paper each time to ascertain the accuracy of their selections.

Igloo walls are often covered with magazine pictures obtained from the trader. These reduce dripping; perhaps they are enjoyed for their colors as well. Some effort is made at vertical rendering but really very little, and the over-all result is haphazard. When the children wanted to imitate me, a sure way to provoke delighted laughter was to mimic my twisting and turning as I tried to look at the *Life Magazine* pictures.

Walrus tusks are carved into aggregates of connected but unrelated figures; some figures face one way, others another. No particular orientation is involved, nor is there a single "theme." Each figure is simply carved as it reveals itself in the ivory.

The value we place on verticality (it influences even our perception) stems from the strength of literacy in our lives. Children must be taught it. Natives do not know it. And when the mentally ill in our society withdraw from the burdens of literate values, and return to nonvertical, nonlineal codifications, we call them childlike, and even note parallels with primitives. To the lack of verticality can be added multiple perspective, visual puns, X-ray sculpture, absence of background, and correspondence between symbol and size: all examples of non-optical structuring of space.

Few examples illustrate this absence of vertical rendering quite so forcefully as visual puns. Eskimos, of course, do not turn them: delight comes from instantaneous perception of multiple meanings. Poems, too, present simultaneously the variations of a character or the diversities of an immediate experience:

Great grief came over me—
Great grief came over me,
While on the fell above us I was picking berries.
Great grief overcame me
My sun quickly rose over it.
Great grief came over me.
The sea out there off our settlement

Was beautifully quiet—
And the dear, great paddlers
Were leaving out there—
Great grief came over me
While I was picking berries on the fell.

The essential feature of sound is not its location, but that it *be* that it fill space. We say, "The night shall be filled with music," just as the air is filled with fragrance: locality is irrelevant. The concert-goer closes his eyes. Auditory space has no favored focus. It is a sphere without fixed boundaries, space made by the thing itself, not space containing the thing. It is not pictorial space, boxed in, but dynamic, always in flux, creating its own dimensions, moment by moment. It has no fixed boundaries; it is indifferent to background. The eye focuses, pinpoints, abstracts, locating each object in physical space, against a background; the ear favors sound from any direction. Here berry-picking is not background for grief, nor are departure and grief causally related; they simply occur together: two independent impressions intersecting, each modified, as in translation, when seen through the other.

I do not think it accidental that we see the closest parallels with Eskimo art in the work of Paul Klee, for in both there is a structuring of space by sound. Klee said his works owed more to Bach and Mozart than to any of the masters of art. He wanted art "to *sound* like a fairy tale," to be a world where "things fall upward."

Literate man often has difficulty in understanding a purely verbal notion. In *Alice in Wonderland* ". . .the patriotic Archbishop found it advisable."

"Found *what*?" said the Duck.

"Found *it*," the Mouse replied rather crossly: "Of course you know what 'it' means."

"I know what 'it' means well enough when *I* find a thing," said the Duck: "it's generally a frog, or a worm. The question is, what did the Archbishop find?"

Literate man feels happier when *it* is visible; then he feels he can understand it, judge it, perhaps control it. In his workaday world, space is conceived in terms of that which separates visible objects. "Empty space" suggests a field in which there is nothing *to see*. We call a fume-filled gasoline drum or a gale-swept tundra "empty" because nothing is visible in either case.

The Eskimos do not think this way. One hunter I knew, when assured by a white man that a gasoline drum was "empty," struck a match and peered inside: he bore the scars for life. With them the binding power of the oral tradition is so strong as to make the eye subservient to the ear. They define space more by sound than sight. Where we might say, "Let's see what we can hear," the Eskimo would say, "Let's hear what we can see."

In handling these tusks I found myself turning them first this way, then that, orienting each figure *in relation to myself*. Eskimos do not do this. They carve a number of figures, each oriented—by our standards—in a different direction, without moving the tusk. Similarly, when handed a photograph, they examine it as it is handed to them, no matter how it is oriented.

The "wrap-around" aspect of auditory space is shown by the manner in which an Eskimo constructs an igloo. Surrounded by space in all its acoustic nondirection, he does not mould his igloo from the outside looking in, but from the inside working out. Working from the center, he builds a series of concentric circles, tapering upwards conically. When the keystone at the apex has been set in place, Eskimo and structure are one. Only then does he cut a small hole at the base, through which he crawls—in effect, doffing his igloo.

Eskimo carvers do not work within borders. The composite nature of their great mobile masks is a deliberate effort to let each mask assert its own dimensions. The familiar Western notion of enclosed space is foreign to the Eskimo. Both snow igloos and skin tents lack vertical walls and horizontal ceilings; no planes parallel each other and none intersect at ninety degrees. There are no straight lines, at least none of any length. Rectangles are unknown. Euclidean space is a concept unique to literate man. Eskimos, with a magnificent disregard for environmental determinism, open up rather than enclose space. They must, of course, create sealed-off heat areas, but instead of resorting to boxes, they build complex, many-roomed igloos which have as many dimensions and as much freedom as a cloud.

I know of no examples of Eskimos describing space primarily in visual terms. They do not regard space as static, and therefore measurable: hence they have no formal units of spatial measurement, just as they have no uniform divisions of time. The carver is indifferent to the demands of the optical eye: he lets each piece fill its own space, create its own world, without reference to background or anything external to it. Each carving lives in spatial independence. Size and shape, proportions and selection, these are set by the object itself, not forced from without. Like sound, each carving creates its own space, its own identity; it imposes its own assumptions.

In the beginning was the Word, a spoken word, not the visual one of literate man, but a word which, when spoken, revealed form: "And God said, Let there be light: and there was light." "By the word of the Lord were the heavens made, and all the hosts of them by the breath of His mouth." The Eskimo speaker imposes his will diffidently upon unbounded reality. Form is temporary, transient; it exists, as the Eskimo poet says, "on the threshold of my tongue."

In literate society, however, to be real a thing has to be visible. We trust the eye, not the ear. Not since Aristotle assured his *readers* that the sense of sight was "above all others" the one to be trusted, have we accorded to sound the role of dominant sense. "Seeing is believing." "Believe half of what you see, nothing of what you hear." "The eyes of the Lord preserve knowledge, and he over-throweth the words of the transgressor." Truth, literate man thinks, must be observed by the eye, then judged by the "I." Mysticism, intuition, are bad words among scientists. Most thinking in literate societies is done in terms of *visual* models, even when an auditory one might prove more efficient. We employ spatial metaphor even for such inner psychological states as tendency, duration, intensity. We say "thereafter," not the more logical "thenafter"; "always" means "at all times"; "before" means etymologically "in front of"; we even speak of a "space" or "interval" of time.

There is a significant difference between Eskimo and Northwest Coast Indian masks. Neither culture is much concerned with change or "becoming," but Northwest Coast artists do emphasize metamorphosis or "coming-to-be." A wolf mask may suddenly open, revealing bear; this springs apart—within is the face of another spirit. Nothing has a definite, invariable shape. Like Echo, the mythical being who successively comes to be all things, the mask is shape-shifting: by a sudden metamorphosis, it is first this, then that. Eskimos, however, emphasize "is"; they depict these elements together, simultaneously, and they accept in the most casual way this blurring of human-animal-spirit forms.

The most interesting Eskimo masks known to me are great composite, mobile puns: the same lines serve to depict Walrus-Caribou-Man; turned slightly, one form may be emphasized, but the others are never lost. There is no need for shape-shifting; all relevant forms are already present. Such a mask expresses the variety and infinite subtlety of personality; its power lies in preserving due proportion between diverse and opposite elements.

To the Eskimo, truth is given through oral tradition, mysticism, intuition, all cognition; not simply by observation and measurement of physical phenomena. To them, the ocularly visible apparition is not nearly as important as the purely auditory one.

> The Eskimo view of self is not as clearly demarcated as ours, and its precise limits often vary according to circumstances. They do not reduce the self to a sharply delimited, consistent, controlling "I." They postulate no personality "structure," but accept the clotted nature of experience—the simultaneity of good and evil, of joy and despair, multiple models within the one, contraries inextricably commingled. Where literate man regards an "alias" as deceiving, representing something other than the "real" self, every Eskimo has several names, each a different facet of himself, for they assert that man's ego is not a thing imprisoned in itself, sternly shut up in boundaries of flesh and time. They say that many of the elements which make it up belong to the world before it and outside it, while the notion that each person is himself and can be no other, is to them impossible, for it leaves out of account all the transitions which bind the individual consciousness to the general. The Eskimo conception of individuality belongs in the same category of conceptions as that of unity and entirety, the whole and the all; and the distinction between spirit in general and individual spirit possesses not nearly so much power over their minds as over ours.

A great proportion of what we recognize as Native American art is inseparable from specified functions—decoration of utensils and clothing or objects intended for ritual or ceremonial use. The significance of Native American functional art forms must take into consideration the intended use and function of the aesthetic item. It may mean that the visual perspective is dynamic as in the Eskimo carvings discussed by Carpenter. There the very dynamics and liveliness of the art object is associated with the absence of a fixed perspective. But it may mean that we must know precisely the visual perspective that must be taken in order to appreciate the intent and meaning of the object. This is the case of effigy pipes and other "self-directed" items that Dr. Ted J. Brasser has discussed.[2]

## SACRED OBJECTS

Sacred medicine bundles are common in a large number of tribes in North America. They are kept by the most responsible members of the community and usually secreted in well-protected locations. The bundles are rarely opened for general view and are subject of the most stringent ritual procedures. The tribes that maintain sacred bundles consider them of the greatest power and significance, often holding that their existence is inseparable from the bundle.

When displayed in museums, there is a radical disparity with the bundles as viewed by the culture from which they came. On display, open for anyone's view, they appear lifeless and often meaningless—an odd assortment of crude objects. Without appreciating the perspectives and actions of the culture that maintains a sacred bundle, there is not even the aesthetic perspective to appeal to Western sensitivities. To appreciate the religious significance of a sacred bundle, we must not examine its contents as they appeal to our own world view, we must place the bundle back in its cultural context and appreciate how it is held by the culture, so that even objects that appear crude and valueless to us may be recognized as embracing meanings of a global and life-giving order.

The following account by a Mandan woman named Scattercorn opens to us something of the origins, functions, and meanings of the corn bundles in Mandan religious life.

## *MANDAN CORN BUNDLES by Scattercorn*[3]

The Corn People were living under the ground by a lake. One day some of the people saw an opening reaching up to the land above, and there was a vine growing in this hole. They asked the Fox to climb up and see this land. He climbed up, but, when he stuck his nose out, he got only a brief look at the beautiful land above because Sun burned his nose.

Then they asked Elk to go up and dig the hole larger with his horns. He made the hole large so the people could get through. The people started up, following the vine. They came up continuously for four days, but on the last day a woman heavy with child broke the vine and ended the migration forever. All these people had been raising the corn on this land beneath the earth.

There were four leaders in the group that reached the earth. They were three brothers and a sister. Their names were Good Furred Robe, Cornhusk Earrings, Uses His Head for Rattle, and a sister named Waving Corn Stalk. Good Furred Robe began to lay out the villages and fields. He laid out the lodges in rows like the rows of corn, and he assigned the garden plots to each family. Then he distributed corn, beans, squash, and sunflower seeds to each family.

In those days the sister would be out in the fields all day overseeing the work. One day a stranger came to the gardens and wanted to talk to her, but she would not see him. He came four times to see her, but each time she refused. That man was Sun. On his fourth visit he said, "What you plant you will not harvest."

The next day when the sun came up, the air was so hot that the corn wilted. After the sun had set, she went through the gardens with her robe singing the holy songs, and the corn plants revived. Sun scorched the gardens four times, and each time she revived them with her robe and songs.

The people were living there when men appeared on the opposite bank and said that they wanted to cross, and the Mandans called them Miditadi after that time. After the Hidatsa crossed the Missouri they camped near the Mandan villages. Some of their young men were foolish, and the customs at that time were quite different, so the older men were afraid that there would be trouble.

Good Furred Robe said, "Our ways are a little different, so I think it would be better if you had villages of your own. If you stay too near us, there will be trouble. If you go too far away, we will be strangers and there will be trouble. The best plan will be for you to travel north until, when you camp, you cannot see our fires. That will be the best place to settle. If you will send your chiefs over in the morning, I will give them all the different seeds we have."

That morning when the men arrived, Good Furred Robe broke an ear in two and said, "My friend, you can take the tip or the butt." The Hidatsa took the tip because he thought that it was the best part. The Hidatsa left that day. The Mandan built fires on the hills, and, when the Hidatsa had traveled until they could no longer see these fires, they stopped and built their village, which was at Knife River.

Good Furred Robe told the people that in the spring they should have certain songs sung when the ducks and other waterbirds came north so that there would be plenty of rain and good crops. He also told them that each family should bring out two kernals of each crop they grew and he would cleanse them so that they would germinate. All that spring and summer, he was painted with red paint and wore moccasins with the fur side on the inside. He wore his sacred robe all that time and could not eat early plums, berries, or garden products until the fall when the corn was ripe and the people announced that they had their seed for the next year. Men brought his meals to him while the crops were growing. He could not sleep with or go near his wives or other women. At the close of these restrictions, those with Corn medicines met, and there was a cleansing feast, after which these restrictions were removed.

Good Furred Robe also told the people that, when working in the gardens, they should burn sage and rub themselves with it to remove the bad spirits of the fields. In those days when he instructed them in that manner, worms and bugs fell from their robes, so the Mandan women set the rule of always burning sage at the close of the day's work in the fields.

Then he organized two societies, one for the men and the other for the women. He called the society for the men "Brave Warrior Society" or "Black Mouths." He brought in the men to dance. Two were given cornstalks, for only the bravest were to carry them, and he told them that these plants represented the bravest men. In war these two men could get a stick and attach raven feathers to represent the corn. If this staff was stuck into the ground, they could hold the enemy back, and, if the Mandan wanted to retreat, they could pull up the staffs and retreat without being killed. The men were between thirty and forty years old.

He organized a women's society and called it the Goose Society. The older ones would be around thirty years of age and would keep the society for five years. He selected two little girls about eight years old and stood them in the middle of the group. One girl's mouth was painted blue, the other's was black, and both represented geese. Each member wore a gooseskin and head for a headdress. Whenever anyone made an offering to the waterbirds when they came north in the spring or in the fall when they returned to the south, this society met and danced. All others with rights in the Corn ceremonies came out at those times also. The leader of the Goose Society and the last woman in the line both carried small clay pots. People could come to these dances and make offerings of horses, guns, or robes which entitled them to dance in the line, going around the Corn Priest four times, which was a sign that the giver would live to be old.

When Good Furred Robe grew old, he told the people to keep his skull and that praying to it would be like praying to him when he was living. There was a little difference in the way that offerings were made to him. I told you today that, when anyone puts on a feast to Old Woman Who Never Dies, an image of her is put up before the giver's lodge so that all will know that the household has made a feast to her. When feasts to the Sacred Robe or the Sacred Skulls are made, the offering is placed on a post on the prairies near the village.

The inheritance of the Sacred Robe bundle was from Good Furred Robe's brother, Uses His Head for Rattle.

## RITUAL ART

There are many visual elements in ritual that have obvious aesthetic value and are therefore usually called "ritual art." While the aesthetic elements of ritual are not to be denied, sometimes such a characterization stands in our way of appreciating the religiousness of these visual elements of ritual.

Navajo sandpainting is well known as a Native American art form, yet it is rarely considered in the context of the curing ceremonials in which sandpaintings are instrumental in the creation of a healthy human being and world rather than the products of aesthetic effort. Visual perspective is an important concern since sandpaintings are placed upon a floor and not displayed against a wall. The unique perspective of the one being treated by the ceremonial is the vantage of one who is sitting in the middle of the painting.

While these visual and functional elements are important to the understanding of Navajo sandpainting, so also is an understanding of the oral tradition in which the story of the origin and intended use of a sandpainting is told. This relationship between ritual objects and actions and oral tradition is commonly found in Native American religions.

In the following selection the familiar Navajo Whirling Logs sandpainting is considered in the context of its story of origin.

## *WHIRLING LOGS AND COLORED SANDS by Sam D. Gill*[4]

I will focus on a single Navajo sandpainting done in an actual ceremonial performance—the Whirling Logs sandpainting of the Nightway ceremonial.* I will view several dimensions of the sandpainting rite considering its construction, the rite performed upon it, elements in the greater ceremonial context, and the associated stories. I want to understand sandpainting as much as possible from the perspective of Navajos and to illustrate aspects of Navajo religious thought.

In preparation for the construction of the Whirling Logs sandpainting the center of the ceremonial hogan is cleared and the fire is moved to the side. A layer of clean sand is spread upon the floor and smoothed out with weaving battens. The sandpainters make a guide for long straight lines by snapping a taut string to make an indentation in the sand base. The sandpainting is constructed from the center outward under the direction of the singer who does not usually participate in the sandpainting. For the Whirling Logs sandpainting, the black cross which represents the whirling logs is constructed first upon the center which may be formed by burying a shallow bowl of water so that the surface is even with that of the painting. The center represents the lake upon which the logs float. The logs are outlined in red and white. The crushed colored materials used in making the sandpainting are held in bark containers.

As the last arm of the cross is being completed, the roots of the corn plants which lay in each of the four quadrants are drawn with their beginning in the central representation of the lake. Navajos have said that this is so because the corn needs water in order to live. The corn plants constructed in each quadrant are of the four colors—white, yellow, blue, and black. Each is outlined in a contrasting color. Two ears of corn are shown on each stalk.

On each of the four arms of the whirling logs sit two *yé'ii* or masked holy people. The outer figures are male and wear helmet-like masks with two eagle plumes and a tuft of owl feathers. They carry gourd rattles and spruce branches. The inner figures are female carrying spruce branches in both hands.

---

*For publications of the Whirling Logs sandpainting see Washington Matthews, *The Night Chant, A Navajo Ceremony* (New York: American Museum of Natural History, Memoirs, vol. 6, 1902), Plate VI; James Stevenson, *Ceremonial of Hasjelti Dailjis and Mythical Sand Painting of the Navajo Indians* (Washington, D. C.: Bureau of American Ethnology, 8th Annual Report, 1891), Plate CXXI; Ruth Underhill, *The Navajos* (Norman: University of Oklahoma Press, 1956), p. 80; and Sam D. Gill, *Songs of Life: An Introduction to Navajo Religious Culture* (Leiden, The Netherlands: E. J. Brill, 1979), Plates XXVa-XXXI.

When the inner portion of the sandpainting is complete, *yé'ii* figures are drawn adjacent to the ends of each of the arms of the cross. To the west is *hashch'é ooghwaan*, or Calling God, who is dressed in black and wears a blue mask ornamented with eagle and owl feathers. He carries in his hands a black wand decorated with representations of feathers of turkeys and eagles. The skins of blue birds are depicted as being attached to the wand. The figure on the east side is *hasch'éłti'i* or Talking God. He is dressed in white and wears a white mask decorated with eagle feathers tipped with breath feathers and a tuft of yellow owl feathers, with a fox skin under the left ear. He carries a gray squirrel skin pouch on a string. His eye and mouth markings are distinctive, but the sandpainting representation does not include the corn symbol on the face as does the mask.

The *yé'ii* to the north and south are *ghwą́ą́'ask'idii* or Humpbacks. They wear blue masks with a zigzag line of white lightning around them and red feathers representing sunbeams radiating out from the masks. The masks are topped with blue horns which identify them with mountain sheep. The hump on the back is a representation of a sack laden with goods. These *yé'ii* carry black staffs. The anthropomorphic rainbow guardian figure circumscribes the painting on all sides but the east. Plumed wands, which represent holy people, are erected around the periphery of the sandpainting.

In the hands of the rainbow guardian are placed cups of herbal infusion which will be used in the sandpainting rite. A cedar twig is laid upon the shell cup with which to administer the medicine. This completes the construction of the sandpainting.

The Nightway ceremonial during which this sandpainting is made is performed according to a Holyway-type ritual process. This indicates that it is performed for a person suffering a predicament whose cause is attributed to one of the *diyin dine'é* or holy people of the Navajo. The ritual process is bent upon reestablishment of proper relationships between the one over whom the ceremonial is being sung, that is, the one-sung-over, and certain of the holy people. The expected results of these renewed relationships are that the malevolence will be withdrawn and the person may then be rightly remade or recreated. The sandpainting rites take place on the fifth through the eighth days of a nine-night ceremonial. It should be noted that Nightway is one of the ceremonials in which the holy people make appearance by means of masked impersonators.

When the rites on the sandpainting are about to begin, the one-sung-over enters the ceremonial hogan and the singer or medicine person begins the whirling logs songs. The one-sung-over, carrying a basket of corn meal, stands to the east of the painting, and sprinkles corn meal upon it. This gesture of blessing is repeated on the south, west and north. Then meal is scattered all around the periphery. While the one-sung-over prepares to enter the sandpainting, a *yé'ii* enters the hogan whooping, and proceeds to sprinkle the picture with the herb medicine using the cedar twig. The application of medicine is done systematically and carefully. The one-sung-over enters the sandpainting and sits down. The *yé'ii* approaches him or her with the shell cup of medicine from which he or she drinks. Some of the medicine is put on the hands of the *yé'ii* and with this moisture he picks up sands from the feet, legs, body, and head of each of the figures in the sandpainting including the cornstalks and applies them to the corresponding body parts of the one-sung-over. After each application, the *yé'ii* lifts his hands toward the smoke hole. When the application is completed the *yé'ii* yells twice into each ear of the one-sung-over and leaves the ceremonial hogan. The one-sung-over then leaves the sandpainting. The plumed wands are removed and what remains of the picture is carefully erased by the singer using a feathered wand. The sandpainting materials are blanketed out of the hogan to be correctly disposed of. The Whirling Logs songs are sung until the *yé'ii* departs.

The stories of Nightway are too extensive and complex to recount in detail. The principal story is about four brothers and a brother-in-law who go on a hunting expedition. The next to the youngest brother is the protagonist and is unique because he is a visionary. His name, *Bitahátini*, means "his imagination" or "his visions." The story begins with a conflict between the visionary and his brothers because they do not believe the authenticity of the vision experiences and refuse to listen to *Bitahátini*. The two eldest brothers and a brother-in-law leave for a hunting trip and the visionary decides to follow them the next day. While camping by himself he overhears a conversation between two groups of crows in human-like forms. He learns that his brothers have killed a crow, a magpie and twelve deer. Since the crow and magpie are the owners of the deer, the crow people decree that the brothers will get no more game. Proceeding the next day the visionary catches up with his brothers and tells them what he has heard. Only the brother-in-law listens to him. The elder brothers continue to hunt for several days, but the visionary's prophecy proves correct; they get no more game. On the way home mountain sheep are spotted and the visionary is sent to kill them. As he attempts to do so, he finds that he is unable to release his arrows and he shakes violently. He makes several attempts until finally, the sheep reveal to him that they are really holy people. They are Fringe Mouths in disguise, and they give him the guise of a mountain sheep and take him into a canyon. The place to which he is taken is no ordinary canyon and here the Fringe Mouths enact the archetypal performance of Nightway and teach *Bitahátini* its songs, prayers, and procedures. In an attempt to help recover their lost brother, the elder brothers have left offerings of jewels and pollens in baskets at the cliff edge. These are used in the ceremonial performance.

During the performance, the visionary is captured by *hasch'é ayói*, or Superior God, and taken to his home in the sky. Talking God is dispatched on a journey to recover the visionary. The ceremonial continues.

Finally, after testing the visionary's powers and his knowledge of Nightway songs and prayers, the holy people allow him to return to his home in order to teach what he has learned to the youngest of the four brothers. After the younger brother becomes proficient in the ceremonial performances, *Bitahátini* disappears and it is believed that he has gone to live in the home of the holy people.

Washington Matthews, who studied the Nightway ceremonial for twenty years during the late nineteenth century, recorded a sequel to this story which he entitled "The Whirling Logs." In many ways it is a more complex and fascinating story than the other. The protagonist, once again, is *Bitahátini*, the visionary. Having seen the picture of the whirling logs when he learned the Nightway, he is driven upon a quest for this place of the whirling logs. The visionary prepares a hollow cottonwood log for travel down the San Juan River in search of this place of the whirling logs. Upon launching his vessel, it immediately sinks and *Bitahátini* fears that he will lose his life. When they find that he is gone, his family seeks the help of holy people in finding him.

Upon rescuing him from the bottom of the river, the holy people ask what he was attempting to do. He reveals his desires to visit the place of the whirling logs and to learn of the mysteries there. His persistence overcomes the reluctance of the holy people to assist him. They prepare a hollow log with crystal windows and launch him down the river. Several holy people accompany his journey to keep him floating in mid-stream and to assist him past obstacles. After a journey of many incidents, the log enters a lake and upon circling it four times, lands on the south shore. The visionary is allowed to leave the log and enter the house of the Fringe Mouths of the Water where he learns from them their sandpainting. He reenters the log and it carries him around the lake four times again to land on the north shore where another sandpainting is revealed to him. Back in the log, he is carried out of the lake and along a stream leading to the whirling lake. Landing on the south shore, *Bitahátini* finally sees the whirling logs upon the lake. The story says, "He beheld the cross of sticks circling on the lake. It did not move on its own center, but turned around the center of the water. The log which lay from east to west was at the bottom; that which lay from north to south was on top. On each of the logs, four holy ones were seated—two at each end. . . . Many stalks of corn were fixed to the log." (Matthews 183–184) As he watches, the log cross lands on the west shore and the holy people who were transported by it enter a house. The visionary proceeds along the shore toward the west and he too enters the house. The holy ones are prepared for him and already have placed the picture of the whirling logs upon the floor. They reveal to him the rites of the painting.

The visionary is then given a ride around the lake on the cross of logs with the holy people.

Taking his leave the visionary starts back to the south shore where he had left his log vehicle, but on the way he discovers an area which would make a good farm. His pet turkey whom he had left behind appears there and produces seeds of four colours of corn and many other plants from various parts of its body. The turkey protects and comforts *Bitahátini*. The seeds are planted and they grow to maturity in four days. Holy people appear to help with the harvest and to instruct the visionary on how to harvest, cook, and eat the foods he has grown. They build him a house and perform a harvest ceremony.

Left alone, the visionary soon becomes lonely, yet he is reluctant to leave his stores of food behind in order to return home. Again the holy people assist him by spreading clouds upon the ground and wrapping his foods in them. This makes several small bundles which he can easily carry home. His journey is made upon a rainbow and he is escorted by Talking God, Calling God, and Water Sprinkler.

Upon his return he teaches his younger brother the mysteries of the whirling logs so that his knowledge of Nightway will be complete and he divides the vegetables and grains among his relatives for use as seeds. The story explains that before this heroic venture the Navajo people had no corn or pumpkins (see Matthews 171–197).

Beginning now with some comments upon these stories, I would like to work my way back to the sandpainting rite, including a discussion of the sandpainting, in an effort to relate more closely the significance this sandpainting rite has for Navajos. An outstanding feature at the surface of these stories which accounts for the tension and drama in them is the existence of two kinds of worlds very different from each other. In the Nightway story there is the world of the hunters and the game animals and there is the world of holy people and the owners of the game. In the whirling logs story there is the world of the visionary's home and family, and there is the mysterious world of the holy people and the whirling lake. From the very beginning of both stories it is clear that the drama is focused upon the visionary because he has some knowledge of both worlds, while other Navajos apparently have little or no knowledge beyond their mundane world. As they unfold, the stories follow similar patterns. The visionary is in the world of ordinary reality and then travels to the other world where he acquires knowledge. In the end he returns to relate this knowledge to those left behind. It seems that the holy people are free to visit the world of ordinary reality, but it is unusual and difficult for an earth surface person to visit the homes and world of the holy people. During the arduous journeys the visionary enters dangerous territories, he undergoes difficult tests, he suffers imbalance and fear. Yet, as a result of his journey he gains knowledge, courage, and balance. Through him knowledge of the other world comes to the Navajo people. This knowledge often reveals facts basic to the subsistence of the Navajo people. It shows that the elements of sustenance—game, corn, and other foods—are ultimately owned by or dependent upon the world of the holy people. The journey of the heroic visionary provides a means by which a complex multidimensional reality as established in the story is integrated and unified.

It is notable that the holy people keep the pictures which are the models for sandpainting on *naskhá*, a cloth or spread, sometimes specified as a cloud. During the archetypal performance, these cloths are spread upon the floor for use and later folded up. In revealing the pictures to *Bitahátini* the holy people explain, "We will not give you this picture; men are not as good as we; they might quarrel over the picture and tear it, and that would bring misfortune; the black cloud would not come again, the rain would not fall, the corn would not grow; but you may paint it on the ground with colors of the earth." (Matthews 165) In another place the visionary is told, "Truly they [Navajo people] cannot draw a picture on a cloud as we do; but they may imitate it, as best they can, on sand." (Ibid. 182–183). Here too the existence of two kinds of worlds, and of two kinds of peoples is emphasized.

This double-imagery is interwoven dramatically throughout the sandpainting ritual. The hogan in which the sandpainting is constructed is blessed at the outset of the ceremonial and set apart from the world outside of it. The ceremonial hogan is identified with the hogan in which the world was created and consequently with the very structure of the universe. The sandpainting, done within this sacred enclosure and in the context of many other ritual acts, provides an identification with the events in the primal era when the heroic visionary lived. It replicates the picture revealed to him in the canyon where he learned Nightway and in the house of the holy people on the shore of the whirling lake. It also represents the whirling logs which he observed on the lake and upon which he rode with the holy people. The very shape and design of the sandpainting echoes the shape of the hogan and the quarternary structure of the universe. The plumed wands erected around it intensify the sacrality of this space.

The design of the sandpainting incorporates a complex dual imagery. On each arm of the log cross sits a male and a female *yé'ii*. By the very nature of the cross, the quarternary division of the world along the cardinal directions, east and west, north and south, is given representation. The paired Humpback *yé'ii* are set across from one another as are Talking God and Calling God. The Navajo colors—white, blue, yellow and black—are set across from their complements in the corn stalks. Contrasting colors are used as outline.

The rainbow guardian and the arc of plumed wands erected around the painting never completely enclose the sandpainting. It is through this opening that the one for whom the ceremonial is performed enters and through which the *yé'ii* enter and leave. This is essential to the purpose of Navajo sandpainting rites and to the very meaning of the Navajo word for sandpainting, *iikháah* which means "they enter and leave." This entryway, sometimes flanked by sandpainted guardian figures, is aligned with the entryway of the ceremonial hogan which faces east. This suggests that the Navajo recognize an essential communication and interdependence between the sacred world of the ceremonial hogan and the ordinary world outside. This is precisely what the stories have shown in a different way.

Stylistically, something may be said about the way in which the double-imagery is presented. In the story the log cross is contained within the sacred lake while in the sandpainted representation it projects out of the lake reaching into the enclosed sphere. This seems to expand the significance of the log cross to more global dimensions and to suggest that it is not limited to the sphere of the lake. Still the major holy people stand beyond it and control its movement with their staffs. The corn plants which appear in the four quadrants are rooted in the lake from which they are nourished, but they project into the areas of each quadrant thus also forming a cross joined at the center in the lake. The details of the story correspond closely with the structure of the sandpainting. The revelation of the whirling logs painting and the origin of agriculture are represented in the picture, one by the cross of logs, the other by the cross of corn. In the story, the log cross on the lake was described as having stalks of corn affixed to it which suggests an interrelationship between the whirling logs and the origin of agriculture. This interrelationship is maintained in the sandpainting, for both crosses are based or rooted in the lake in the center.

The sandpainting is, at one level, a visual reminder of the events of the story of a heroic adventurer who obtained knowledge of the Nightway ceremonial, who experienced the mysteries of the whirling logs, and who introduced agriculture to the Navajos. At another level, the sandpainting is a geometric projection of the essential pattern of order in the world.

The tension of the double-imagery gains further complexity in the rite which takes place on the sandpainting. The earth surface person walks upon the painting and sits amidst the holy people. This entry to the sandpainting reenacts the visionary's journey in that it brings the two worlds together. A *yé'ii* enters the hogan and walks on the sandpainting to administer the rite. The masked appearance is another instance of the coincidence or integration of the two worlds. The *yé'ii* offers to the one-sung-over the medicines that have been fed and applied to each of the holy people in the surrounding picture. Then with the aid of the moisture of the medicine on the hands of the *yé'ii*, the person being treated is ritually identified with each one of the holy people by being pressed at the sacred spots on his or her body with sands from the corresponding parts of all of the surrounding holy people. This act of identification is described in a common prayer segment which goes:

> His feet have become my feet, thereby I shall go through life.
> His legs have become my legs, thereby I shall go through life.
> His body has become my body, thereby I shall go through life.
> His mind has become my mind, thereby I shall go through life.
> His voice has become my voice, thereby I shall go through life.

In this way the person is identified with the very forces of the universe. He or she becomes one with the gods.

It is too little to say that for the person involved this identification with the gods must be a very significant event. The position on the logs identifies the person treated with the hero as he was escorted on the primordial ride around the lake. The suffering person too can experience this mystery. While it may well be beyond all description, his or her experience surely must be related to the position in the center of the sandpainting which is symbolically the center of the world. The visual perspective of one sitting in the center of a sandpainting is unique. From this vantage, only portions of the sandpainting may be seen at any one time and these only from the center outward, and perhaps upward. This visual perspective introduces a depth and movement to the picture that cannot be enjoyed from any other place. The person being treated has a heightened experience of truly being at the center. And by being at the center of the sandpainting, this map of cosmic dimensions, the person who perceives its cosmic design becomes the integrative element within it. In the person on the sandpainting the complexly dual aspects of reality and their tension is resolved. To sit upon the sandpainting and to be identified with its many elements is to experience the point common to all of them and therefore to see the unity and wholeness of the universe. The sandpainting event accomplishes a re-creation of the person and the universe. The world which may have seemed at odds with itself, experienced in the person as physical or mental suffering, is unified and reintegrated in the sandpainting rite where it is acknowledged that the whole drama of the universe is repeated in the human being.

In the complex representation through the double-imagery in the sandpainting and the ritual acts, the person who is the subject in the ritual may achieve a unity transcending this duality, an integration of the many to the one. This opens to the person an experience of reality in which he or she may grasp the spiritual powers which are present in it and one with it.

In the sandpainting rite, the person comes to experience the truth in the stories, which is that there are not two worlds, but one world composed of parts which are complexly interrelated and interdependent. Order and disorder (*hǫźhǫ́* and *hǫ́chǫ́* in Navajo) are interdependent as are health and sickness, life and death, spiritual and material.

Once this truth is experienced the sandpainting can no longer serve as a map. The person being treated has found his or her way from within the sandpainting and by becoming a part of it it has disappeared by becoming a part of him or her. With the experience of the unity of the world, the sandpainting, as a depiction of the order of the world, cannot exist. So the destruction of the sandpainting which always occurs during its use corresponds with the dissolution of the double-imagery it presents. When a person arises and leaves the sandpainting his or her experience of unity is confirmed in a way by the destroyed sandpainting. The many colors have dissolved into one as the sands and the renewed Navajo person return to the world.

## DANCE

Dance is a form commonly recognized as being inseparable from the performance of Native American religions. While our perceptions may center a bit too strongly on Native American dance performances done to entertain either themselves or others, the observation is nonetheless accurate. Indeed, even some of the grandest of Native American religious performances are referred to primarily as dances, for example, the Sun Dance, the Hopi Snake Dance, Pueblo Kachina Dances, the Iroquois Feather Dance. Also familiar are the many animal and bird dances that are performed by many tribes such as the Deer Dance and the Eagle Dance, and there are widespread performances of dances associated with agriculture such as the Bean Dance and the Corn Dance. While these dances vary from tribe to tribe, there is commonly nonetheless a strong association between dance and religious world views.

In the following selection, Lewis Henry Morgan describes in considerable detail the Iroquois Feather Dance as he observed it in the mid-nineteenth century. The importance of the performance is appreciated even in Morgan's admission of the impossibility of adequate description. His description may convey to us something of the mood and effect such dances may so powerfully evoke.

### *IROQUOIS FEATHER DANCE by Lewis Henry Morgan*[5]

The Feather dance and the War dance were the two great performances of the Iroquois. One had a religious, and the other a patriotic character. Both were costume dances. They were performed by a select band, ranging from fifteen to twenty-five, who were distinguished for their powers of endurance, activity and spirit. . . .

Second in the public estimation, but first intrinsically, stood the great Feather dance, *O-sto-weh'-go-wä*, sometimes called the Religious dance, because it was specially consecrated to the worship of the Great Spirit. . . . It was performed by a select band, ranging from fifteen to thirty, in full costume, and was chiefly used at their religious festivals, although it was one of the prominent dances on all great occasions in Indian life. This dance was the most splendid, graceful and remarkable in the whole collection, requiring greater powers of endurance, suppleness and flexibility of person, and gracefulness of deportment, than either of the others. The *saltandi ars*, or dancing art, found in the Feather dance its highest achievement, at least in the Indian family; and it may be questioned whether a corresponding figure can be found among those which are used in refined communities, which will compare with it in those particulars which make up a spirited and graceful dance.

The music was furnished by two singers, seated in the centre of the room, each having a turtle-shell rattle. . . . It consisted of a series of songs or measured verses, which required about two minutes each for their recitation. They were all religious songs, some of them in praise of the Great Spirit, some in praise of various objects in nature which ministered to their wants, others in the nature of thanksgivings to *Ha-wen-né-yu*, or supplications of his continued protection. The rattles were used to mark time, and as an accompaniment to the songs. In using them, they were struck upon the seat as often as twice or thrice in a second, the song and the step of the dancers keeping time, notwithstanding the rapidity of the beat.

The band arrayed themselves in their costumes in an adjacent lodge, came into the council-house. . . . Instead of grouping, however, within the area of a circle, they ranged themselves in file, and danced slowly around the council-house in an elliptical line. When the music ceased, the dance also was suspended, and the party walked in column to the beat of the rattles. After an interval of about two minutes, the rattles quickened their time, the singers commenced another song, and the warriors, at the same instant, the dance. The leader, standing at the head of the column, opened, followed by those behind. As they advanced slowly around the room, in the dance, they gestured with their arms, and placed their bodies in a great variety of positions, but, unlike the practice in the War dance, always keeping their forms erect. None of the attitudes in this dance were those of the violent passions, but rather of the mild and gentle feelings. Consequently, there were no distortions either of the countenance or the body; but all their movements and positions were extremely graceful, dignified and imposing. . . . Each foot in succession is raised from two to eight inches from the floor, and the heel is then brought down with great force as frequently as the beat of the rattles. Frequently one heel is brought down twice or three times before it alternates with the other. This will convey an impression of the surprising activity of this dance, in which every muscle of the body appears to be strung to its highest degree of tension. The concussion of the foot upon the floor served the double purpose of shaking the rattles and bells, which form a part of the costume, and of adding to the noise and animation of the dance.

The dancers were usually nude down to the waist, with the exception of ornaments upon their arms and necks, as represented in the engraving, thus exposing their well-formed chests, finely rounded arms, and their smooth, evenly colored skins, of a clear and brilliant copper color. This exposure of the person, not in any sense displeasing, contributed materially to the beauty of the costume, and gave a striking expression to the figure of the dancer. Such was the physical exertion put forth in this dance, that before it closed, the vapor of perspiration steamed up, like smoke, from their uncovered backs. No better evidence than this need be given, that it was a dance full of earnestness and enthusiasm. One of their aims was to test each other's powers of endurance. It not unfrequently happened that a part of the original number yielded from exhaustion before the dance was ended. Nothing but practice superadded to flexibility of person and great muscular strength would enable even an Indian to perform this dance. When the popular applause was gained by one of the band for spirited or graceful dancing, he was called out to stand at the head of the column, and lead the party: in this way several changes of leaders occurred before the final conclusion of the figure.

In this dance the women participated, if they were disposed. They wore, however, their ordinary apparel, and entered by themselves at the foot of the column. The female step is entirely unlike the one described. They moved sideways in this figure, simply raising themselves alternately upon each foot from heel to toe, and then bringing down the heel upon the floor, at each beat of the rattle, keeping pace with the slowly advancing column. With the females dancing was a quiet and not ungraceful amusement.

As a scene, its whole effect was much increased by the arrangement of the dancers into column. In this long array of costumes, the peculiar features of each were brought more distinctly into view, and by keeping the elliptical area around which they moved, entirely free from the pressing throng of Indian spectators, a better opportunity was afforded to all to witness the performance. To one who has never seen this dance, it would be extremely difficult to convey any notion of its surprising activity, and its inspiring influence upon the spectators. Requiring an almost continuous exertion, it is truly a marvellous performance.

## ACTS OF REVERSAL

Among the most creative of Native American actions are those which gain their significance because of what by contrast they set off or distinguish. A range of figures from clowns to fools and tricksters gain their character and the potency of their action by various principles of symbolic reversal. Not only do acts of reversal establish the character of these religious figures, they are often associated with the symbolization of special religious modes of being. The following brief examples illustrate two cultural situations in which acts of reversal have important religious significance.

Emory Sekaquaptewa, a professor at the University of Arizona, maintains an active religious life at his home at Hopi. Based on his own experience and the stories related to him by his elders, Sekaquaptewa describes, in the following essay, the broad historical and ideological context in which Hopi clowning is performed and from which it draws its religious value. His presentation describes the extended scenario that unfolds throughout the two-day public dance performance of kachinas and clowns. Reflection upon the story that concludes Sekaquaptewa's essay allows one to appreciate the layer upon layer of meaning expressed throughout the symbolic acts of reversal that characterize Hopi clowns.

### *ONE MORE SMILE FOR A HOPI CLOWN by Emory Sekaquaptewa*[6]

The heart of the Hopi concept of clowning is that we are all clowns. This was established at the very beginning when people first emerged from the lower world. In spite of the belief that this was a new world in which no corruption and immorality would be present, the people nevertheless took as their own all things that they saw in the new world. Seeing that the people still carried with them many of the ways of the corrupted underworld, the Spirit Being divided them into groups and laid out a life-pattern for each of them, so that each would follow its own life-way.

Before the Hopi people left from the emergence place, one man chosen by them as their leader went up on a hill. I can just imagine the throng of his people around him who were excited and eager in getting ready to be led out to the adventures of a new world. The leader gets up on his hill and calls out, "yaahahay!" four times. Thus gaining their attention he said, "Now you heard me cry out to you in this way. You will hear me cry in this way when we have reached the end of our life-way. It will be a sign that we have reached the end of the world. We will know then whether we have fulfilled our destiny. If we have not we will see how it is to be done." The leader who was a visionary man chose this way of reminding his people that they have only their worldly ambition and aspirations by which to gain a spiritual world of eternity. He was showing them that we cannot be perfect in this world after all and if we are reminded that we are clowns, maybe we can have, from time to time, introspection as a guide to lead us right. From this beginning when we have been resembled to clowns we know that this is to be a trying life and that we will try to fulfill our destiny by mimicry, by mockery, by copying, by whatever.

This whole idea of clowning is re-enacted at the time of the *katsina* [commonly *kachina* in English] dances. When they are dancing in the plaza the *katsinas* represent the spiritual life toward which Hopi destiny is bent. The *katsinas* dance in the plaza at intervals throughout the day and sometimes for two days. When the clowns come they represent man today who is trying to reach this place of paradise. That is why the clowns always arrive at the plaza from the rooftops of the houses facing the plaza where the *katsinas* are dancing. The rooftops signify that even though we have reached the end, we are not necessarily ready to walk easily into the spiritual world. The difficulties by which clowns gain the place of the *katsinas* make for fun and laughter, but also show that we may not all be able to make it from the rooftop because it is too difficult. We are going to clown our way through life making believe that we know everything and when the time comes, possibly no one will be prepared after all to enter the next world. We will still find the way difficult with obstacles in front of us. Maybe some of us won't make it.

The clowns come to the edge of the housetops around noon and they announce themselves with the cry "yaahahay!" four times. This announces as foretold at emergence the arrival at the end of the life-way journey. And then they make their way into the plaza with all sorts of antics and buffoonery representing the Hopi life quest. In their actions they reveal that we haven't yet fulfilled our destiny after all. By arriving at the late hour, noon, they show that we are lagging behind because we think we have many things to do.

Once in the plaza they act just as people did when they emerged in this world. They presume that they are in a new world, clean and pure. They are where they can finally have eternal life like the *katsinas*; indeed, this is the day all Hopi look forward to. But as they are remarking on the beauty of this place filled with plants and good things they hear the *katsina* songs. They grope around the plaza looking for someone. They pretend they cannot see them because they are spirits. Finally, one of the clowns touches a *katsina* and upon his discovery of these beautiful beings, the clowns immediately try to take possession of them. "This is mine!" "This is mine!" They even fight each other over the possession of the *katsinas* and over the food and things they find.

The remainder of the afternoon is filled with all sorts of clown performances, many of which are planned in advance. Others just happen. These are satires focused on almost anything whether it be in the Hopi world or in the non-Hopi world. Clowns make fun of life and thereby cause people to look at themselves.

Imagination is important to the clown. There are good clowns and not so good clowns when it comes to being funny and witty. But all clowns perform for the smiles and laughter they hope to inspire in the people. When the clowns leave the kiva on their way to the plaza the last request by each is a prayer something to the effect, "If it be so, may I gain at least one smile."

The clown skits and satiric performances done throughout the afternoon are reminiscent of the corruption that we experienced in the underworld, where we presumably had Conscience as a guide. We chose not to follow the Conscience and it comes into play during the clown performances in the form of *katsinas* that visit the plaza. The Owl *katsina* on his first visit comes with a handful of pebbles, carrying a switch. He appears at each corner of the plaza presumably unseen by the clowns and throws little pebbles at the clowns, occasionally hitting them. These pangs of Conscience are felt but not heeded by the clowns. Owl *katsina* returns to the plaza later accompanied by several threatening *katsinas* carrying whips. And this time, instead of pebbles, he may brush up against one of the clowns. He may even knock him down. Conscience keeps getting stronger and more demanding and insistent. On Owl's third visit, the clowns begin to realize that they may suffer consequences if they don't change their ways. Still, they try to buy their safety by offering Owl a bribe. On the sly, the head clown approaches Owl, presumably unseen by anyone, but, of course, they are in the middle of the plaza and are witnessed by all the spectators. Those two kneel together in an archaic conversation modeled upon an ancient meeting.

Owl finally accepts the bribe of a string of beads and thus leads the clown to believe that he has bought his safety. The head clown asks Owl to discipline the other clowns so as to get them back on the right road, but he thinks he will be safe.

With each of Owl's visits more and more *katsinas* accompany him. They do not come as one big group, but in groups of two or three. Throughout the afternoon the tension builds with the threatening presence of the whip-carrying *katsinas*. All of the spectators begin to identify with the plight of the clowns. You feel like you are the one who is now being judged for all these things.

Owl's fourth visit may not come until the next day. On this visit he brings with him a whole lot of warrior *katsinas*. The atmosphere is one of impending catastrophe. They move closer and closer, finally attacking the clowns, who are stripped and whipped for all they have done. In this way they force the clowns to take responsibility for their actions. After they are whipped, water is poured on them and sprinkled about the audience to signify purification.

When it is all over the threatening *katsinas* come back to the plaza again, but this time they are friendly. They shake hands with the clowns signifying that they have been purified. Then they take each clown the length of the plaza and form a semi-circle around him. At this time the clowns make confessions, but even here they are clowns for their confessions are all made in jest. Having worked up satires for the occasion they jump and sing before the *katsinas*. Their confessions usually are focused on their clan, who, by way of being satirized, are actually honored.

I'll tell you one I heard not long ago. When it was time for this young clown man to make his confession he jumps up and down in front of the *katsina* and says, "ah ii geology, geology, ah ii." Then he made a beautiful little breakdown of this word so that it has Hopi meaning. "You probably think I am talking about this geology which is a white man's study about something or other. Well, that's not it," he says. "What it really is is that I have a grandmother, and you know she being poor and ugly, nobody would have anything to do with her. She is running around all summer long out in the fields doing a man's job. It breaks her down. She would go out there every day with no shoes and so her feet were not very dainty and not very feminine. If you pick up her foot and look at her sole, it is all cracked and that's what I am talking about when I say geology." Every Hopi can put that together. *Tsiya* means "to crack" and *leetsi* means things placed "in a row," so these cracks are in a row on the bottom of the feet, geology. Things like that are what the confessions are like.

There is a story about the last wish of a Hopi man who died many years ago that shows the character of clowning.

In those days the clown society was very much formalized. It was a practice for men who had great devotion for their ritual society to be buried in the full costume of their office. Of course, this was not seen by the general public since Hopi funerals are rather private affairs.

This story is about a man who had gained great respect for his resourcefulness and performance as a clown. Clowning had become a major part of his life and he was constantly attending to his work as a clown by thinking up new skits and perfecting his performance. As he reached old age he decided that clowning had made his place in this world and he wanted to be remembered as a clown. So he made a special request for what was to be done with him at his death as he realized his time was short. He made his request to his family very firmly.

When he died his nephews and sons began to carry out his request. In preparation for burial the body was dressed in his clown costume. Then the body was carried around to the west side of the plaza and taken up on a roof. While this was being done the town crier's voice rang out through the village calling all the people to the plaza. Everybody was prompt in gathering there. I can just see the women, as with any such occasion, grabbing their best shawl on their way to the plaza. It didn't matter whether they were dressed well underneath the shawl.

When the people arrived they saw this unusual sight on the roof of the house on the west side of the plaza, men standing around a person lying down. When all of the people had gathered, the attendants—pallbearers I guess you could call them—simply, quietly, picked up the body and took it to the edge of the house near the plaza. They picked it up by the hands and legs and swung it out over the plaza as if to throw it and they hollered, "Yaahahay!" And they'd swing it back. Then they'd swing it once more. "Yaahahay!" Four times! On the fourth time they let the body go and it fell down, plop, in the plaza. As they threw the body the pallbearers hollered and laughed as they were supposed to. It took the people by surprise. But then everybody laughed.

The Huichol of northern Mexico engage in an annual pilgrimage to the place of their origins, Wirikuta, where they collect peyote and spend a night experiencing the oneness of the many elements within their world—the peyote, the deer, and the maize—as well as a union with their deities. The special status of the pilgrims, who personify deities during the journey is signified by a complex set of inversions of actions. In a remarkable statement obtained by Barbara Myerhoff during her important study of the Huichol pilgrimage, a *mara'akáme* or pilgrimage leader describes these acts of reversal and their importance and significance to the Huichol pilgrimage.

## *HOW THE NAMES ARE CHANGED ON THE PEYOTE JOURNEY by Ramon Medina Silva*[7]

Well, let's see now. I shall speak about how we do things when we go and seek the peyote, how we change the names of everything. How we call the things we see and do by another name for all those days. Until we return. Because all must be done as it must be done. As it was laid down in the beginning. How it was when the mara'akáme who is Tatewarí* led all those great ones to Wirikuta. When they crossed over there, to the peyote country. Because that is a very sacred thing, it is the most sacred. It is our life, as one says. That is why nowadays one gives things other names. One changes everything. Only when they return home, then they call everything again that it is.

When everything is ready, when all the symbols which we take with us, the gourd bowls, the yarn discs, the arrows, everything has been made, when all have prayed together we set out. Then we must change everything, all the meanings. For instance: a pot which is black and round, it is called a head. It is the mara'akáme who directs everything. He is the one who listens in his dream, with his power and his knowledge. He speaks to Tatewarí, he speaks to Kauyumari.† Kauyumari tells him everything, how it must be. Then he says to his companions, if he is the leader of the journey to the peyote, look, this thing is this way, and this is how it must be done. He tells them, look, now we will change everything, all the meanings, because that is the way it must be with the *bikuritámete* (peyote pilgrims). As it was in ancient times, so that all can be united. As it was long ago, before the time of my grandfather, even before the time of his grandfather. So the mara'akáme has to see to everything, so that as much as possible all the words are changed. Only when one comes home, then everything can be changed back again to the way it was.

"Look," the mara'akáme says to them, "it is when you say 'good morning,' you mean 'good evening,' everything is backwards. You say 'goodbye, I am leaving you,' but you are really coming. You do not shake hands, you shake feet. You hold out your right foot to be shaken by the foot of your companion. You say 'good afternoon,' yet it is only morning."

So the mara'akáme tells them, as he has dreamed it. He dreams it differently each time. Every year they change the names of things differently because every year the mara'akáme dreams new names. Even if it is the same mara'akáme who leads the journey, he still changes the names each time differently.

And he watches who makes mistakes because there must be no error. One must use the names the mara'akáme has dreamed. Because if one makes an error it is not right. That is how it is. It is a beautiful thing because it is right. Daily, daily, the mara'akáme goes explaining everything to them so that they do not make mistakes. The mara'akáme says to a companion, "Look, why does that man over there watch us, why does he stare at us?" And then he says, "Look, what is it he has to stare at us?" "His eyes," says his companion. "No," the mara'akáme answers, "they are not his eyes, they are tomatoes." That is how he goes explaining how everything should be called.

When one makes cigarettes for the journey, one uses the dried husks of maize for the wrappings. And the tobacco, it is called the droppings of ants. Tortillas one calls bread. Beans one calls fruit from a tree. Maize is wheat. Water is tequila. Instead of saying, "Let us go and get water to drink," you say, "Ah, let us take tequila to eat." *Atole* [maize broth], that is brains. Sandals are cactus. Fingers are sticks. Hair, that is cactus fiber. The moon, that is a cold sun.

On all the trails on which we travel to the peyote country, as we see different things we make this change. That is because the peyote is very sacred, very sacred. That is why it is reversed. Therefore, when we see a dog, it is a cat, or it is

---

*Huichol name for the deity with whom the shaman has a special affinity, roughly translatable as Our Grandfather Fire.

†Kauyumari is a trickster hero, quasi-deified and roughly translatable as Sacred Deer Person.

a coyote. Ordinarily, when we see a dog, it is just a dog, but when we walk for the peyote it is a cat or a coyote or even something else, as the mara'akáme dreams it. When we see a burro, it is not a burro, it is a cow, or a horse. And when we see a horse, it is something else. When we see a dove or a small bird of some kind, is it a small bird? No, the mara'akáme says, it is an eagle, it is a hawk. Or a piglet, it is not a piglet, it is an armadillo. When we hunt the deer, which is very sacred, it is not a deer, on this journey. It is a lamb, or a cat. And the nets for catching deer? They are called sewing thread.

When we say come, it means go away. When we say "shh, quiet," it means to shout, and when we whistle or call to the front we are really calling to a person behind us. We speak in this direction here. That one over there turns because he already knows how it is, how everything is reversed. To say, "Let us stay here," means to go, "let us go," and when we say "sit down," we mean, "stand up." It is also so when we have crossed over, when we are in the country of the peyote. Even the peyote is called by another name, as the mara'akáme dreamed. Then the peyote is flower or something else.

It is so with Tatewarí, with Tayaupa.* The mara'akáme, we call him Tatewarí. He is Tatewarí, he who leads us. But there in Wirikuta, one says something else. One calls him "the red one." And Tayaupa, he is "the shining one." So all is changed. Our companion who is old, he is called the child. Our companion who is young, he is the old one. When we want to speak of the machete, we say "hook." When one speaks of wood, one really means fish. Begging your pardon, instead of saying "to eat," we say "to defecate." And, begging your pardon, "I am going to urinate" means "I am going to drink water." When speaking of blowing one's nose, one says "give me the honey." "He is deaf" means "how well he hears." So everything is changed, everything is different or backwards.

The mara'akáme goes explaining how everything should be said, everything, many times, or his companions would forget and make errors. In the late afternoon, when all are gathered around Tatewarí, we all pray there, and the mara'akáme tells how it should be. So for instance he says, "Do not speak of this one or that one as serious. Say he is a jaguar. You see an old woman and her face is all wrinkled, coming from afar, do not say, 'Ah, there is a man,' say 'Ah, here comes a wooden image.' You say, 'Here comes the image of Santo Cristo.' Or if it is a woman coming, say 'Ah, here comes the image of Guadalupe.'"

Women, you call flowers. For the woman's skirts, you say, "bush," and for her blouse you say "palm roots." And a man's clothing, that too is changed. His clothing, you call his fur. His hat, that is a mushroom. Or it is his sandal. Begging your pardon, but what we carry down here, the testicles, they are called avocados. And the penis, that is his nose. That is how it is.

When we come back with the peyote, the peyote which has been hunted, they make a ceremony and everything is changed back again. And those who are at home, when one returns they grab one and ask, "What is it you called things? How is it that now you call the hands hands but when you left you called them feet?" Well, it is because they have changed the names back again. And they all want to know what they called things. One tells them, and there is laughter. That is how it is. Because it must be as it was said in the beginning, in ancient times.

---

*Our Father Sun.

## *NOTES*

1. Edmund Carpenter, "Image Making in Arctic Art" in *Sign, Image, Symbol*, ed. Gyorgy Kepes (New York: George Braziller, 1966), pp. 206–225. Reprinted by permission of George Braziller, Inc. See also E. Carpenter, *Eskimo Realities* (New York: Holt, Rinehart & Winston, 1973).
2. Ted J. Brasser, *"Bo'jou, Neejee!" Profiles of Canadian Indian Art* (Ottawa: National Museum of Man, 1976).
3. Alfred W. Bowers, *Mandan Social and Ceremonial Organization* (Chicago: University of Chicago Press, 1950), pp. 194–96. Reprinted by permission of the University of Chicago Press.
4. A revised version of Sam D. Gill, "Whirling Logs and Coloured Sands," in *Native Religious Traditions*, ed. Earle H. Waugh and K. Dad Prithipaul (Waterloo, Ontario: Wilfrid Laurier University Press, 1979), pp. 151–63. Used by permission of Wilfrid Laurier University Press.
5. Lewis H. Morgan, *League of the Ho-De-No Sau-Ne or Iroquois* (first published 1851; new ed. edited and annotated by Herbert M. Lloyd, New York: Dodd Mead and Company, 1901; reprinted New Haven: Human Relations Area Files, (1954), vol. I, pp. 252, 257–72. Notes omitted.
6. Emory Sekaquaptewa, "One More Smile for a Hopi Clown," *Parabola*, vol. IV, no. 1, pp. 6–9. Reprinted by permission of Emory Sekaquaptewa.
7. An appendix to Barbara G. Myerhoff, "Return to Wirikuta: Ritual Reversal and Symbolic Continuity on the Peyote Hunt of the Huichol Indians," in *The Reversible World: Symbolic Inversion in Art and Society*, ed. Barbara A. Babcock, (Ithaca: Cornell University Press, 1978), pp. 236–239. Copyright © 1978 by Cornell University. Reprinted by permission of Cornell University Press.

# CHAPTER 5

# *Religion and the Life Cycle*

## INTRODUCTION

The life cycle or the road of life, as it is so often called by Native Americans, is a journey marked by many formal religious occasions and by a host of principles that dictate actions or avoidances. From conception through death, for every moment of transition from stage to stage in life, and for most occasions of crisis and accomplishment, religious beliefs prescribe the actions to be taken or avoided and the attitudes and ideas to be held. While formal rites of the life cycle may be understood from one perspective as celebrative in character, it is often more accurate to recognize that these religious acts bring about the transitions from stage to stage and that they meet and effectively resolve the many crises, such as sickness and bad luck, that confront one during life. For Native Americans, life's road is a journey powered by the hand of religious traditions.

## PREGNANCY, BIRTH, CHILDHOOD, AND NAMING

The beginning of life is a most important time. Although it is not often the occasion for large formal public ritual, the prenatal period and the event of birth are religiously important for most Native American peoples. Since this period is one in which the individual is formed, many Native American peoples pay careful attention to social, psychological, and religious, as well as physical, development. Often the prenatal period is one during which the expectant mother is heavy-laden with restrictions and special observations. These may extend to the father and the immediate family and some even to the entire community. While at the surface these restrictions may appear to the outsider as mere superstition, they are linked with beliefs, values, and world views that must be communicated to the forming child and which must be reaffirmed by the family and community into which the child will be born. These special actions are linked with the understanding that the future of the community depends upon the children, whose responsibilities for their heritage must be constantly nurtured from the moment of conception.

Many Native Americans begin their own life stories with the account of their births and even their prenatal existence. In such stories we can often appreciate the religious importance of birth and how it is closely observed for signs of the person's future life. In the following account, Don Talayesva, a Hopi, begins his life story with his prenatal existence. The account is a richly detailed description of the Hopi practices associated with the event of birth and it illuminates the religious importance of these careful actions. For the Hopi, birth is something of a two-stage affair. First, coincident with physical birth, one is born into one's mother's clan. Here in the darkened clan house, womb-like in atmosphere, the infant is nurtured for a period of time by its clan mothers. Later it is taken from the clan house at dawn to greet the rising sun, to receive its baby names from women in its father's clan, and to be received by the larger community.

## *TWINS TWISTED INTO ONE by Don Talayesva*[1]

When we were within our mother's womb, we happened to hurt her. She has told me how she went to a medicine man in her pain. He worked on her, felt her breasts and belly, and told her that we were twins. She was surprised and afraid. She said, "But I want only one baby." "Then I will put them together," replied the doctor. He took some corn meal outside the door and sprinkled it to the sun. Then he spun some black and white wool, twisted the threads into a string, and tied it around my mother's left wrist. It is a powerful way to unite babies. We twins began, likewise, to twist ourselves into one child. My mother also helped to bring us together by her strong wish for only one baby.

My mother has described how carefully she carried me. She slept with my father right along, so that he could have intercourse with her and make me grow. It is like irrigating a crop: if a man starts to make a baby and then stops, his wife has a hard time. She had intercourse only with my father so that I could have an easy birth and resemble him.

She refused to hold another woman's child on her lap and took care not to breathe into the face of small children and cause them to waste away. She had nothing to do with the tanning of skins or the dyeing of anything lest she spoil the goods and also injure me. When she grew big, she was careful to sit in such a way that other people would not walk in front of her and thus make my birth difficult. She would not look at the serpent images displayed in the ceremonies, lest I turn myself into a water snake while still in her womb and raise up my head at the time of birth, instead of lying with head down seeking a way out.

My father has related how he took care to injure no animal and thus damage my body. If he had cut off the foot of any living creature, I might have been born without a hand or with a clubfoot. Any cruel treatment of a dumb beast would have endangered my life. If he had drawn a rope too tightly around the neck of a sheep or burro, it might have caused my navel cord to loop itself about my neck and strangle me in birth. Even if I had been able to free myself from the cord, I might have remained half choked and short of breath for a long time.

Whenever I made movements in the womb, my mother was encouraged to expect an early and easy birth. She worked hard at cooking, grinding corn, and bringing water, so that her baby would be in trim for labor. My father fed her the raw flesh of a weasel and rubbed the skin on her body so that I could be active and come out swiftly, in the way that sly little animal slips through a hole.

I have heard that I had a hard birth. It began in the early evening of a day in March, 1890. Since the exact date was not remembered, I could never have a birthday. When my mother's face darkened and she felt the expected pains, she settled down on the earthen floor in the third-story room of her Sun Clan house. She had sent my five-year old sister Tuvamainim with my little brother Namostewa to a neighbor's house. Namostewa was about two years old and still nursing.

My grandfather (mother's father, Homikniwa of the Lizard Clan), who lived in the same house with my mother and father, has told me how he climbed the ladder to the third floor where my mother lay. There he rubbed her belly and turned me straight to come out. The power in his hands helped her womb. His presence encouraged her, too, because he was the best medicine man in Oraibi. My father, Tuvanimptewa of the Sand Clan, also came in to help, which was rather unusual for a Hopi husband. He soon sent for Nuvaiumsie, an experienced old midwife and a member of his father's linked Water-Coyote Clan. As soon as she came, she heated water in a clay pot over coals in an old-fashioned fireplace in the southwest corner of the room.

In labor, according to all reports, my mother moved over on a pile of sand which was especially prepared for my birth, rested herself on hands and knees, raised her head a little, and began to strain downward. My father and her father took turns standing over her with their arms around her belly, pressing down gently and trying to force and shake me out. If I had refused to come, more and more pressure would have been applied, but no Hopi doctor would have opened her body to get me.

I was a big baby. I caused a lot of trouble and took a long time coming out—head first. Old Nuvaiumsie is said to have taken me fresh and crying from my mother. She cut my navel cord on an arrow to make me a good hunter, folded back my end of the cord, and tied it about a finger's length from the navel to keep out any fresh air. She used a piece of string from my mother's hair, which was the proper thing to do. If she had not tied the cord securely, fresh air would have entered my belly and killed me. My mother was given some small twigs of juniper to chew and some juniper tea, in order to strengthen her and to hasten the discharge of the afterbirth.

My grandfather, my father, and Nuvaiumsie examined me closely. Sure enough, I was twins twisted into one. They could see that I was an oversize baby, that my hair curled itself into two little whorls instead of one at the back of my head, and that in front of my body I was a boy but at the back there was the sure trace of a girl—the imprint of a little vulva that slowly disappeared. They have told me time after time that I was twice lucky—lucky to be born twins and lucky to just miss becoming a girl.

In Native American cultures, names are usually not simply labels that help to distinguish one person from another. They often are consciously used and understood as shaping or reflecting the very identity and character of a person. Some names are given with the intent that the bearer should aspire to live according to the attributes of the name. In other instances, names may be given to reflect character faults or unacceptable behavior, often with the explicit intent at criticism. Often individuals receive a succession of names during their lifetime. This is reflected in the following comment on names by Long Lance, a member of the Blood Band of Blackfeet.

## *WHAT'S IN AN INDIAN NAME? by Long Lance*[2]

In the civilization in which we live, a man may be one thing and appear to be another. But this is not possible in the social structure of the Indian, because an Indian's name tells the world what he is: a coward, a liar, a thief, or a brave.

When I was a youngster every Indian had at least three names during his lifetime. His first name, which he received at birth and retained until he was old enough to go on the war-path, was descriptive of some circumstance surrounding his birth. As an instance, we have a man among the Blackfeet whose name is Howling-in-the-Middle-of-the-Night. When he was born along the banks of the Belly River in southern Alberta, the Indian woman who was assisting his mother went out to the river to get some water with which to wash him. When she returned to the teepee she remarked: "I heard a wolf howling across the river." "Then," said the baby's mother, "I shall call my son 'Howling-in-the-Middle-of-the-Night'."

This birth name of the youngster was supposed to be retained by him until he was old enough to earn one for himself; but always when he grew old enough to play with other children his playmates would give him a name of their own by which he would be known among them, no matter what his parents called him. And this name often was not flattering; for we Indian boys were likely to choose some characteristic defect on which to base our names for our playmates—such as Bow Legs, Crazy Dog, Crooked Nose, Bad Boy, or Wolf Tail. Instances are known where these boyhood nicknames have been so characteristic of the youngster that they have superseded his birth name and stuck with him throughout his life, if he was not able to earn a better one on the war-path.

But the real name of the Indian was earned in the latter instance: when he was old enough to go out for his first fight against the enemy. His life name depended on whatever showing he should make in his first battle. When he returned from the war-path the whole tribe would gather to witness the ceremony in which he would be given his tribal name by the chief of the tribe. If he made a good showing, he would be given a good name, such as: Uses-Both-Arms, Charging Buffalo, Six Killer, Good Striker, Heavy Lance, or Many Chiefs. But if he should make a poor showing his name might be: Crazy Wolf, Man-Afraid-of-a-Horse, or Smoking-Old-Woman. Thus, an Indian's name tells his record or what kind of man he is.

But a man was given many opportunities to improve his name as time went on. If he should go into some future battle and pull off some unusual exploit against the enemy he would be given a better name. Some of our great warriors have had as many as twelve names—all good names, and each one better than the one that preceded it. No matter how many names were successively given to him, all of his past names belonged to him just the same, and no one else could adopt them. These names were just as patently his as if they had been copyrighted; and even he, himself, could not give one of them away. Indian names were handed out by the tribe, not the family, and no man could give his name even to his own son, unless the chief and the tribe should ask him to, as a result of some noteworthy deed his son had performed. I know of only three or four instances where this has happened, and it is the rarest honour that can befall a person—the honour of assuming one's father's name. In my day every son had to earn his own name.

The foregoing is the reason why no old Indian will ever tell you his own name. If you ask him he will turn to some third person and nod for him to tell you. The reason for this is that he is too modest to brag of his exploits on the war-path. His names are like decorations in the white man's army, and the Indian has a certain reticence against advertising his bravery by pronouncing his own name in public.

There are certain 'Chief Names' among the Indians which the original owners made so distinguished that the tribe never allows them to pass out. These names are perpetuated in successive generations, and after a while they become a dynastical name, such as 'Ptolemy' in the Egyptian line of rulers. One of my names, Chief Buffalo Child, is a dynastical name and title among the Blood Band of Blackfeet living at Cardston, Alberta. The original Chief Buffalo Child was killed in battle, in what is now Montana, more than eighty years ago; and years ago when I became a chief of this band his name was resurrected and perpetuated in the present holder of the title—thanks to our war chiefs, Mountain Horse and Heavy Shields, and to the Blood Missionary, the Reverend Canon S. Middleton.

I have four other names: Night Traveller, Spotted Calf, Holds Fire, and Long Lance. Of these latter four I valued Spotted Calf the most, because it was given to me by my adopted mother, Spotted Calf, wife of Sounding Sky, father and mother of the famous Indian outlaw, Almighty Voice—whose lone-handed battle against the Royal North-West Mounted Police has become a conspicuous page in northwestern history. This wonderful woman, Spotted Calf—daughter of the renowned Chief One Arrow—who stuck to her son throughout his sensational siege and shouted advice to him through a rain of bullets, is still living (1928) on the One Arrow Indian Reserve at Duck Lake, Saskatchewan. I think her name ranks with those of great warriors, and that is why I value it, and her motherhood.

## ACQUIRING RELIGIOUS KNOWLEDGE AND COMING OF AGE

For most Native American peoples, the acquisition of knowledge is an open ended affair that extends throughout one's life. Still, there are the occasions of formal rites of passage when new religious knowledge is obtained as one is inducted into a new stage of maturity. In such rites one often acquires a new name and a whole set of new relationships and responsibilities. There are many types of these ritual passageways, rich and complex in appearance and significance.

Widely practiced in North America until recently was the vision quest. Youths went into isolation to fast and to humble themselves in preparation for receiving their visions. Their vision experiences often allied them with guardian spirits and the substance of their visions served as models for their future lives. Vision experiences gave access to knowledge and power. While visions were often sought in the process of entering adulthood, they were also sought on many other occasions.

At present, fewer tribes and communities continue to send their youths in quest of visions. A remarkable account of a recent vision quest is that of Arthur Amiotte who, upon reaching adulthood, acquiring a university education, and after gaining employment as an artist found that his way of life was undirected and could not be fulfilled without undergoing the vision quest, a tradition of his people, the Sioux. He describes the first of several annual fasts.

### *EAGLES FLY OVER by Arthur Amiotte*[3]

*Petaǧa is a medicine man of the Sioux people. He lives in a little hut of logs and mud near the white sandstone buttes of Payaba Community on the Pine Ridge Reservation. His face is noble, deep-lined with age and bold with wisdom tempered by hard work, weather and uncompromising devotion to living out his vision.*

*His large rough hands tell the story of a man whose youth was spent in labor yet who in his time has touched and guided saint and sinner to enlightenment with gentle and self-sacrificing effacement.*

*Petaǧa Yuha Mani—He Walks with Coals of Fire.*
*I sought him out and he spoke to me like this:*

. . .Life is like a huge design. Each part of the design is made up of the happenings, acts and interactions of people with each other and the world. You must know that this design is completed by the intervention of Wakan Tanka. People and this world and all that is in it are only a part of Wakan Tanka, the lesser part when you consider the limitlessness of eternity and the universe, and the limits and relative insignificance of matter as we know ourselves and this world to be.

Yet from the holy goodness of Wakan Tanka a way was given us—for he loves his children and this creation—that we may pray, and have a glimpse, a little knowledge, of the Great Mystery that is this life. He has given us a way that we may be reminded regularly of our obligations as *ikće wicasa*—original man—and what we must do in this life to be good people, men, women, and children, and how to remember our origins and to honor our creator. He has given us a way that we may ask his help in times of need and also give thanks in times of joy. Wakan Tanka is all that is wondrous, awesome, powerful, and infinite, and yet he is also personal, compassionate, loving and tender. Perhaps this is why we call him Great Mystery.

Look at the tiny ants going about their business on the ground in front of us. In this world, everything has its purpose, its time and its place, from the smallest particle to the powerful storms as they sweep and wash the face of the land. Men also come and go, but man is different from the ants for he must learn where his place is and what his life means. That we may do this, our people were given a way of prayer that is called the Buffalo Calf Pipe. We were given ceremonies in which we pray with the pipe, ways that we may stand before Wakan Tanka so that he will instruct us about our place in his design.

You must know that a medicine man among our people is in possession of a special office. He is a servant of the people and of the gods. He enters upon a way that is sometimes not of his choosing, sometimes because he chose. I have known people who have bought their office. Some are good and some use it to their own advantage.

I did not ask for my office. My work was made for me and given to me by the other world, by the Thunder Beings. I am compelled to live this way that is not of my own choosing, because they chose me. I am a poor man; see how I dress and the house I live in. My whole life is to do the bidding of the Thunder Beings and of my people and to pay heed to what the Grandfathers tell me. You have come to see me, but did you know how to come?

To enter into any ceremony is a most sacred act. It begins in the mind of a person either by himself or because other beings chose him for their purposes. When it is clear that a man has an intention, he must prepare himself by being honest within himself about what it is he desires and intends to do. If after he has examined himself well he feels confident that he wants and needs the help of a counsellor, an intercessor, he must fill a good pipe with red willow bark tobacco and seek out the medicine man he wishes to see and whose help he wants. When he approaches the home of the medicine man he should rid himself of all undesirable thoughts so that his mind might be clear to utter his request as a petition prayer.

As a man with a filled pipe approaches a medicine man, he should realize that this man, depending on his predilections and his ability to read the intent of his visitor, has the right to refuse the offered pipe. A petitioner should be prepared to offer the filled pipe four times, each time stepping back and extending the pipe at arm's length. It is important also to hold the pipe bowl in the left hand when offering the pipe as this signifies that the intent is coming from the heart, and is a sign of sincerity and honesty. If the medicine man accepts the pipe on the first or any other offering, it means he is willing to listen to your request, but it does not mean he will grant it. He will either light the pipe himself or ask you to light it. While he smokes the pipe, you must make your request. Since the pipe is being smoked in a sacred manner, you must make your petition as simply and as honestly as you can, for depending on what you say and how you say it, the medicine man will deliberate and make his decision. When the smoking is finished and after the bowl has been emptied of its ashes, a less formal conversation will follow.

This filled pipe is called an *opaği*. Long ago, smoking materials were not always available, and the host who wished to show his high regard for a guest and to express his hospitality offered him smoke from a pipe. Since we medicine men are servants of the Powers and the people, we own little or nothing and sacrifice our whole lives that our people may live; so tradition has granted us this one pleasure that as old men we may smoke and pray while preparing to do our work. But what is more important than this is that what is said while the pipe is smoked is included in the prayers, and that while the medicine man smokes he unites his words and yours with the smoke as it rises through the air to the always-listening ears of Wakan Tanka.

This is the beginning and how it should be done. Go now, prepare yourself, think things through in your mind. In a month you may come back prepared to do things in the proper way. . . .

A storm was coming and there were still a lot of things to do. It had been a very unsettling day, full of anticipation and dread. It had begun with a dream in the early hours: I was sitting against a white chalk cliff—a place that I have seen before, perhaps in my early childhood while exploring near my grandparents' home here on the reservation. In the dream, as I sat, two eagles were soaring in the distance and then began to approach me. As they came closer and swooped down I saw they had huge beaks and large eyes that seemed to penetrate my mind. Diving down in front of me they said, "We have come for you now." Then they swerved and flew upward and away and the dream ended.

When I woke I pondered the meaning of this dream and decided the ceremony had begun and the eagle nation was already waiting for me.

I had to go in to Pine Ridge and set up an account at a local store so my relatives would be able to buy meat and other food for the ceremonial meals that would take place while I was gone. I also had to find a wooden bowl, twine, colored cloth, and tobacco to take to the medicine man so his wife could make the rosary-like strings of tobacco offerings wrapped in tiny cloth squares, to enclose the sacred area where I would stand for the Pipe Fast. The day seemed to pass too quickly; I couldn't find a decent wooden bowl, and kept mentally telling the eagles, "I'm coming, I'm coming." Finally I had to settle for an old bowl that I sanded down to the unused wood. Somehow I collected the other things I needed: a quilt and a blanket that had never been used, a large knife, a pail and dipper, yard squares of red, yellow, green, and white cloth, Bull Durham tobacco, an eagle feather attached to a conch shell disc, and of course my pipe, sage, and a braid of sweet grass. One thing that was hard to find was wild chokecherry juice; fortunately one of my neighbors found a jar of canned chokecherries and I could use the juice from that.

The storm was getting closer and there was more sage to gather and four chokecherry trees to cut. My aunt and my grandmother drove with me to my cousin's place and we picked sage. Before we picked it I offered pinches of tobacco and addressed the gray grass, our oldest plant relative, asking it to help me in the task I was going to undertake. I asked it to forgive me for uprooting it and I asked the creation to accept the tobacco as an offering:

> Peji ȟota, my relative,
> from time immemorial you have helped us.
> It is said you are one of our first and oldest medicines.
> Peji ȟota, I have come to get you now
> for I wish you to help me and protect me.
> You were here first and know many things.
> I am only a man seeking a way and a place.
>
> Peji ȟota, forgive me for taking you away from this place.
> You will be put in another one
> in which you will be recognized
> by those who already know you.
> You will become a ceremony.
>
> Peji ȟota, accept this offering and help me
> in the way that is your way
> that my relatives and I may know and live.

I had yet to cut the four cherry trees. I wanted them to be fresh, so I would have to cut them the next morning, but I wanted to find them now. I drove towards Wounded Knee, and along the road by Jumping Eagle's place there was a nice stand of bushes. I crawled into them and chose four straight trees and marked them with yellow ribbon so I could find them easily at dawn when I went to cut them. As I tied each ribbon I addressed the trees asking them to forgive me for doing this: I was going to sacrifice them, but they would be serving the order of things in a different way, and helping to bring life to a person, and to the people, otherwise than by giving their fruit to eat.

I had just gotten back to the house when the rain started. Some relatives came to visit and stayed very late. I had wanted to sit down at the sewing machine and hem a piece of cloth for my ceremonial breech cloth, but the electricity went off and we spent most of the night by candle light. Finally I began to fix the cloth by hand and my aunt finished it when the power came back on again about one o'clock in the morning.

I had gotten a puppy from my grandmother's sister for the sacrifice that had to take place on the evening of the first day of my fast. After we had kept it for about three weeks, my little son Andrew had become as fond of it as I had, but I told him that I would have to take it home later on and that we couldn't keep it or name it. This night the puppy slept soundly; but in the distance, yet seemingly close at hand, another puppy was crying. It reminded us of the one that was sacrificed at the first Eagle Ceremony at Pete Catches'* place, at which the time and day of my fast was designated for me. That puppy had not been cooked for the feast following the ceremony proper, but was put in an old car until the next day. During the ceremony it yelped and cried; we were told that it wanted to be

---

*Pete Catches is Petaġa's everyday name. He is called Petaġa only when ritually addressed.

inside where we were, but since it could not it was crying and praying that I would have good weather when the time of my fast arrived. The voice of that pup was just like the one we were hearing tonight, nearby yet far-off; and now we felt confident that the weather would be good in the following days, since my first puppy was still crying and praying for me from wherever it is that sacrificed puppies go.

We slept for an hour or two and were up again a little after three. Andrew was sound asleep; he had been told that his father was going away to a meeting. I felt that it was indeed to be the meeting of myself with the richest traditions of our people, a meeting that would begin my spiritual journey through a timeless place; for here were to be joined the ritual and wisdom of the ancients and a contemporary soul adrift in a chaotic world. I hoped I would be worthy and would recognize and understand the truth in the newness and strangeness of what was to come.

My grandmother cooked breakfast and we were on our way before four. We stopped along the road and I chopped down the four cherry trees and put them in the car. At one point a porcupine crossed the highway in front of us, and a little later, three deer.

The ceremony was to take place at Pete Catches' (Petaġa's) country place at Payaba Mission. We found the road passable, even though it had rained very hard the night before. Shortly after we arrived, Catches' brother drove up and began to get the fire ready to heat the stones for the sweat bath. The men all went up to the sweat lodge on the hillside, and the women stayed down by the house.

By this time the fire was burning hard and Catches was now ritually filling his pipe and mine and offering them to the four quarters, the sky and the earth. I was to take mine with me to the hilltop. His would be left filled inside the sweat lodge for the duration of the fast. His brother tore pieces of the red cloth I had brought and prepared four little tobacco offerings—flags attached to short sticks, which were placed on the earth altar in front of the door which faced west and towards the fire where the rocks were heating. Sage had already been spread on the floor of the lodge. The four colored cloths I brought were also tied on sticks and stuck in the ground outside the door near the earth altar, after they had been purified inside the sweat lodge over the first steam, before the door was closed.

I had already attached the feather to the shell disc, and now Catches tied it to my hair on the back of my head. We stripped and entered the lodge. I hadn't brought a towel so I used my shirt to wipe myself during and after the bath.

Inside I was seated facing the door with the fire pit between me and the door. Catches sat to my left, or on the right as one entered the lodge. Catches' brother placed the rocks in the pit in the center of the lodge with a pitchfork, after which he entered and sat on my other side. A pail of water, the wooden bowl, dipper, knife, and pipes were now arranged in their proper places, my pipe being set before me on the sage. Before the door was closed some prayers were said and the bowl, the knife, and the bowls of the pipes were touched to the heated stones.

After the door was closed, Catches prayed and told of his power, and then told from the beginning the story of my coming there. He repeated my prayer of supplication from the first time I offered him the pipe, before and during the Eagle ceremony. Then the singing began and the Eagle's wings touched me.

Water was poured on the hot stones and steam arose with the praying.

I think it was then that the little bird sound was in the lodge; and now Catches' brother repeated my prayer to Red Hawk, Petaġa's intercessor; then the wings touched me again.

Four times, water was poured on the stones and steam filled the lodge and sweat poured from me as I have never known it to do before.

At the end of some prayers the door was opened and a dipper of water was passed out of the door to someone—I think it was Catches' wife—and when it was handed back, water was offered to me and then to the others, and we drank.

The door was closed again and there were more prayers and again water was poured on the rocks.

When this time was over, before the door was opened again, I was asked if I had anything to say. I was overwhelmed by everything that had happened and had been said and could only ask the Grandfather Great Spirit to have mercy on me, as I was now coming before all that is, that I might know and understand better as a humble man. Then the door was opened and the dipper passed out and back in. I was offered a drink of water from the wooden bowl; this was to be my last until the fast was over. What I didn't drink from the bowl was poured on the rocks.

Catches said that the door was opened only twice as the number two lies between one and three, which was the number of days I would be on the hill. I did not understand this as I was actually there three days and two nights.

We then all came out of the lodge and wiped ourselves. I put on my dark blue breech cloth and moccasins and trousers, and was handed my pipe. I felt that a new kind of existence had begun and that an invisible wall had come between me and the people around me. All I wanted was to be alone.

The cars were now parked by the lodge. My grandmother and aunt were in my car, my aunt driving. I got in and Catches and his group got in their car and led the way to the place. We drove until we came to a windmill near the base of the little range of hills where I was to go. Before we started up the hill I wrapped my pipe in the sage where the bowl and stem come together. Then I wrapped it with two strips of red flannel. The rest of the party each took some of the other things, the blanket, quilt, sage, bowl, and knife. Catches led the way, carrying his suitcase of paraphernalia; I followed him and the rest walked behind us. We stopped four times climbing the hill. About halfway up were four large cherry trees that Catches had cut earlier; we didn't use the ones I had taken. He picked up two of them and his brother the other two, and they dragged them the rest of the way up the hill.

The sky was now light with scattered clouds from behind which the sunshine was occasionally reaching past to touch the earth. A slight wind was blowing and changing directions every now and then. As we reached the place I was rather surprised to see an elongated willow structure about the length of a man and three feet high, made of little arches tied with strings of yellow cloth.

We stopped and stood while Catches and his brother prepared the place. With a crowbar apparently brought up the day before, Catches' brother made four holes about ten feet apart, forming a square. Into these holes the cut ends of the cherry trees were placed so they stood erect but not firm. A bed of sage was then laid out in a little circle where I was to stand. In front of the sage, an altar was erected, made of two forked sticks about a foot high with a crosspiece of fourteen inches. The bowl and the knife were set to the left of the altar.

I took off my trousers and moccasins and was led counterclockwise around to the front of the square, which faced west. I was stationed holding my pipe and standing facing the west on the bed of sage. Catches then took a rosary of tobacco bags which his wife had prepared the previous day, and wound on a piece of cardboard. He began unwinding it, first tying it to the cherry tree on the west on which the yard of red cloth had also been tied, then to the tree on the north which had the yard of white cloth on it, to the tree on the east with the yellow cloth, and the one on the south with green. The little red tobacco flags that had been used on the altar before the sweat lodge were stuck in the ground on either side of the stick altar. The tobacco rosary, stretching from tree to tree, reached back to the west tree and surrounded the square defined by the trees standing at each of its corners.

Catches then laid a row of single sage stems in front of the altar. He paid great attention to this and laid them very exactly. When he had finished he lit a braid of sweet grass and sent the smoke over the entire area and the rosary surrounding the space where I was standing. He then backed out of the space and tied the loose end of the rosary to the west tree, thus closing the space. Then he smoked the entire rosary from the outside, going clockwise until he came to the west. When he had done this, the people started to leave, going over the hill and down out of sight. Catches walked clockwise around the square, and as he approached the top of the knoll, a short distance from where I was standing, he sang a short song in an imploring, mournful tone and then disappeared down the hill.

I stood alone with the cool breeze gently blowing, I could not tell from what direction. A warm sense of well-being came over me, and a comfort in my solitude welled up from within. At last what I had longed for since leaving the sweat lodge was a reality. I was alone and quiet, naked before the creation. Catches' words spoken in the sweat lodge floated through my consciousness: "He comes to you young and innocent. Have mercy on him and give him what he seeks." Indeed I felt as though I were newly born. Yet there was a foreboding, a strong feeling of the presence of some other being, as I stared in one direction over the hills and into the sky. I was not sure if all that I was sensing was real.

The sun breaking through the clouds for a moment and warming my back brought me back to what I must now do. Holding my pipe, the bowl in my right hand and my left hand on the stem, I first asked that my prayer be heard, and because I had never prayed in this way I asked that my inexperience and possible mistakes be overlooked and my heart read, for I was there to learn and for that I was offering my prayers in these days of my fast.

Standing facing the west, I first addressed those powers, praying that the forces of the west, of thunder, lightning and the storm, hear me and lend me their strength to have courage in the face of what opposed me; should they wish to come to test me I would accept the challenge, but if not, I asked to be spared suffering from the storms while I was in this place. I asked them for courage and wisdom to face the trials of living and contending with my own ignorance. I asked for clarity of mind and good judgment so that the difference between right and wrong, good and evil, should be as plain to me as the difference between day and night. I asked all this also for all our people, so that they might see their way out of all their difficulties. I asked that the children especially be given strength to grow and become good people who will preserve our ways and take care of the land. To my amazement a wind began blowing from the west and made the red flag and all the others flutter as I completed that prayer.

Facing the north, I addressed those powers and asked them also to hear me and grant me strength to face all storms, and to receive with thankfulness the cleansing winds and snows that purge and wash away the old, preparing a way for the new. I asked that their harshness brace my weakness and make me strong and persevering, just as after the winter has come wrapping the world in cold our old selves are washed away and we can be new again in the spring. I asked that all our people be made strong to stand against what is harsh in life.

Facing the east, I asked these powers to hear me, and that the light which is the day that comes from the east should enter me and light my mind to its fullest power. I asked for the light of wisdom to see and understand what I must do and become so that my people may live. I asked for enlightenment for all the people, that they may discover the wisdom and peace of our religion as a light to guide them and bring day where there is so much darkness. I asked for the new life of spring to come to the people so that they may meet life with hope, as the earth greets spring in regeneration.

To the south I prayed that those powers of everlasting spring and summer grant me health to reach my life's harvest and full potential. I asked them to enter me and bring my life's tasks to fruition just as the summer matures the production of the earth. I asked for this power of accomplishment so that my people may live, and I asked for the people that they also may reach their highest and bear their fruit and accomplish what must be done in their time.

Pointing my pipe to the sky, I asked that the mystery of creation, reaching into infinity, bring together all of life in peace. I asked for wisdom to know and understand my part and place on this earth with other people. I asked to know humility and to become a better man so that my people may live better through my efforts and my work as a teacher. I asked for mercy and to be worthy to know the Spirit as it makes itself known to man.

Pointing my pipe to the earth I prayed the earth to give bodily health to all her children. I asked that the powers that live there manifest themselves in me so that I may be healthy and not be hungry. I asked for health for our people and that the babies and children reach old age, that life be long and good for all the people. I asked earth to be generous to her children and I repented that we have not cared for her nor her creation as we should.

At the end of this prayer I faced the west once again and asked that my prayer be heard.

Shortly after I had finished, a yellow butterfly came from behind the square area where I was standing and flew counter-clockwise to the tree on the west. It circled the tree and then fluttered back and forth in front of it, inside the square. I had been told to offer my pipe to any creature that might come to me while I was in that place; so addressing it, I pointed my pipe toward it and said, "My friend, I offer you this pipe in respect for your presence. If you come with good will, to help me, accept this offering; if you are here for other reasons, you should know that this is a sacred place and I beg you to leave it."

I said this while the butterfly circled the tree. When it fluttered to and fro in front of the tree, I somehow knew it had heard me, for it then flew to the tree on the north and circled it and then did the same with the other two trees. Then it came and circled me and almost lit on my pipe but instead left the place, fluttering clockwise around the square and leaving over the hill.

Soon after this I had to leave the enclosure to relieve myself. Catches had told me that when this was necessary I was to open the rosary attached to the tree on the west, as though it were a little gate, and to go a distance away from the sacred place. I did this and then returned and closed the gate again. Being out of the square for a few minutes was an experience of difference; I knew that I had left a place that was sanctified and was treading on ground that was ordinary and common. I was glad to come back in to the security of the enclosure.

Catches had said that during the days of the fast, the sacred power of all holy places, the sites of other Pipe Fasts and of the Sundance of times past, would be brought together and centered in this place which would henceforth always be sacred. No one who believed this could be harmed or touched by anyone while he was there; it is said that even the rain and the hail sometimes do not touch such a spot, while falling all around it. As I stood thinking about this and other things, a little brown bird flew close and sat in a pine tree about ten feet from the square. I addressed it as I had the butterfly; there were other birds in the trees to the north, east and south, and they chirped as though in response. A feeling of communication and of being a natural part of that place made me feel that I wanted to stay there forever. One of the birds, a blue one, remained long after the others flew away, and returned daily for the next two days, always coming by itself to the same tree where it sat for hours regarding me. I offered it the pipe each time. I did not know then that it would return for the next three years to sit in a tree to the east of me and, in the third year, sing me a song of encouragement, the words of which I would understand on my third pipe fast and sing on my fourth.

As the sun travelled across the sky that day, the wonder of the creation entered my awareness, the relation of microcosm and macrocosm; and I felt the connectedness of everything, as Catches had said, like a massive design woven by a sacred power, constantly breathed into by the breath of the Great Spirit.

I stood for what seemed a long time, yet in a way time no longer existed as there was nothing with which to compare the length or breadth of my experience, other than the changing appearances of things as they were touched by the changing light of the sun.

For a long time I had had the strange feeling that somebody was approaching me or looking at me, but I was startled to hear from behind me the sound of a man walking. Not quite knowing if it was someone of this world or another, I waited. Presently a man approached on my right side; it was Catches. He had brought up the buffalo skull to be placed on the altar. Very slowly he lit the sweet grass he had brought and going clockwise, smoked the entire rosary again. When he finished he untied the end of the rosary that was fastened to the cherry tree, opened it and came in and asked me how I was. I told him I was fine. He said that the buffalo skull should have been brought up when we first came but no one was available to carry it to the sacred place, as only those who had fasted before were qualified. So he had brought it now because the day was approaching its end and it would remain with me for the duration of the ceremony. He then placed the skull in front of the little rack facing me and proceeded to smoke the interior of it and then to smoke me, with the sweet grass. Then he smoked the tiny flags and the rack and the inside of the rosary, and backed out of the opening, tying it shut. Then he went to the back, standing in approximately the same place where he had stood before he left for the first time, and sang the same song he had sung earlier.

Shortly after he had gone, I began my second round of prayers to each of the quarters of the earth, beginning at the west, as I had been instructed. I went through the entire round as I had done before, and at the end of that prayer it sounded as if a gun had been shot off in the valley below; it reverberated and echoed through the valleys below me. A little later a host of hawks came flying up from the south, near where I was, and hovered there and then headed west. Once again I had the awesome feeling that Nature or the great powers had responded in an unusual way to what I had said, and I knew that my prayers were being answered.

As the sun began to set I heard a strange noise coming from beneath the earth, approaching from the south. At first I thought perhaps it was something digging under the ground, but I didn't know, so I offered it my pipe, as I had been told; and shortly thereafter it stopped. When the sun had sunk a little lower, there was a clopping sound that came nearer; once again, not knowing what it was, I waited, and it was a line of cows going by. Two of them, very curious, stopped and looked at me, so I offered them the pipe also. No sooner had I finished the first prayer, the offering to them, than one turned its head and mooed and went the other way; but the other, a black one, a little bit more curious, stood and looked at me for a long time before it turned finally and left.

I sat and waited until the sun was just touching the horizon and I began my third round of prayers, once again beginning at the west and continuing around. By the time I had finished, the day had almost disappeared and the moon was beginning to rise, so I began my fourth round while the blueness of the day was still there on the horizon. When I had finished the fourth round the moon was quite high. I put my pipe on the pipe rack as I had been told to do, and gathered my blanket around me, and sat, again thinking about all that had happened. It was then that an owl began hooting and a woman's voice, rather mournful, began to come from the hill across the valley that began on my right. I didn't know the meaning of this; I wouldn't know till three years later when things I had seen and heard were finally clarified and their meaning revealed.

As the moon rose higher I sat with my blanket gathered around me and imagined what was happening back at Catches' little mud and log house. I could picture in my mind my relatives and Catches' relatives gathered there, the preparations that had been made for the feast that evening, the sacrifice and cooking of my second pup that would be offered that night as a companion to the first one, in order that there might be good weather and a successful vision quest.

When the moon was quite high I decided it was time to make my first round of the night, as I had been instructed also to make four rounds of prayers also during the night. The night is considered one day in Indian tradition: that is, two nights and two days would actually be thought of as four days. In this case I was fasting five days; three days and two nights. I got my pipe from the rack and began my round. Once again, upon completion of the round, the woman's voice, this time very plainly crying, came from the same place where it had come from before. Knowing that I was in a sacred place and that nothing could harm me as long as I was there, I was not afraid; in fact I was very glad I had received a sign that was so clear to my understanding, so that I knew the fulfillment of my quest was beginning.

I then placed the pipe on the rack and crawled into the little willow lodge to stretch out and rest. My back was a little warm from the day's exposure to the sun, and oddly enough the insteps of my feet were also quite burned. My face felt hot. I hardly knew whether I was asleep or awake, and I had no mysterious dreams that night, except that the eagles that I had dreamed about the night before I began the fast came again soaring, but this time turned abruptly and flew over me. I don't know how long I had been there in either a dreaming or waking state when I decided it was time to make my round again. This I did three more times that night, and by dawn I was surprisingly very relaxed and prepared to meet the sun.

Shortly before I climbed out of the willow structure to get my pipe and begin my morning round and the greeting to the sun, I had the feeling that I was being watched; but I continued anyway and when I finished I stood facing the west, holding my pipe. The sun was now above the horizon and at my back. I decided to sit for a while, and when I placed my pipe on the rack I saw out of the corner of my eye what looked like a hunched-over eagle form. Turning and looking at it closely I saw that it was Catches sitting on the hill behind me, hunched over, with his eagle-bone whistle in his mouth. When I had put my pipe on the rack, he stood and faced the sun and sang a song that morning to the sun, and waved his eagle wing fan in the air above his head and blew the whistle four times. Then he came down to the sacred place, smoked the outside, untied the string and came in, smoked the whole area and then me. Then he asked if I had to relieve myself, which I did, so he walked in front of me, making a little path and waving the smoking sweet grass. He took me some distance from the sacred area and waited till I was finished and then returned me to the place. When we had gotten back he stood on the sage pallet that had been prepared and checked the tiny sage stems that he had arranged the day before, and examined the flags and the tobacco rosary that enclosed the place like a fence, and then asked me again if I was all right, and I told him once again that I was fine. He backed out then, tied the rosary shut and smoked it, and then returned to the hill where he had sung the last two songs; but this time he faced the west as he had done the first day, and sang the same song that he had sung the day before. Then he went away over the hill.

I began my second round of prayers, but this time I took off my blanket as the morning sun was bright enough now to warm me. I went on through that day; and upon the beginning of my third round, I noticed a strange appearance in the sky to the south. It was like two parallel rolling clouds that stretched far into the south and far above me. They were not jet streams; they were much larger, and rolling within themselves. It was at this time then that my vision began. I had thought it would be a very mystical experience, one that would be perhaps more of a dream than a vision, and my first reaction was: "How strange! This is not at all what I thought a vision was like." I felt I was perfectly clearheaded; I had not been deprived of food nor of water for that great a length of time. It lasted for what seemed the greater part of that day, gradually revealing a changing series of distinct forms and figures, like a panorama of shifting scenes, whose meaning once again would be revealed to me only upon the completion of my fourth pipe fast.

I cannot tell this vision here, for there is a time and a place reserved for the telling of visions: a sacred setting, the proper songs, the proper preparations. It lasted, as I said, quite a long time: and by the time it was finished I was thoroughly exhausted. I lay down to rest and covered my head because the day was now very hot; and I knew that something had happened to me because I was alternately sweating and very cold. I wanted to protect myself from the hot sun, for every ray that touched my body burned almost as if it were focused on my skin with a magnifying glass; yet when I covered myself, I became so hot I had to take off the blanket, and yet after I had it off for a while I got very cold alternately with being burned by the sun. It was a very strange sensation.

It was then I noticed the wind blowing. I don't understand or know how it blew that way, but all the flags would be blowing inward at one moment and then outward at another moment. I covered my head again and prayed that what was happening to me was a sacred and good thing and I asked for help that I could endure this.

Gradually I fell asleep and when I awoke it was late in the day and everything was very peaceful. What awakened me was the little blue bird that had returned to the tree and was singing the song that I spoke of before. Once again I picked up my pipe, only this time I added to my prayers thanks for that vision that had been given to me, and I prayed at the same time that through it and from it good and understanding would come to me and my people, and that the purpose of my fast would be fulfilled.

When I had finished that round, I was doubly exhausted and very weak. I placed my pipe on the pipe rack and sat once again, slipping in and out of sleep. When I drifted into sleep it was not total unconsciousness but was more like dreaming; it was as though there were multitudes of children playing around me and making a lot of noise, and I would wake up to find I was alone still in the sacred place. Then I would doze again and a phase of my childhood would return: myself as a child speaking with my grandmother and my grandfather. There were also times when in the dreams I walked in very strange places, places I don't remember as a child. Eventually I must have rested, because by the time I awoke again the sun was just beginning to set on the horizon, so I began my fourth round for the day. Upon finishing that I was exhausted once more and I put my pipe on the rack and returned to the willow lodge. Just as I was about to enter it, Catches came again to check to see if I was all right. He went through the same ritual that he had done before, and when he asked me how I was, he could see there was something strange about me and asked me if I should go down now. I told him no, I had this night and the next day still to go and I preferred to stay them out. I told him that I had had visitors and that something mysterious occurred. He saw my swollen feet and my burned back and my burned chest and my burned face; the skin was beginning to peel. That evening when he sang the departing song, the man cried with such compassion that I cried also, not knowing whether it was for him, the song or myself.

That night was a very restless one. I prayed four times. Catches did not come the next morning which was the beginning of my final day. I began the day greeting the sun, before and at the moment of its climbing over the horizon. I was very weak and my lips were very dry and felt swollen. As I returned my pipe to the rack and stood, I noticed there were two cloud banks, one to the east and one to the west, like huge cliffs, and they were moving towards each other, so that in my reckoning they would collide right above me. I prayed to each of them and told them that if this was the test that was being given me, I was ready to endure it, for I knew these things were necessary and a part of nature; for just as there is sunlight and good weather, there is also the wind and the rain which are also needed for life on this earth. Besides, I was very hot and dehydrated; I thought if it rained I would thankfully get some moisture. But these cloud signs were so forceful they made me fearful also, because only two or three weeks before the torrential rains in the Black Hills had caused floods and the loss of many lives. In our part of the country we frequently have tornadoes and strong wind storms. So I prayed and asked that I would be strong enough to endure what was to happen.

It was then that a nausea and a tremendous weakness came over me, and with that I heard the sound of wind in the pine trees and the sound of wind at a great distance and also the sound of the two approaching storms above. I put my pipe on the rack and lay down on the ground and covered my head, and I must have fainted. I don't know how long I was lying there; but on awakening I was lying on my side with my head in the dirt, and directly opposite my eyes, the tobacco rosary had been broken in one place. I staggered to my feet and picked up my pipe, and pointing it toward that place where the rosary was broken I offered it to whatever force it was that had broken through, and reminded it that this was a sacred place. I said that if the intentions it had here were good, it should accept this pipe and all it represents, but if they were evil it must depart. On completing that pipe offering, a certain strength and well-being returned to me, but I was becoming very apprehensive about that place.

It was then I began another round of prayers and while I was making it I saw that the cloud banks, which had subsided somewhat from the time I first saw them, now were beginning to build power again and to move toward each other. I thought that certainly this time I was going to be in the eye of a tornado. Upon completion of that round of prayers I became again very weak and nauseated. I returned my pipe to the rack and lay down and covered my head. That time there was a rushing sensation, almost as if I were in the middle of a whirlwind. I didn't know what caused me to cover my head—I would not know that until later—but for some reason I did and lay there praying all the while that I would be strong enough to endure whatever it was that was happening. I lost consciousness again and as I awoke I saw directly in my line of vision that the tobacco rosary had been broken in two more places. I felt very much afraid and I knew that something extraordinary had happened. Then I thought, "Now it is over. The Pipe Fast is finished." Suddenly I had a surge of energy and a strong sense of well-being. I rose and took my pipe and made my round, that time in a kind of joyous thanksgiving for all that had taken place. Indeed a part of what I had seen during the vision prompted me on this final round to make at each quarter, in gratitude, the dance steps up and down of the Sundance, for I felt a great sense of joy but also one of responsibility and of awe, almost as if an obligation had been laid upon me.

As I returned from that round to face the west, the eagles flew above, one from each quarter; not all at once, but beginning from the west an eagle flew over me, then one from the north, one from the east, and one from the south. Soon afterward the butterfly that I had seen on the first day returned, and danced about the trees as it had done before, and disappeared. It was after all that that I noticed that the cherry trees had bent over and that the flags were now touching the ground; and it was a verification that the ceremony had indeed come to an end.

I stood then for the remainder of the day until later afternoon with my pipe and as I examined the area around me and myself, it seemed I was in a pitiful condition. Finally I heard steps approaching from the rear, and there was a procession of people coming to take me down. Catches and his brother came around in front of me. I didn't look back to see who was in the group, but stood and held my pipe.

First Catches untied the rosary and went around rolling it up. When he came to the broken parts he stood and pondered for a while and then went on rolling them into a ball. He pulled out the cherry trees and took them and the tobacco pouches and laid them over in the little gully to my right, where the valley began. He took down the willow frame and put that over there also, as well as the rack and the little flags. He smoked me with the sweet grass and then took his eagle wing fan and beating it on his leg several times, very carefully began to wipe me with the fan, making quick brushing motions as if to dust or wipe something off. Then he stood and addressed the west and prayed and gave thanks that this process had gone this far. He gave instructions to his brother to hand the things that I had used to the people that had come with him. Then he told my grandmother to come and put on my feet the moccasins she had brought. She could hardly get them on because my feet were so swollen with sunburn, and the poor little bent-over woman cried very hard. Then out of the corner of my eye I could see that my mother had arrived also. She lived 120 miles from there, and they had called her once I had been placed upon the hill. I am sure she would have objected at first, which is why I had told them not to tell her until after I had been put on the hill. We went then in a procession: Catches first, then a man with the buffalo skull, and after him I walked carrying my pipe. We went down the hill stopping four times, and each time Catches sang a song of thanksgiving.

When we reached the bottom of the hill cars were there waiting, but I told him that I preferred to walk the rest of the way. He asked me if I could, and I said yes. So the rest got in the cars and he walked ahead of me leading the way, and we went back to the sweat lodge.

When we arrived, the rest had already gotten there, and all the ceremonial paraphernalia was gathered by the sweat lodge, because it had to be purified once again. By that time the fire was roaring and the rocks were heating, and I was placed in the lodge to wait. After the rocks had been put in the men entered, once again sitting in the places they had sat in before. I was at the very back facing the door which opened to the west, Catches at my left and his brother at my right.

First of all the bowl and blanket and knife I had used were held above the hot rocks as water was poured on them, so that the spiritual residue could be washed away and they too could return to the world of men. Those things were passed out the door and then the door was closed and the ritual began. This time Catches took sage and wiped my eyes, my nose, my mouth and my ears. Then he blew in my eyes, he blew on my nose, my mouth and my ears, so that they too would be made ready for the common world again. During the ritual the cherry juice was poured into the wooden bowl, and taking the sweet grass Catches painted the parting in my hair with cherry juice; this is symbolically my red road. Then he painted four times down the back of my hair, somehow setting the pattern that I would do this three more times to complete the cycle that had begun there.

Then he began his telling of visions—that is, the story of his power as a man and his qualifications to conduct such rites; and the little bird sound came, his intercessor, Red Hawk, arrived; and it was time for me to tell now of the things I had seen and heard and experienced on the hill. Starting from the beginning and not leaving out anything that might have meaning, I began to tell of all that had happened. The intercessor heard this and left for a while; the door was opened, and I had my first drink, which was cherry juice. Catches first dipped a braid of sweet grass in the cherry juice and I sucked the juice from the end of the sweet grass. This he did four times. After that I took four sips of the cherry juice. Next I was given four drinks of water. Then the intercessor returned, the door was closed and the singing began: translated from the sacred language into one I could understand, it was said that indeed a legitimate spiritual event had taken place, and that I was now committed for the next four years to fasting and participation in the rituals so that my vision might be fulfilled and made efficacious.

The responsibility weighing on me made me very sad but also very happy, for I had gone there seeking something and had come away with something very wonderful, very powerful yet also very hard to live by. I had something difficult to do in the years to come.

The door was opened once more, then Catches explained that the sweat lodge is a true part of the whole rite. He explained that it was only opened four times in all, twice the first time and twice the second, and it is the beginning and ending of the ceremony. As before, at the ending the water was passed out first to the helper and then back in and then to me. Then it was time to come out and wipe ourselves and prepare ourselves for the breaking-of-the-fast meal which had been prepared and was waiting.

As we emerged from the sweat lodge, gliding in and hovering over us came the hugest eagle I have ever seen, and the people down by the house below the sweat lodge had seen it also. It circled and hovered and slowly, slowly passed over the pine trees, and the blessing rain came. There were some broken clouds in the sky, but it was sunlight; and yet a slight little rain came at that moment and a very tiny little rainbow opened up on the hillside across the valley from where we were; and we knew again that it was good and that our prayers had been heard.

We went down to the house then where I went among my relatives and shook their hands and embraced the womenfolk; it was such a happy reunion, coming back from a journey so very far away in time, since where I had gone was actually four generations back. We assembled inside the little house and a very traditional meal was served. The first dish that was brought around was the *wasna*, the dried and pounded pemmican mixed with chokecherries. I gave my first handful to the spirits that they might be fed, and it was taken out and offered to them.

I had thought of food occasionally when I was on the hill, but not very much; and now when the time came that I could eat again, I was hardly hungry, and all I could take was a small amount of soup and a little bit of *wasna*.

Later the people began to leave, to return that night for the final ceremony, the one that was to be held in the dark. And I went out and sat on a stump by the woodpile and thought, and thought, and thought: how wonderful it was to be alive in this century yet also able to experience the sacred traditions from the past and to know that the Great Spirit still responds to his twentieth-century children by giving them visions and signs, and a sense of peace, and the knowledge of an all-enduring faith.

The vision quest was usually practiced by men and boys, although women and girls sometimes entered such quests. Whereas the acquisition of a vision was associated with attaining maturity for the boys of many tribes, the beginning of menstruation often signaled maturity for the girls. Special observations such as the isolation of a girl during her first period of menstruation are widely practiced. Such practices show that the female at sexual maturity is perceived as potentially harmful. Because she may be a pollutant or impure during menstruation, she must be isolated in order to protect her community. During isolation the initiate must carefully follow many restrictions associated with eating, sleeping, drinking, touching herself, and bathing. These restrictions are linked with attaining desirable attributes and avoiding undesirable ones during her adult life. A public event, like a feast or giveaway, often concludes the period of isolation, serving as the debut for the new woman.[4]

The Navajo and Apache, southern Athapascan tribes, have extensive puberty rites in which the onset of menstruation and the ritual process of entering womanhood invest the pubescent girl with creative powers that extend from her to her family and community in a positive way. Contact with the girl during this time is considered a blessing. For the Apache, the rite not only inducts a girl into womanhood, it renews the community in which she lives, and recreates the Apache world.[5]

The Navajo girls' puberty rite, *kinaaldá*, is modeled upon the puberty rite of the mythic figure, Changing Woman, when she came of age. Consequently, the guide and prototype for all performances of *kinaaldá* is the story of Changing Woman's *kinaaldá*, a story known by Navajo singers (medicine persons) who perform the puberty rite. The following selection is a version of the story as told to Charlotte Frisbie in 1963.

## *NAVAJO KINAALDÁ STORY, by Frank Mitchell*[6]

I am going to tell the story I know about the beginning of the Kinaaldá ceremony, its purpose, and why such things were laid down for the people.

### *Kinaaldá of Changing Woman*

It was a long time ago that Changing Woman had her Kinaaldá. She made herself become kinaaldá. This happened after the creation of the Earth People. The ceremony was started so women would be able to have children and the human race would be able to multiply. To do this, women had to have relations with men. The Kinaaldá was created to make it holy and effective, as the Holy People wanted it to be. They called many meetings to discuss how they should do this ceremony.

In the beginning, there was fog at the top of Blanca Peak. After four days, the fog covered everything down to the base. Coyote, of course, went there to find out what was happening. When he went running over there, he saw a baby floating on the lake which was at the top of Blanca Peak. He wanted to pick up the baby and bring it back, but he was not able to. So he came back and reported it to Hashch'éhooghan (Calling God). Hashch'éhooghan went over there and could not get it either. Then Talking God went there, got the baby out of the lake, and brought it to the top of Gobernador Knob.

The one who was picked up as a new baby was 'Esdzą́ą́nádleehé (Changing Woman). She was taken home to be raised. In four days she grew up and became kinaaldá. When this happened, they decided to have a ceremony for her.

At this time, the Holy People were living on the earth. They came to her ceremony, and many of them sang songs for her. They did this so that she would be holy and so she could have children who would be human beings with enough sense to think for themselves and a language with which to understand each other.

The first Kinaaldá took place at the rim of the Emergence Place in the First Woman's home. All kinds of Holy People were there. The first time that Changing Woman had it, they used the original Chief Hogan Songs. The second time, they used the Hogan Songs which belonged to Talking God.

The first ceremony took place at Cho'óol'į́í (Gobernador Knob); this is a place that is now on the Jicarilla Apache Reservation. When Changing Woman became kinaaldá, Salt Woman, who was the first White Shell Woman, gave her her own name, "White Shell Woman." She dressed her in white shell clothes. Changing Woman was also painted with white shell; that is why she was called "White Shell Woman."

The Kinaaldá started when White Shell Woman first menstruated. It is still done the same way today. At her first ceremony, White Shell Woman ran around the turquoise that was in the east. That is why the kinaaldá today wears turquoise.

During her second ceremony, she started from the west, where there was white shell. The second menstruation was connected with white shell.

Nine days after that, Changing Woman gave birth to Naaghéé' neezghání (Monster Slayer) and Tó bájíshchíní (Born for Water), twin boys. These two were put on earth so that all the monsters which were eating the human beings would be killed. They rid the earth of all these monsters; that is why they were called Holy People. As soon as they had done this, their mother, Changing Woman, who was then living at Gobernador Knob, left and went to her home in the west, where she lives today.

After she moved to her home in the west, she created the Navaho people. When she had done this, she told these human beings to go to their original home, which was the Navaho country. Before they left, she said, "After this, all the girls born to you will have periods at certain times when they become women. When the time comes, you must set a day and fix the girl up to be kinaaldá; you must have these songs sung and do whatever else needs to be done at that time. After this period, a girl is a woman and will start having children."

She also told the people to make a round cake representing Mother Earth during the Kinaaldá. She said that this cake should be given to the singers who helped with the singing during the ceremony. She told the people how to make the cake; one of the things that she mentioned was that the cornhusks were to be placed in the east, south, west, north (in the four directions) and in the center of the pit.

That is what 'Esdzą́ą́nádleehé told the people she made in the west. She told them to go to their own country and do this.

When 'Esdzą́ą́nádleehé created the people in the west, she made four groups. These were the four original clans of the Navaho people: Tó díchi'íini, Bitter Water Clan; Kiiya'áani, Tall House Clan; Tó'áháni, Short Distance to Water Clan; and Hashtł'ishni, Mud Clan. They were told to go to their own country.

When the four clans were created by 'Esdzą́ą́nádleehé, pairs, male and female, were made in each clan. They were ordered to be man and wife so there would be more children. The first child that was born was a girl.

When the people were ready to leave, 'Esdzą́ą́nádleehé said, "You must go right back to my first home (Gobernador Knob), There is a cornfield there by the name of Dá'ák'eh jigishí (Where One Gazes on a Cornfield). That field is mine; when you go back, you are to settle there and let it be yours."

## *The First Kinaaldá of the First Girl Born on Earth*

These people did what 'Esdzą́ą́nádleehé told them to do; they went to Gobernador Knob to the cornfield and settled there. They were living there when the first-born girl became kinaaldá. That was where the first Kinaaldá, which was directed by 'Esdzą́ą́nádleehé, took place. She came there supernaturally and directed the making of the cake.

The only songs that have come down to this day from the first ceremony over that girl without being changed are the Hogan Songs which were sung by the Holy People who were there. After these songs, the Holy People sang others about fabrics, jewels, journeys, mountains, and other things they happened to have in their possession.

When this girl was being prepared for her Kinaaldá, 'Esdzą́ą́nádleehé directed how she was to be fixed. Of course, 'Esdzą́ą́nádleehé had gone through the same things when she had hers for the first time, and she did the same things for the first-born girl. She combed her hair, fixed it in a pony tail, and dressed her in her ceremonial clothes.

After these things had been done, the girl lay on her stomach, and she was molded and pressed so she would have a good figure. When she got up, she ran to the east for her first run. At that time, just as now, anyone could run with her.

When she returned from her first run, she started grinding corn for the cake. The people were told to shell the corn, winnow it, bring it in, and start grinding. 'Esdzą́ą́nádleehé said, "For two full days, the girl shall do this grinding." The first-born girl spent all her time grinding.

On the third day, they started preparing the mush for the cake. The first thing they were told to do was to dig a pit, build a fire in it, and let it get hot. They kept the fire going all day long, so the pit was hot when the mush was ready. Dry corn meal was stirred into the hot water. Then they rubbed the mixture between their hands to get the lumps out of the mush. Late in the afternoon, at sundown, all of the mush was ready to be taken out to the pit.

They cleaned all the ashes and charcoal from the pit. The four cornhusks were put down to the east, south, west, and north. A middle piece was then put on. After this had been done, they started to pour the mush in. Cornhusks were put down at the same time so that no mush would get on the bare earth. They started from the center and worked out to the edges of the pit; then they went up the sides, busily putting husks down all the time. When all the mush had been poured in, the girl stood with a basket of corn meal in the east and tossed a pinch of corn meal to the east, to the west, and back to the east, and then to the south, to the north, and back to the south. Then she took a handful of corn meal and sprinkled it in a circle around the pit.

After she had done these things, anyone who wanted to was allowed to take a pinch of corn meal and do what she had done, while praying for good luck, plenty, good vegetation, and no hunger, hardships, or suffering. When this had been done, husks were placed, starting from the edge of the pit and going into the center. Then the gap was closed and husks were put in the center as had been done earlier. The pit was covered with more husks and then with dirt. That is the way they were told to do it in the beginning, and that is how they have been doing it since.

The cake was covered with a thin layer of dirt because the mush was too soft to have any weight put on it in the beginning; twigs and little pieces of wood were used until the mush had settled and hardened. Then more dirt was put on, and a big fire was built. The fire was kept going all night so the cake would cook.

In the evening, the original Chief Hogan Songs were sung; then the singing was turned over to the people. After all these songs, at that time, the Twelve Word Songs were not sung.

The cake was cut up and given to the singers. The last thing that the people did after cutting the cake was to take four pinches of the cake from the four directions, east, south, west, and north. These pinches were buried in the center of the pit where the cake had been baked. They offered these to Mother Earth, who produces vegetation and makes it possible to grow corn. This was done to say thanks to the Earth. It is done today. After this, the people ate. Lots of prayers were offered for good luck and good life.

That is what happened at the first ceremony. From then on, these things have been carried on by the Navaho. When a girl has her period, she becomes kinaaldá and has the ceremony.

In the days when the first girl born on earth had her ceremony, the Holy People were still on the earth. Sometimes they would come around and check on the Earth People to see if they were following the rules laid down for them. As time passed, they realized that the Earth People were getting careless about these things. When this happened, 'Esdzą́ą́nádleehé decided to take two young boys of the Tó'áháni Clan, the original clan made by 'Esdzą́ą́nádleehé in the west, to her home in the west. There she taught them about everything in the past, present, and future.

The boys were given the power to make Blessing Way Songs. They became good at doing this. It was at this time that the Blessing Way Ceremony was started. The Blessing Way Ceremony concerns everything good for the people to live by.

Terms like "medicine" and "medicine person" invariably have a religious connotation as used by Native Americans. Quite clearly, matters of health and healing are not restricted to conditions of a simple physiological and biological order, but rather these matters are laden with meanings and concerns that reach the highest cultural, even cosmological, levels. The state of health speaks to Native Americans of the conditions of the world in which they live. Consequently, matters of health and healing are commonly central to the religious concerns of many Native American tribes. Health and healing constitute a symbolic form of expression, which is a portion of a symbolic language of place. We will fail to understand even the simplest level of Native American medical practices and much of Native American religion if we do not appreciate this important point.

Perhaps no tribe in North America is more extensively concerned with religious healing than the Navajo. In the following selection, I have attempted to state briefly the religious ideology associated with Navajo ceremonial cures.

## *RELIGIOUS IDEOLOGY OF NAVAJO CEREMONIAL CURES by Sam D. Gill*[7]

It is commonly known that most Navajo ceremonials are performed for the purpose of curing a sick person. But I believe that the failure to place this expressed purpose in the context of Navajo religious thought . . . has led to much misunderstanding of Navajo ceremonialism. The performance of the song ceremonials must be seen as a positive and essential part of living a full and meaningful life as a Navajo, and not solely as a means for ridding oneself of unwanted suffering from illness. It is surely accurate to say that in Navajo culture, never to have been the one over whom a ceremonial is sung is not necessarily a lauded cultural position. Certainly it is not comparable to the pride in a "no cavities" dental report. And even though it is generally recognized that a person often becomes ill because of some trespass or transgression committed, there are never any negative social connotations associated with the person on whom the ceremonial is focused. Shame and guilt are not suffered. The error is not simply of a legal or ethical nature.

Still, the ceremonials are never sung without purpose and that purpose is commonly to administer to a suffering person. As with the hero in ceremonial origin mythology, suffering a predicament is the occasion for having a ceremonial performed. Illness is an occasion to learn the Navajo way of life, to learn the significance of relationships, to appreciate the meaning of time and space as defined in the acts of creation. As the created world is not appreciated without the constant presence of the threat of it collapsing into disorder, so is the Navajo way of life not fully understood, or for that matter even known, without the presence of the sickness which threatens to destroy it. Navajo life is maintained in the tension between health and sickness, between observing and trespassing boundaries, between pleasantness and adversity, between *hózhǫ́* and *hóchǫ́*, for it is only when the tension is drawn to the point that the balance is threatened that the ceremonials are performed.

Much effort has been expended on the consideration of the medical efficacy of the curing ceremonials. Theories of magical control, of psychological techniques, of physical therapeutics, and of folk pharmacology have been advanced. All of these have merit. But when the ceremonials are placed in the light of religious thought as revealed in the whole fabric of Navajo mythology, it must be recognized that the ceremonials are primarily religious acts which serve to reveal the power and knowledge of a way of life to the Navajo people. I believe that the therapeutic and prophylactic effects of a ceremonial on a person are not actually most central and in many cases not even expected.

It is a common practice to perform a ceremonial for a person long after the physical aspect of their illness has been cured. It is increasingly common to perform a ceremonial for a person who has gone first to a hospital to receive treatment by European-American scientific medical practices. It is common to perform trial versions of ceremonials to see if a person responds. The full ceremonial must still be performed for him at a later time. Certain sicknesses if contracted in the summer may not be treated immediately because of seasonal restrictions on ceremonial performance. Were the person to regain his health before the proper season, he still will have the ceremonial. There is mounting evidence that the performance of the ceremonial is not solely tied to the cure of a physical or mental illness even though that is the stated motivation for many ceremonial performances.

The majority of studies of Navajo ceremonialism have focused on an understanding of Navajo medical ideology against a background of Western scientific thought. This approach is fraught with difficulties. Some ceremonials do not perform cures in any sense of the word. In accounting for the medical efficacy of the huge variety of carefully performed ritual acts, some have yielded to either the rationalization of these practices from some aspects of medical science, while many others have expressed an appreciation of the complexity of Navajo thought patterns but have consigned them to the arenas of magic, and cite the principles of "like produces like" and "the part stands for the whole."

Only from a religious perspective can the adversity or sickness which motivates so much of Navajo ceremonial practices be adequately appreciated and understood. The essential pragmatic element in the ceremonial performances is the revelation and maintenance of proper relationships among the living entities in the world. They are performed not only to reveal these relationships, but to establish them, inner life form to inner life form, on a person to person basis. The pragmatic goal toward which the ceremonials are aimed, as stated by Navajos, is the acquisition of *hózhǫ́*. The very meaning of the word *hózhǫ́*, an environment of beauty and pleasantness, suggests that the ceremonials are primarily interested in establishing the proper relationships of the individual to his environment, and this will consequently be reflected in a healthy condition regained by his physical body. It has commonly been shown that there is not a necessary correspondence between the physical ailment suffered and the ritual cure recommended. Indeed, all of the theories of disease that I know which have been described for the Navajo focus upon etiology as the primary means to correlate types of illness with curing methods. But the etiology has to do with religious and moral categories, that is, with trespass, taboos, and spiritual relationships, more than with physiology. Hence, explanations of ceremonial practices which are concerned with the pragmatic effect they have upon physical and psychological health will always be very limited. The significance of illness is far greater for the Navajo.

If we hold that shamanism is distinguished by techniques through which the shaman enters ecstatic or entranced states, then Navajo ceremonial cures are not technically shamanic, for Navajo singers do not ordinarily enter such states. Navajo singers are commonly, yet incorrectly, referred to as shamans as are a great variety of curing specialists in many other tribes. Another overused term is "medicine man," which is often incorrect in both its sexist designation and in its collapsing of a variety of types of curing specialists, usually distinguished even in a single tribe, into one overly simplistic term.

Recalling the selection given in Chapter Two that presented the ecstatic performances of the Bear River shaman, we may observe how shamanic performances, as in the Bear River example, are distinct from medicine powers presented in the following selection on Omaha Buffalo medicine men. The medicine powers of these Omaha medicine men are inseparable from songs and the powers of an initiatory experience. The richly dramatic character of these accounts is not unusual among hundreds of tribes in North America.

## *THE OMAHA BUFFALO MEDICINE-MEN by Francis LaFlesche*[8]

Among the bluffs of the Missouri River valley, there stood an Indian village, the inhabitants of which were known as the Omahas. . . .

In this village many of the days of my childhood were spent. By the lodge fire I have often sat, with other little boys, listening to the stories handed down by my forefathers, of their battles with the Sioux, the Cheyennes, and the Pawnees; to the strange tales told of the great "medicine-men," who were able to transform themselves into wild animals or birds, while attacking or fleeing from their enemies; of their power to take the lives of their foes by supernatural means; and of their ability to command even the thunder and lightning, and to bring down the rain from the sky. Like all other little [boys] of my age, I, too, loved to dream of the days when I should become a warrior, and be able to put to shame and to scalp the enemies of my people. But my story is to be about the buffalo medicine-men.

It was on a hot summer day that a group of boys were playing, by the brook which ran by this Omaha village, a game for which I cannot find an English name. I was invited to join them; so I took part in the gambling for feathers, necklaces of elk-teeth, beads, and other valueless articles which were the treasures of the Indian boy. In the village, preparations were going on for the annual summer hunt, and all the people were astir in various occupations. Here and there sat women in the shade of their tents or sod houses, chatting over their work. Warriors were busy making bows and arrows, shaping the arrowshafts, and gluing the feathers to them; while in the open spaces or streets a number of young men were at play gambling as we were, but using a different game. Now and then a noisy dispute arose over the game of the young men, but by the interference of the older men peace would be restored.

Towards the afternoon, our game grew to be quite interesting, there being but one more stake to win, and the fight over it became exciting, when suddenly we were startled by the loud report of a pistol. We dropped our sticks, scrambled up the bank of the brook, and in an instant were on the ridge, looking in the direction of the sound to see what it meant. It was only a few young men firing with a pistol at a mark on a tree, and some noisy little boys watching them. One of our party suggested going up there to see the shooting, but he was cried down, as he was on the losing side of our game, and accused of trying to find some excuse to break up the sport. We were soon busy again with our gambling, and points were made and won back again, when we heard three shots in succession: we were a little uneasy, although the shouts and laugh of the men, as they joked, quieted us, so that we went on with the game. Then came another single loud report, a piercing scream, and an awful cry of a man: "Hay-ee!" followed by the words, "Ka-gae ha, wanunka ahthae ha! O friends! I have committed murder!" We dropped our sticks, and stared at one another. A cold chill went through me, and I shivered with fright. Before I could recover myself, men and women were running about with wild shouts, and the whole village seemed to be rushing to the spot, while above all the noise could be heard the heartrending wail of the man who had accidentally shot a boy through the head. The excitement was intense. The relatives of the wounded boy were preparing to avenge his death, while those of the unfortunate man who had made the fatal shot stood ready to defend him. I made my way through the crowd, to see who it was that was killed. Peering over the shoulders of another boy, I saw on the ground a dirty-looking little form, and recognized it as one of my playmates. Blood was oozing from a wound in the back of his head, and from one just under the right eye, near the nose. The sight of blood sickened me, as it did the other boys, and I stepped back as quickly as I could.

A man just then ordered the women to stop wailing, and the people to stand back. Soon there was an opening in the crowd, and I saw a tall man come up the hill, wrapped in a buffalo robe, and pass through the opening to where the boy lay; he stooped over the child, felt of his wrists, then of his breast. "He is alive," the man said; "set up a tent, and take him in there." The little body was lifted in a robe, and carried by two men into a large tent which was hastily erected. A young man was sent in haste to call the buffalo medicine-men of another village (the Omahas lived in three villages, a few miles apart). It was not long before the medicine-men came galloping over the hills on their horses, one or two at a time, their long hair streaming over their naked backs. They dismounted before the tent, and went in one by one, where they joined the buffalo doctors of our village, who had already been called. A short consultation was held, and soon the sides of the tent were thrown open to let in the fresh air, and also that the people might witness the operation. Then began a scene rarely if ever witnessed by a white man.

All the medicine-men sat around the boy, their eyes gleaming out of their wrinkled faces. The man who was first to try his charms and medicines on the patient began by telling in a loud voice how he became possessed of them; how in a vision he had seen the buffalo which had revealed to him the mysterious secrets of the medicine, and of the charm song he was taught to sing when using the medicine. At the end of every sentence of his narrative the boy's father thanked the doctor in terms of relationship. When he had recited his story from beginning to end, and had compounded the roots he had taken from his skin pouch, he started his song at the top of his voice, which the other doctors, twenty or thirty in number, picked up and sang in unison, with such volume that one would imagine it could have been heard many miles. In the midst of the chorus of voices rose the shrill sound of the bone whistle accompaniment, imitating the call of an eagle. After the doctor had started the song, he put the bits of root into his mouth, grinding them with his teeth, and, taking a mouthful of water, he slowly approached the boy, bellowing and pawing the earth, after the manner of an angry buffalo at bay. All eyes were upon him with an admiring gaze. When within a few feet of the boy's head, he paused for a moment, drew a long breath, and with a whizzing noise forced the water from his mouth into the wound. The boy spread out his hands, and winced as though he was again hit by a ball. The man uttered a series of short exclamations, "He! he! he!" to give an additional charm to the medicine. It was a successful operation, and the father, and the man who had wounded the boy, lifted their spread hands towards the doctor to signify their thanks. During this performance all of the medicine-men sang with energy the song which had been started by the operator. There were two women who sang, as they belonged to the corps of doctors.

The following are two of the songs sung at this operation:—

Thae'-thu-tun thae'-aw thae
Thae'-thu-tun thae'-aw thae
Thae'-thu-tun thae'-aw thae
Thae'-thu-tun
Thae'-aw thae

Ae'-gun ne'-thun thae'-aw thae tae'-aw ma
hun-aw-dun thae-aw thae
Ae'-gun thae'-thu-tun thae'-aw thae
Shun' thae'-aw thae

*Translation*

From here do I send,
From here do I send,
From here do I send,
I send.

Thus, the water to send, I'm enjoined,
Therefore do I send,
Thus, from here do I send,
Therefore do I send

The first four lines of this song can be readily understood, but the last four need an explanation. The meaning is, Because I am commanded, or instructed (by the buffalo vision), to send the water (the medicine) from this distance, therefore I do so.

Ne-thun tha-dae-aw ma,
Ne-thun tha-dae-aw mae,
Ou-hae ke-thae e-thae-aw mae tho hae,
Ne-thun tha-dae e-thae-aw mae tho hae.

*Translation*

The pool of water, they proclaim,
The pool of water, they proclaim,
Yield to his entreaties, they declare they will,
The pool of water, they proclaim, sending their voices to me.

The composer of this song is said to have seen in a vision a number of buffalo attending one of their number who was wounded. The vision was given to the man to reveal to him the secret of a healing potion. The first two lines mean that the attending buffalo, the doctors, have indicated a pool of water in a buffalo wallow as the place where the wounded one shall be treated; the third line, that they assent to the entreaties of the injured animal to be taken to the water, that his wounds may be healed in it. In the fourth line the word "ethae" has a different meaning than in the third line, and is not quite the same pronunciation. In the fourth line the word signifies to send in this way or in this direction. As all the words that the visionary animals uttered were directed to the dreamer's ears, the last line of the song is intended to convey this meaning. The round pool of water* they proclaim sending this way; that is, their voices to me.

This song is quite poetical to the Indian mind. It not only conveys a picture of the prairie, the round wallow with its gleaming water, and the buffalo drama, but it reveals the expectancy of the dreamer, and the bestowing of the power of the vision upon him for the benefit of sufferers.

Although there were twenty or thirty doctors in attendance, only four of them operated upon the patient in the manner above described. In a severe case like this one, all of the medicine-men unite in consultation, and each man is entitled to his share of the fees. When the case is not so severe, the relatives of the patient select one or two of the doctors to attend the wounded person. The buffalo doctors are organized into a society, and treat nothing but wounds. It is seldom that they lose a patient, but, when called to a person in a critical condition, they declare the hopelessness of the case, so that no blame may be attached to them should the sufferer die. All night the doctors stayed with the patient, the four men taking turns in applying their medicines, and dressing the wound.

The next morning the United States Indian agent came into the village, driving a handsome horse, and riding in his shining buggy. He first went to the chief, and demanded that the wounded boy be turned over to him. He was told that none but the parents of the child could be consulted in the matter; and if he wanted the boy, he had better see the father. The agent was said to be a good man, and before he offered his services to the government as Indian agent he had studied medicine, so that he could be physician to the Indians as well as their agent. I had attended the mission school for a while, and learned to speak a little of the white man's language; and as the government interpreter was not within reach, the agent took me to the parents of the boy, who were by the bedside of their sick one. On our way to the place we heard the singing and the noises of the medicine-men, and the agent shook his head, sighed, and made some queer little noises with his tongue, which I thought to be expressive of his feelings. When our approach was noticed, every one became silent; not a word was uttered as we entered the tent, where room had already been made for us to sit, and we were silently motioned to the place. We sat down on the ground by the side of the patient, and the agent began to feel of the pulse of the boy. The head medicine-man, who sat folded up in his robe, scowled and said to me, "Tell him not to touch the boy." The agent respected the request, and said that unless the boy was turned over to him, and was properly treated, death was certain. He urged that a

---

*Water seems to hold an important place in the practice of this Medicine Society, even when roots are used for the healing of wounds. The songs say: "Water was sent into the wound," "water will be sent to his wound," etc. It is said the buffaloes heal their wounds with their own saliva, and there are Indians who declare that they have actually seen a wounded buffalo being doctored by others of the herd, who would lick the wound, and blow through their nostrils what seemed to be saliva, and the men who tell of seeing such scenes do not belong to the Medicine Society, or lay any claim to visions concerning the buffalo. I have myself shot more than one buffalo which had had its leg bones shattered by a bullet, but the wounds had healed, and the animal had been able to rejoin the herd to fall by my hand.

sick person must be kept very quiet, and free from any kind of excitement, for that would weaken him, and lessen the chances of recovery. All this I interpreted in my best Omaha, and the men listened with respectful silence. When I had finished, the leader said, "Tell him that he may ask the father of the boy if he would give up the youth to be cared for by the white medicine-men." The question was asked, and a deliberate "No" was the answer. Then the medicine-man said, "He may ask the boy if he would prefer to be doctored by the white man." While I was translating this to the agent, the boy's father whispered in his child's ear. I then interpreted the agent's question to the boy. He held out his hand to me, and said with an effort, "Who is this?" He was told that it was "Sassoo," one of his friends. I held his hand, and repeated the question to him, and he said, "My friend, I do not wish to be doctored by the white man." The agent rose, got into his buggy, and drove off, declaring that the boy's death was certain, and indeed it seemed so. The boy's head was swollen to nearly twice its natural size, and looked like a great blue ball; the hollows of his eyes were covered up, so that he could not see; and it made me shudder to look at him.

Four days the boy was treated in this strange manner. On the evening of the third day the doctors said that he was out of danger, and that in the morning he would be made to rise to meet the rising sun and to greet the return of life.

I went to bed early, so that I could be up in time to see the great ceremony. In the morning I was awakened by the singing, and approached the tent, where already a great crowd had assembled, for the people had come from the other villages to witness the scene of recovery. There was a mist in the air, as the medicine-men had foretold there would be; but as the dawn grew brighter and brighter, the fog slowly disappeared, as if to unveil the great red sun that was just visible over the horizon. Slowly it grew larger and larger, while the boy was gently lifted by two strong men, and when up on his feet, he was told to take four steps toward the east. The medicine-men sang with a good will the mystery song appropriate to the occasion, as the boy attempted this feeble walk. The two men by his side began to count, as the lad moved eastward, "Win (one), numba (two), thab'thin (three):" slower grew the steps; it did not seem as if he would be able to take the fourth; slowly the boy dragged his foot, and made the last step; as he set his foot down, the men cried, "duba" (four), and it was done. Then was sung the song of triumph, and thus ended the first medicine incantation I witnessed among the Omahas.

Before the buffalo medicine-men disbanded, they entered a sweat lodge and took a bath, after which the fees were distributed. These consisted of horses, robes, blankets, bears' claw necklaces, eagle feathers, beaded leggings, and many other articles much valued by Indians. The friends of the unfortunate man who shot the boy had given nearly half of what they possessed, and the great medicine-men went away rejoicing. One or two, however, remained for a time with the boy, and in about thirty days he was up again, shooting sticks, and ready to go and witness another pistol practice.

It is only recently that I have been able, through inquiry, to find out two of the most important roots used in the healing of wounds, but how they are used is known only to the medicine-men. And to obtain that knowledge one would have to go through various forms of initiation, each degree requiring expensive fees. One of these medicines is the root of the hop vine, *humulus lupulus*, and the other the root of the *Physalis viscora*.

## DEATH AND DESTINY

Since the state of health is a major religious concern to many Native Americans, the total failure of health resulting in death is one of the most serious of situations, and is commonly reflected upon for its religious meaning.[9] For many tribes, the way one states the goal of life, the conditions of life's fulfillment, is in the simple terms of a healthy life reaching to old age, or death in old age. The Ojibwa term *pimadaziwin* expresses this idea as does the Navajo term *są'ah naagháii bik'eh hózhǫ́*.

As conception and birth are moments in the life cycle that reflect how a people understands the nature and character of being human, so too, death is an occasion when ideas and conceptions about the fulfillment of human life and the ultimate destiny of being human are expressed. Indeed, the destiny of the human soul is usually inseparable from the practice of funerary rites and mortuary customs.[10]

The subject of death is very common in the oral traditions of most Native American tribes. Perhaps stories of the origin of death are most common and they take a variety of forms. Other stories deal with the visit to the land of the dead and the Orpheus-Eurydice type story, which tells of a man who seeks the return of his dead wife or lover from the domain of the dead. The following selections offer a sampling of Native American oral traditions dealing with the subject of death and destiny.

### *THE ORIGIN OF BIRTH AND DEATH (Tahltan)*[11]

Once the Tree and the Rock were pregnant and were about to give birth. The Tree woman held on to a stick or bar, as Indian women do, while the Rock woman used nothing to hold on to. Her child, when half born, turned into a rock and died. Raven came along shortly afterwards, and found the women. He said, "I am very sorry. I have come too late. Had I been here, this would not have happened. Now people must die, because Tree gave birth, and Rock did not." If Rock had given birth, and Tree had not, people would never die. People would then have been like rocks, and lasted forever. As it is now, people are like trees. Some will live to be very old, and decay and die, as some trees do; while others, when only partly grown, will die like young trees that die without decay and fall down. Thus death comes to people at all ages, just as among trees, and none lives very long.

### *COYOTE AND THE ORIGIN OF DEATH (Caddo)*[12]

In the beginning of this world there was no such thing as death. Every one continued to live until there were so many people that there was not room for any more on the earth. The chiefs held a council to determine what to do. One man arose and said that he thought it would be a good plan to have the people die and be gone for a little while, and then to return. As soon as he sat down Coyote jumped up and said that he thought that people ought to die forever, for this little world was not large enough to hold all of the people, and if the people who died came back to life there would not be food enough for all. All of the other men objected, saying that they did not want their friends and relatives to die and be gone forever, for then people would grieve and worry and there would not be any happiness in the world. All except Coyote decided to have the people die and be gone for a little while, and then to come back to life.

The medicine-men built a large grass house facing the east, and when they had completed it they called all of the men of the tribe together and told them that they had decided to have the people who died come to the medicine-house and there be restored to life. The chief medicine-man said that he would put a large white and black eagle feather on top of the grass house, and that when the feather became bloody and fell over, the people would know that some one had died. Then all of the medicine-men were to come to the grass house and sing. They would sing a song that would call the spirit of the dead to the grass house, and when the spirit came they would cause it to assume the form that it had while living, and then they would restore it to life again. All of the people were glad when the medicine-men announced these rules about death, for they were anxious for the dead to be restored to life and come again to live with them.

After a time they saw the eagle feather turn bloody and fall, and so they knew that some one had died. The medicine-men assembled in the grass house and sang, as they had promised that they would, for the spirit of the dead to come to them. In about ten days a whirlwind blew from the west, circled about the grass house, and finally entered through the entrance in the east. From the whirlwind appeared a handsome young man who had been murdered by another tribe. All of the people saw him and rejoiced except Coyote, who was displeased because his rules about dead were not carried out. In a short time the feather became bloody and fell again. Coyote saw it and at once went to the grass house. He took his seat near the door, and there sat with the singers for many days, and when at last he heard the whirlwind coming he slipped near the door, and as the whirlwind circled about the house and was about to enter, he closed the door. The spirit in the whirlwind, finding the door closed, whirled on by. Death forever was then introduced, and people from that time on grieved about the dead and were unhappy. Now whenever any one meets a whirlwind or hears the wind whistle he says: "There is some one wandering about." Ever since Coyote closed the door the spirits of the dead have wandered over the earth, trying to find some place to go, until at last they find the road to spirit land.

Coyote jumped up and ran away and never came back, for when he saw what he had done he was afraid. Ever after that he ran from one place to another, always looking back over first one shoulder and then over the other, to see if any one was pursuing him, and ever since then he has been starving, for no one will give him anything to eat.

## *THE ORIGIN OF DEATH (Sahaptin)*[13]

Coyote's married daughter was accidentally burned to death. Her husband moved away, and left Coyote alone. One night, as Coyote was sleeping, his daughter came and talked to him. "I have just come to see you," she said. "I am going on to where the dead people live. You cannot go with us, because you are alive, and we are dead." Coyote said that he would follow her. "You can come along if you throw yourself into the fire," the girl told him. Coyote threw himself into the flames; but as soon as he felt the pain, he jumped out again. He was so badly blistered, however, that his daughter allowed him to go along. "You will never see us again," she told him, "but you will hear us later. There is nothing to eat on the trail. You must stick your hand in your mouth. That will satisfy you."

The girl led the way, and Coyote followed her voice. It often led him into rocks and trees. There was the noise of laughter ahead of him, and Coyote followed the sound. Though it was daylight, Coyote could see nothing. They talked only when evening came, and then Coyote would follow the sound. They travelled for five days. At the end of that time Coyote could almost see them. In five days more they would be like people to him.

When they finally arrived at the land of the dead, they feared they would have to bar him from it, because he was alive. They made him sleep at some distance from the others. The land of the dead was very close to the sea. All about him Coyote saw all kinds of eggs. They gave him a bag full of holes in which to gather eggs. He filled the bag, and saw that all the eggs fell through the holes. Therefore he did not even tie it up. When he came back to his daughter, he had nothing at all. The girl then said to him, "Next time fill up the bag; and even if it falls together, as if there were nothing in it, be sure to tie it up. Then it will be full."—"That is what I thought," replied Coyote. He went back to gather more eggs. He filled the bag and tied it up. He threw it on his back, but it seemed as though there were nothing in it. Soon, however, it grew heavy: and when he reached the house, it was quite full. Henceforth it became his duty to gather eggs.

Though he heard people talk, he could not see them. He would laugh over their jokes, and they would talk about him. They said that they would put themselves into a bag, which he was to carry home. When they were ready, they told him to start. He travelled over five mountains. The girl said to him, "Father, now we are going home. Four of the mountains will be easy to climb, but the fifth one will be hard. You will hardly be able to climb it, but do not under any circumstances open your pack. When you have reached the side of the last mountain, untie the bundle, and there will be people in it. When later others die, they too will come back in a little while." Coyote promised not to untie the bag. "I may be able to cross the mountains in two days," he said. He threw the pack on his back and started on his journey. This time he had a little food with him. He crossed three mountains, and the load began to get heavy. He heard the people laugh and talk, and he was very glad. He crossed the fourth mountain, and now there was only one more to climb. He started to climb it, and managed to get within a few feet of the top. He was very tired, still he forced himself to go about four feet more, but that was as far as he could go. Though he had only about six feet to travel, he opened his pack. Those in the pack then said to him, "Father, now we must go back, and you will have to go home. Henceforth when people die, they will be dead forever." Then Coyote cried, and said, "I shall not be the only one to mourn a child. All people shall do the same as I. When a person dies, they shall never see him again." Thus he said, and went home. That is the end.

## *TIMTIMENEE OR THE ISLAND OF DEATH (Sanpoil)*[14]

There was once a camp by a river. Among the people there was a handsome man, who was a brave warrior and a great hunter. He had two children. His wife was beautiful, and he loved her dearly. One day he met a very plain maiden. She attracted him. He took her for his wife, and put her in another tent. He took most of his meat to her.

Then the first wife and his children grew hungry. The younger child cried. Then the mother sent her son to his father for meat. The boy went to the tent and stood in the doorway. When his father asked him what he wanted, he said that they were hungry. He was sent back without any food, and the new wife laughed.

The boy returned, and told his mother that he had been rebuffed and scolded, and that his father's new wife had laughed at him. His mother listened to his words, took a deer's antler, and whittled three sharp bones out of it. With two of these she killed her children while they were asleep. The last one she drove into her own breast.

In the morning the grandmother of the children came with food, and found them dead. She raised a wail, and the people came to see what had happened. Then the father was grieved. He took his bow and arrows and left the camp.

He crossed the plain, and came to a river in which was a large island. He saw canoes and camps on it, but he did not see any signs of life. He became sleepy. One tent on the island was open. A woman came out, boarded a canoe, and paddled across. He recognized his first wife, who took him across. They landed, and she pulled the canoe up on shore. She took him into the large tent. Inside there were only skeletons. He saw his children's skeletons. Then he saw that his wife too was a skeleton. He looked at himself, and he saw that he had no flesh. He had crossed the River of Death.

## *NOTES*

1. Don C. Talayesva, *Sun Chief: The Autobiography of a Hopi Indian*, ed. Leo W. Simmons (New Haven: Yale University Press, 1942), pp. 25–27. Reprinted by permission of Yale University Press.
2. Chief Buffalo Child Long Lance, *Long Lance* (New York: Farrar & Rinehart, Inc., 1928), pp. 41–45. Copyright 1928 by Cosmopolitan Book Corporation. Copyright © 1956 by Holt, Rinehart and Winston. Reprinted by permission of Holt, Rinehart and Winston, Publishers.
3. Arthur Amiotte, "Eagles Fly Over," *Parabola*, vol. I, no. 3 (1976): 29–41. Reprinted by permission of Arthur Amiotte.
4. See Harold E. Driver, *Girls' Puberty Rites in Western North America*, Anthropological Records Series (Berkeley: University of California Press, 1941).
5. See Sam D. Gill, *Native American Religions*, pp. 92–97 for a discussion of the Apache girls' puberty rite.
6. Charlotte J. Frisbie, *Kinaaldá: A Study of the Navaho Girl's Puberty Ceremony* (Middletown, Connecticut: Wesleyan University Press, 1967), pp. 11–15. Notes omitted. Copyright © 1967 by Wesleyan University Press. Reprinted by permission of Wesleyan University Press.
7. Sam D. Gill, *Songs of Life: An Introduction to Navajo Religious Culture* (Leiden, The Netherlands: E. J. Brill, 1979), pp. 9–10. Reprinted by permission of E. J. Brill.
8. Francis LaFlesche, "The Omaha Buffalo Medicine-Men," *Journal of American Folklore* 3(1890): 215–21.
9. For an excellent narrative account that demonstrates this reflective atmosphere on the occasion of death, see Dennis Tedlock, "An American Indian View of Death," in *Teachings From the American Earth: Indian Religion and Philosophy*, ed. Dennis Tedlock and Barbara Tedlock (New York: Liveright, 1975), pp. 248–71.
10. See Harry C. Yarrow, *A Further Contribution to the Study of Mortuary Customs of the North American Indians* (Washington: Bureau of American Ethnology, Annual Report No. 1, 1881), pp. 91–205.
11. James A. Teit, "Tahltan Tales," *Journal of American Folklore* 32(1919):216. Reprinted by permission of the American Folklore Society.
12. George A. Dorsey, *Traditions of the Caddo* (Washington, Publications of the Carnegie Institution of Washington, no. 41, 1905), pp. 15–16.

13. Livingston Farrand, "Sahaptin Tales" in *Folk-Tales of Salishan and Sahaptin Tribes*, collected by James A. Teit, Livingston Farrand, Marian K. Gould, and Herbert J. Spinden, ed. Franz Boas (New York: American Folklore Society, Memoirs, vol. XI, 1917), pp. 178–79. Reprinted by permission of the American Folklore Society.
14. Marion K. Gould, "Sanpoil Tales," in *Folk-Tales of Salishan and Sahaptin Tribes*, p. 112. Reprinted by permission of the American Folklore Society.

# CHAPTER 6

# *Sustaining Life*

## INTRODUCTION

For millennia Native Americans have sustained life by the fruits of the land, by gathering, by fishing, by hunting, and by planting and harvesting domesticated plants like maize (corn) and beans. While the land was often bountiful, life nonetheless depended upon delicate relationships between human beings, the land, and plants and animals. In such a crucial domain of life, it is not surprising that the labors of sustaining life were for Native Americans works of a highly sacred character. In few other areas of life may we see so clearly Native American conceptions of reality and their understanding of the nature of human existence.

## HUNTING

While by the time of European contact corn had for many centuries been grown throughout much of the area we now know as the United States, hunting and gathering had been the main sources of sustenance for millennia before corn and other plants were domesticated. Native Americans share strongly in this worldwide hunter-gatherer legacy of human history. Even with the introduction of agriculture, hunting has remained widely practiced and of importance even to those tribes who are most involved in agriculture, for they practice hunting on a seasonal or occasional basis to supplement their food crops. Hunting remains the principal means of sustenance among tribes in areas north of the United States.

The Eskimo hunters in the far north tell stories of a goddess, Sedna, to relate the origins of the game animals of the sea. These complex stories attribute the origins of these animals to the mistreatment and mutilation of the goddess, Sedna. The story explains why the Eskimo shamans must travel in spirit journeys to the bottom of the sea to the home of Sedna, the mistress of the game animals. The shaman appeases Sedna by combing her hair for her. She cannot comb her own hair because her fingers were lost in the act that created the animals. In this way the livelihood of the Eskimo is enriched, for when she is pleased, Sedna releases her animals to be hunted by the Eskimo.

## *SEDNA AND THE FULMAR (Eskimo)*[1]

Once upon a time there lived on a solitary shore an Inung with his daughter Sedna. His wife had been dead for some time and the two led a quiet life. Sedna grew up to be a handsome girl and the youths came from all around to sue for her hand, but none of them could touch her proud heart. Finally, at the breaking up of the ice in the spring a fulmar flew from over the ice and wooed Sedna with enticing song. "Come to me," it said; "come into the land of the birds, where there is never hunger, where my tent is made of the most beautiful skins. You shall rest on soft bearskins. My fellows, the fulmars, shall bring you all your heart may desire; their feathers shall clothe you; your lamp shall always be filled with oil, your pot with meat." Sedna could not long resist such wooing and they went together over the vast sea. When at last they reached the country of the fulmar, after a long and hard journey, Sedna discovered that her spouse had shamefully deceived her. Her new home was not built of beautiful pelts, but was covered with wretched fishskins, full of holes, that gave free entrance to wind and snow. Instead of soft reindeer skins her bed was made of hard walrus hides and she had to live on miserable fish, which the birds brought her. Too soon she discovered that she had thrown away her opportunities when in her foolish pride she had rejected the Inuit youth. In her woe she sang: "Aja. O father, if you knew how wretched I am you would come to me and we would hurry away in your boat over the water. The birds look unkindly upon me the stranger; cold winds roar about my bed; they give me but miserable food. O come and take me back home. Aja."

When a year had passed and the sea was again stirred by warmer winds, the father left his country to visit Sedna. His daughter greeted him joyfully and besought him to take her back home. The father hearing of the outrages wrought upon his daughter determined upon revenge. He killed the fulmar, took Sedna into his boat, and they quickly left the country which had brought so much sorrow to Sedna. When the other fulmars came home and found their companion dead and his wife gone, they all flew away in search of the fugitives. They were very sad over the death of their poor murdered comrade and continue to mourn and cry until this day.

Having flown a short distance they discerned the boat and stirred up a heavy storm. The sea rose in immense waves that threatened the pair with destruction. In this mortal peril the father determined to offer Sedna to the birds and flung her overboard. She clung to the edge of the boat with a death grip. The cruel father then took a knife and cut off the first joints of her fingers. Falling into the sea they were transformed into whales, the nails turning into whale-bone. Sedna holding on to the boat more tightly, the second finger joints fell under the sharp knife and swam away as seals (*Pagomys fœtidus*); when the father cut off the stumps of the fingers they became ground seals (*Phoca barbata*). Meantime the storm subsided, for the fulmars thought Sedna was drowned. The father then allowed her to come into the boat again. But from that time she cherished a deadly hatred against him and swore bitter revenge. After they got ashore, she called her dogs and let them gnaw off the feet and hands of her father while he was asleep. Upon this he cursed himself, his daughter, and the dogs which had maimed him; whereupon the earth opened and swallowed the hut, the father, the daughter, and the dogs. They have since lived in the land of Adlivan, of which Sedna is the mistress.

When considering Native American hunting practices, it is most important to understand that hunting is not an economic and occupational activity with religious overtones or with religious elements; hunting is first and foremost a religious activity based on a spiritual view of reality and of the relationship between humans and animals. Commonly game animals are under the care of a spiritual master or mistress, such as Sedna, who controls and releases them to be hunted. The hunt, the kill, the dressing of the carcass, the distribution of the meat, and the disposal of the bones usually follow a carefully prescribed and often ritual procedure.[2]

Unfortunately, we commonly categorize Native American peoples on the basis of sustenance practices. We divide the hunters from the agriculturalists. While some tribes have exclusive modes of sustenance, this is an unusual exception rather than the rule. For example, the Pueblo tribes of the Southwest are commonly identified as corn growers, agriculturalists, to the total exclusion of hunting, yet this view is inaccurate. Hunting is of considerable importance to all Pueblo tribes and it is not without influence in the religious world views of the Pueblo tribes. The following selection is an account written by an Acoma Pueblo man that describes the Acoma practice of deer hunting. It is not only an informative, but a beautifully written, account.

### *DEER HUNTING (Acoma), by James Paytiamo*[3]

Let me take you to an Indian deer hunt.

First we get our men together. Four is enough in a bunch. We start out from home with a song. The song is translated:

> From Acoma I am going to put the sewed-up moccasins on my feet. I, the man, do put on the moccasin heel-piece.
> Painting my body with yellow, red, blue and white clay color,
> Then clothing myself with an apron round my waist with designs on,
> Then round my knee the colored yarn,
> Then the colored yarn around my wrist,
> Then around my arm green bands with fir tree branches stuck in them.
> Next I paint my face red and black.
> I tie an eagle feather on top of my hair.
> I pick up my arrows. The bow made of a rainbow, and the arrows representing the lightning flash.
> I travel sometimes with song to attract deer with my singing.

After a whole day's travel we camp. For a whole day's trip I travel south from Acoma, and reach a place for my prayer-sticks. I lay them down carefully, and bury them, as if there were strange gods near to hear my prayers; and each one of the party does the same. After we bury our prayer-sticks, we all gather round the campfire.

We have started out with a supply of food and ready baked bread to last us for two weeks, the same amount of blue cornmeal to make our gravy, and such things as lard, onions, potatoes, coffee and sugar. We do not need any meat, as we will be killing rabbits on our way.

When we reach our camp, the first evening after dark, each one goes off in some direction by himself, to pray to strange gods. We pray towards any direction in which we think there may be some god listening to hear our prayers. We pray to the mountain lion, eagles, hawks, wolves, and other wild beasts. Then we bury our prayer-sticks and pick up a piece of log and sprinkle it with cornmeal, and say to it: "You be the deer which I expect to bring into camp," and then we carry this piece of wood in and place it on the campfire, and blow our breath on a pinch of cornmeal in our hands and throw it on the flames. Doing so we receive power, and hunt well.

Then each is seated on his rolled-up blanket around the campfire. The next thing we do is to choose our officers. First we choose the field chief, *Tsa-ta-ow-ho-tcha*. He has to see that all the hunters get their deer. If one of the hunters is unlucky enough not to get a deer, he has to divide up with him. Next we elect our governor, *Dta-po-po*. He is to see that the camp is in order, and keep peace in the camp. The youngest one is always elected as the cook, and also has to look after the horses and burros, and get wood for the fire. If he has any time, after the dishes are washed, and there is plenty of wood and water, and the stock has been watered, he can hunt right around the camp.

After these officers are elected, the field chief gives orders to put down as an altar, between us and the fire, the flint and other stone animals which every hunter carries with him to the hunt, and which are handed down in each family. After all of these little animals are placed on the level ground, they sprinkle white cornmeal over them, and around them, forming a circle of cornmeal. Then a song is sung which means: "We welcome this altar into our camp. Come and take a place with us." Then they sing to the mountain lion to take its place, then the wolf, then the man himself, then the owls, then the hawks. Song after song continues through the night until dawn. In the morning, each one picks up his little hunting animal, and ties it in the handkerchief around his neck, and takes his cornmeal from the little bag at his side. Praying to the strange gods, and breathing his breath on the cornmeal, he sprinkles it out to the east to the sun.

The hunters are ordered to pack up for another day's trip. All are feeling happy, and they are not supposed to make one complaint about anything, which is strict orders. They sing softly all the way they travel.

We reach the second camp on the second evening. This time after our meal each one sings a new pretty song that he prepared before starting. We practice these songs all night, until they are well learned. We get on our feet and dance around the fire. The songs are all about something nice that gives us hopes of getting a deer. Then we go to sleep for an hour or two before daybreak.

About three o'clock in the morning the cook is up. He has breakfast ready long before dawn, so as to have the hunters off while the animals are roaming the woods. The hunters get up and eat their breakfasts, and start on climbing the mountains without any lunch, and without knowing whether there is any water in the direction in which they are going.

We are climbing through thick brush on tiptoe. If you meet an Indian hunter, he will not speak to you. He is taught to keep quiet. When a deer starts off, he always heads for a canyon, which he descends. Then the Indian seeing the deer, starts at full speed for the canyon, because the deer will cross the canyon, and ascend the opposite side, and will stop and look back on top of the ridge. Then the hunter will have a chance to shoot the deer, as he stops in full sight on the ridge.

When an Indian has hit a deer, he runs to the fallen animal. First he takes a small branch of a tree and brushes him off, as he has a religious belief that the deer is made of sheets of clouds, and he has to brush off the clouds to get at him. Then he reaches down in his pocket for the yellow pollen he has collected from flowers, takes it between his thumb and forefinger, drops a little on the deer's mouth, then carries it to his own breath, and makes a sign with the pollen towards the hunter's camp, which is supposed to lead the spirit of the deer to the camp.

Then he pulls the deer around by the forelegs, until he lies with his head towards the camp. The next thing is to take the little flint animals in the shapes of lions, wolves and bears, as many as he carries, and place them on the deer to feed and get back the power they gave him. They always come first. While these animals are on the deer, the hunter rolls a cigarette of cornhusks, and while he smokes he talks to the dead creature just as if he were telling a human where to go. When he finishes he gathers his flint animals, carefully places them in his bag, and talks to them while he puts them in the bag, telling them that he hopes for the good luck of another deer. Then he ties the bag with these animals round his neck under his shirt.

He pulls out of his pocket a flint arrowhead, and, starting from the deer's neck pretends to cut it. In olden days they really cut with the spear head, instead of knives. Then he cuts off juniper pine twigs and lays them as thick as he can alongside of the deer, ready to be placed upon it after it is skinned, to keep the blood off the hide and the dirt off the meat.

After skinning the deer and placing the meat on these juniper twigs, the hunter starts to cut the animal into parts like a beef. He is always sure that he takes the entrails out first. He digs in the ground a shallow hole, and washes his hands. If there is no water nearby, he wipes his hands on a cloth. He reaches down with his hands into the blood and dips it up four times, and places it in the shallow hole on the earth. This is to feed the mother earth. Then he takes out the spleen, and places it nearby on a twig of a tree to feed the crow. Then he cuts him up.

The hind legs are taken off first, then the front quarters. Then he strips the meat off the bone from the hoofs to the first joint, and ties these muscles together, front and hind legs, so as to hang the deer over the saddle without any rope. Next the ribs are taken off in such a way as to hang over the saddle without being separated. This leaves the breast connected with the meat of the stomach, and in this way all the parts will balance on a burro's back, and the backbone and fur and head are still together, and are easily balanced on the saddle.

Now the deer is prepared to carry to the camp. The fur is placed over the limb of any tree nearby and the meat is placed on the fur. The Indian hunter takes off his shirt, or some other article of clothing, and places it near the meat somewhere, as this will keep away all animals while he goes back to the camp for his horse and saddle.

When he reaches camp, the cook is always ready to feed him no matter what time he arrives. While the hunter is eating, the cook is ordered to bring his horse and have it saddled as soon as he is done with his meal.

He goes back to his meat, and has no trouble getting it on his horse's back, unless the horse isn't used to carrying deer meat, then he will have all kinds of trouble. When the horses smell the deer meat, they will buck and whirl.

To the Indian hunter, so long as he is getting his game, it matters not how far from camp he goes, nor how late he comes in, nor how dark his travel will be through forest and mountain, cold or fair weather: he does not make camp, but returns to the big camp. And every brave that comes in with a load on his horse, they serve as if he were a chief. All he carries in the camp is his gun. The others unload the burden on the horse. They always do this, as every hunter knows how tired they get wandering around in the deep canyons, no water and no food, on foot.

First he is called to his meal, and when all have arrived at the camp, they have a fine time. When there is one absent, they all worry, for there is danger in the forest:—a mountain lion might have gotten him, or he might have fallen off a cliff, and they will sit up all night if a hunter is absent from the camp, but if all are there, they are happy through the night, singing, laughing and dancing, and feasting on the meat.

After each hunter gets one deer, they agree on a day to start home. Coming home they will all join in on their new songs, singing as loudly as they can, and if they camp again before reaching home, the burdens of the burros and horses are placed in line, so as to be easy to repack in line in the morning.

When they are within a mile from home, each of the hunters loads his gun with one shot, and they are fired off, one by one, so that each family by counting the shots, can tell which group of hunters is returning. As they come home each hunter makes a round circle from fir trees, to fit his head, puts evergreens on his horse's bridle, and around the deers' heads. Even the burros' heads are decorated with fir twigs.

When they arrive home there will be relatives there to take charge of the meat, and see to the unsaddling and feeding of the animals. All the hunter does is to tell his wonderful story.

The very next day after the hunter arrives, his wife or mother, or some member of his family, goes to invite all the relatives to dinner on the following day, and every one of these relatives who comes to the dinner brings along some food to replace what he will eat, and the hunter is there to receive this food. He breaks off a little chunk from each piece of bread, and the end of the tongue and the tenderloin are cooked especially for this hunter. The men in the meantime roll cigarettes of cornhusks. They make as many as the number of places the hunter is going to. He lays out fifteen cornhusks, and on them places these cigarettes, a small amount of the deer tongue hash, and wraps them up. With these he is going to pray to the strange gods, and thank them for the help they have given him.

As we have seen hunting is commonly a highly religious practice, extending well beyond the actual pursuit and killing of the game. Magical practices often accompany the hunt in the form of medicines and formulas. In the following account by a Menomini woman, the origins of a special deer hunting medicine are told. This native account is followed by a brief description of the use of this hunting medicine.

## *SPOTTED FAWN DEER HUNTING MEDICINE (Menomini)*[4]

Some Menomini Indian people, long ago, were moving about on the fall hunt. The woman of the family had a child, a little girl five years old. The child was continually fretting and crying because it was lonely, as it had neither brothers nor sisters. In order to quiet it, its mother was in the habit of telling it that she would be thrown outside for the owls.

Now all the Great Birds Above heard this said by the mother, and they spoke to the owl. "Why don't you take the child given you, it has been offered you many times."

To this the owl replied: "I heard all that, but it was only said to the child to scare it, because I look so ugly. That's why I don't go and take it, for all parents say that to their children to frighten them."

But the little girl kept on crying at night, and so, one night, to punish her, her mother said, "Child, I will throw you out doors for the owls to come and take you away."

Then she opened the mat door and threw her daughter out, saying, "Now Owl, come and get her, she is yours."

The child stayed outside for some time crying, and then she ceased and was not heard any more. Her mother went out to see what was the matter, but she could not find her. She looked all around the lodge, but the child was not there. She went to every wigwam to enquire for her, but she could not learn anything of her, for it had come to pass that the owl had come and taken the child away secretly. Then the mother ran into her own wigwam and told her husband about the matter, what she had said and done in giving the child to the owl. Her husband was very angry at her, and they quarrelled and fought over the child.

When the little girl was taken away to the owl's den in the wilderness, she found that one was her grandmother, and she was placed in a fancy wigwam and kept there in comfort all winter. Every once in a while the owl, her grandmother, would say "My grandchild, tomorrow I will take you home, for your parents live nearby. I will dress you up to look beautiful. I will give you some of my medicine and I will take you back where I got you. The medicine I shall give you is called *Kītag'asa Musk'iki*[u] (Spotted fawn medicine), and is intended to charm deer and other game so that they may be killed. Medicine of this kind must be kept wrapped in a spotted fawnskin, and is named on that account. It is very powerful, this medicine I shall give you, grandchild, for you and your parents and great grandparents to use in the future among all your people as long as the world shall last."

When it drew near spring the parents of the lost girl were making maple sugar at their sugar bush. Only a little snow remained here and there, and in the evenings the owls begin to whoop and sing to show that they are at last awake, for the Indians know that winter is but a short night to all the Sacred Powers.

In the meantime the parents of the little girl had given her up as lost, but the owl said to her grandchild, "Now I will take you home, and land you at the limits of your parents' work on the trees they have tapped, surrounding their sugar camp. Stand there silently until your mother comes and finds you. Don't allow her to touch you at all for four days. Then you must tell her to go and prepare a tiny wigwam for you to remain in for four days. This must be away from the sugar camp in a clean place where no one has done any trampling on the ground, and you shall remain there, silent."

So owl did leave her grandchild where her mother could find her, and her mother did come. When the woman first caught sight of her daughter, she cried out:

"Oh my! Is it my lost daughter or am I imagining or dreaming? Oh yes it is my daughter! Come my dear daughter, to me!"

But the girl said: "Do not grasp me, for I am forbidden to allow you to touch me for four days."

The mother then ran back to the sugar camp to tell her husband and they both went back and met the girl. Their daughter said to them:

"Make a tiny wigwam here and place me in it to remain for four days by myself, to be clean and pure as I was instructed by my grandmother owl. In the course of the four days my father must come to me frequently and I will instruct him how to use the medicine given me by my grandmother."

So the wigwam was made according to her instructions and the girl showed her father how to use the fawnskin medicine, for it had sacred songs which had to be repeated as the owl had ordered.

*This medicine was and is always prepared by a pure young girl. It is made up when a number of hunters wish to use it. The girl who has it has to build a tiny wigwam, and the men have to have sticks made in the shape of deer's legs with their hooves to beat upon in the lodge.*

*The men, clad only in their shirts, enter the lodge and sit in a circle, in the center of which is strewed a number of cedar boughs. Stones, heated in a fire outside are rolled in, in front of the hunters, and medicine which has been prepared is poured over the stones to make a medicated vapor. While the steam saturates each hunter, the songs are sung, and the sacred power of the owl is invoked. The other Sacred Powers hear it too, and send the aid to the hunters. Several tiny boys and girls are called into the lodge in memory of the little girl and their purity attracts the aid of the Sacred ones.*

*All wild animals are called by the spell and approach the wigwam. The hunters meet the game coming to them. The medicine must always be kept and guarded by a pure young girl.*

## FISHING AND WHALING

Fishing is an important sustenance activity among many tribes. A whole genre of stories tell of how the fish or game were released so that they might be fished or hunted by human beings. In the following Tahltan story, Raven, a common protagonist in northwest area stories, is a culture hero who releases the olachen so that they become available for people to eat. This story, appealing to peoples who depend upon the presence of fish, reflects community and cosmic relations that are essential for life.

### *THE ORIGIN OF OLACHEN (Tahltan)*[5]

Raven now went to a village of people, and asked them if they had any olachen. They answered, "No, we have no olachen. It is in possession of a man who lives a little distance from here." Raven went to the house that had been pointed out to him, and entered. The owner believed that Raven was a distinguished person, and treated him hospitably. Plenty of food was placed before him, but very little olachen. Raven went out, and went to Sea-Gull, who had eaten olachen, and to Heron, who had also eaten olachen. He said to Sea-Gull, "Heron talks evil of you, and calls you bad names." Then he went to Heron, and told him that Sea-Gull called him bad names. Thus he caused them to quarrel. He told Heron he would help him fight Sea-Gull. Heron said, "I push back the heads of people when I fight, and break their necks. I have done that often." Heron attacked and fought Sea-Gull, and broke his neck. Sea-Gull then vomited up all the olachen that he had in his stomach, and Raven gathered it up and put it into his canoe. He also gathered up broken shells, and put them into his canoe to make it look greasy and as if covered with fish-scales. He also rubbed shells on his arms to make them look as if they were covered with fish-scales.

Now he went to the owner of the olachen, and entered his house. No one spoke to him. At last Raven said, "I am tired," and Olachen-Man asked what he had been doing. He answered, "I have been working at olachen." The man inquired where he had found them; and Raven answered, "You are not the only person who has olachen. I have plenty at my place." Olachen-Man sent down some men to look at his canoe. They saw the olachen there, and what looked like the scales of fish all over the inside of his canoe. They came back and reported that the canoe must have been full of olachen. The houseowner then thought that Raven must be a great man, and that it would be better to treat him well. He placed before him as much olachen as he could eat. He took the precaution, however, of locking him up in the house, intending to keep him until he had digested all the olachen that he had eaten; but Raven flew out of the smokehole and over to a tree near a stream. Here he vomited, and threw the olachen into the mouth of the stream, saying, *"Henceforth olachen shall frequent the mouths of rivers, and all the people may eat them."*

The drama and danger of the whale hunters of the Olympic Peninsula of Washington can scarcely be fully appreciated. In light canoes, armed with harpoons and weapons made largely from the bones and sinew of the whale, the hunters required the finest skills, enormous knowledge, and the greatest strength to even survive the hunt, much less to be successful. While we must recognize that the whale hunters spent years to become fully adept at the practical side of hunting, they considered the ritual and ceremonial elements as necessary as any other element for success in hunting. This view is shown in the following selection, which describes Quileute whale hunting as it was practiced around the beginning of this century.

## *WHALING METHODS AND CEREMONIES (Quileute), by Albert B. Reagan*[6]

Thirty-six miles down the Pacific coast southeast of Cape Flattery is the Indian village of Quileute. It is situated on a point of land flanked by a giant forest on one side and the pounding ocean on the other. To the west of it is James Island in the shape of a giant lobster's claw reaching toward the setting sun. Southeast of it the hissing, seething surf beats against the world-foundation stones of the Giant's Graveyard.

In this village from time immemorial have lived the Quileute Indians, a coastal people that engage in whaling. The whale principally pursued is the California gray.

The aspiring whale hunter, especially the harpooner, must first obtain a knowledge of the sea folk-tales of the tribe, which are many and varied. These include the account how Kwatte, the creator god, the transformer and trickster, deliberately paddled his big dugout canoe toward the great whirlpool that was caused by Subbus, the whale, as, lying on the bottom of the sea, he drew the surface water down through his mouth. To the very edge of the great funnel Kwatte paddled the canoe. Its prow went forward and projected over the great hollow space above Subbus' mouth. For a moment it remained suspended there. Then it went down edgewise, right down through Subbus' mouth into his gigantic stomach, with Kwatte lying snugly in its bottom.

Then Kwatte set to work. He used the big canoe as a ladder, climbing to its top in the huge stomach. With clamshell knives he cut at the inner linings and muscles of Subbus. From side to side he moved the canoe and cut and cut. The infuriated monster plunged and pitched in his death agony but he could not get rid of his enemy. At last Subbus made one powerful lunge, but in vain. Then he rose to the surface and floated there, dead.

The huge lifeless bulk drifted to shore. There the Indians found it and started to cut it up. As they began to remove the blubber, they heard someone talking inside the carcass:

"Be careful! You people will wound me with your knives. Don't hurt me! Ouch! Look out!"

A knife penetrated the body wall into the body cavity. Another thrust of the knife made a large hole in the great stomach. And Kwatte came up through this gash and stepped out on the beach.

We may turn at this point to another myth. It tells how in a wrestling match between the sea animals and those of the land, Bear threw Whale down and scratched him on the breast. These scratches are still to be seen on the fore part of the pectoral surface of the huge monster.

The Thunder Bird is represented as engaged in dreadful battles with whales. Once this bird, after killing the powerful ocean monster, was nearly robbed of its prey by a group of people who came to the scene and cut up the whale. But scarcely had they done so when it began to rain, snow, and hail. The Thunder Bird, the flash of whose eyes is the lightning and the flapping of whose wings produces the mighty winds, came flying up in anger. Soon he caused great chunks of ice to fall. The people were scared. Some tried to flee, others concealed themselves under logs and rocks to escape the wrath of this god of the air. But all were stricken and turned to stone as was also the meat of the whale. Whoever visits the scene of their fatal gathering may view their remains, represented by the great blocks that form a ridge from one end of Beaver Prairie to the other. One may even see the ribs of the whale's carcass and its massive head.

When these myths and many others of a similar nature have been learned by the harpooner, he must undergo curious and weird ordeals. He must bathe his body in the cold salt water of the ocean two or three times each night for several moons, beginning usually in the month of December before the whaling season opens. For the purpose he selects some rock that juts out of the water and around it he swims the hours away. He pretends that the rock is a whale that has come to the surface to get air and that he is attacking it. Then, in turn, he makes believe that he himself is a whale: he tries in every way to imitate a whale's motion, diving, coming to the surface, spouting, and the like. After a time he comes ashore from his whale-killing play and dries himself with a blanket or a bear skin. He then rubs himself with the twigs of a tree that his family has held sacred for generations. In doing so he must take care that the head of this body brush is pointing to the region where the sun rises. His task completed, he must not throw the brush away heedlessly, as that would bring great misfortune in addition to shortening his life. While he thus rubs himself he prays to Se-kah-til, the mother earth, who especially aids whalers in their quest for the king of the sea. In addition to bathing, he also wanders about graveyards and secluded places at night. Often he gathers a number of human skulls and trails them behind him on a rope made of whale sinew, or practices similar gruesome rites.

While he is thus engaged out of doors, other members of the respective whaling crews are going through various incantations indoors to invoke the aid of the gods in the coming whaling season. They shake whale rattles and crawl and flounder around on the floor in imitation of the movements of a whale, especially those of a whale in his dying struggles. The bathing and other rites they indulge in so that the whale may not detect them and also to gain the good will of the deities.

Thereupon a whaling canoe and the prerequisites for the whaling trip are secured. The harpoon and attached gear, a few buoys, a sufficient supply of paddles, and food enough for eight men—the complement of a canoe—are essentials in a venture on the deep that has for its object the killing of the largest animal of the seas.

The harpoon head is a piece of whale rib, or a flat piece of copper, iron, or steel, according to the hunter's choice. Attached to it are two barbs made of elk or deer horn, or of steel. These are fitted together very tightly and fastened in place by cords. The entire harpoon, including the barbs, is then covered with spruce gum to protect it and to aid in holding the parts in place. When this gum is sufficiently hardened, the harpoon is scraped and ground until it is very sharp and will penetrate flesh easily.

To the barbed head of the harpoon is attached a lanyard from thirty to forty feet in length. This lanyard is made of whale sinew or cedar twigs or roots twisted into a rope. To make it still stronger, twine of whale sinew is wound very tightly around it throughout its entire length.

The staff is usually composed of two pieces of yew wood, which are spliced together neatly and firmly with bark or sinew. It is from eighteen to twenty feet in length, being thickest in the middle and tapering off toward each end. It is inserted in the harpoon head, and the end of the lanyard is fastened to a buoy.

Each buoy is a sealskin that has been taken off whole with the hair left inside, as in skinning small fur animals for market. The holes left by the removal of the head, flippers, and tail are tied up perfectly tight; and then the skin bag thus formed is inflated.

When the harpoon is driven into the whale, the barbs to which the lanyard is attached, penetrate the animal and remain firmly fastened. The staff is then removed from the harpoon and put into the canoe. To the floating end of the lanyard is attached a long rope on which buoys have been fastened to keep the whale from sinking. Often as many as forty buoys are thus employed. The more buoys, the more difficult it is for the struggling monster to plunge beneath the surface, and the easier for the whalers to attack it with their spears and lances. The rope to which the buoys are attached is usually made of spruce limbs, which have been split into fibers and then twisted into rope.

The paddle of yew wood has a broad blade that tapers to a point; to the other end is fitted transversely a headpiece that is sufficiently long to enable the paddler to use it freely and comfortably as a hand-hold piece. Furthermore, the whole paddle is usually blackened in the fire and then polished with a vegetable compound. The canoe is a dugout that, with the exception of its prow, which is fashioned to represent the mythical river deer, is made from a single log.

When the whaling season arrives and all the preparations are completed, the weather being favorable, the whaling canoes are dragged to the beach in the gray of the early morning long before the blazing orb of day looks down into the valleys from the heights of the Olympic Mountains. There is wild excitement as the Indians haul the boats to the water's edge. The whale dancers go through their antics, shout and sing around their respective canoes as they carry the weapons of whaling out to them. In this ceremony the actors wear a black blanket, or one on which a whale has been painted. They also grease themselves with whale oil and wash their faces in it. They dance in imitation of a whale that is diving, swimming, and floundering in his last efforts before dying.

At last the boats, with the hunting equipment and whale rattle, are launched. In another moment each of the crews is off, the man who has convinced his fellows that he has "bathed good" and that he "can catch the whale easy" being the harpooner. When they are out some distance from shore, the spouting of a whale may be seen. The crew in the boat nearest to it paddles swiftly but cautiously to the attack, while all chant in long-drawn-out crescendo to induce the whale to head toward the canoe or toward the shore. Usually, however, it submerges before they can reach it.

When it disappears, the whalers shake their rattles for a moment as they sing. Those in the foremost boat then cease singing and row their canoe swiftly over the water to the spot where the whale is likely to come to the surface again. Everyone now nerves himself for the attack as one of the hunters signals with uplifted paddle that the decisive moment has arrived. This news is transmitted in like manner to other canoes, and also to the shore. The spectators on James Island build huge bonfires on the southeast corner of the island if the whale is seen southeast of the village; and on the southwest corner if it happens to be seen southwestward of it. This is for the purpose of advising all the whaling canoes of the approximate location of the whale to be attacked.

The whale comes to the surface again, and the native navigator has not miscalculated the probable place of emergence; he seldom does. As soon as the huge head makes its appearance, the action begins. With measured dip the paddles move the canoe noiselessly up to within a few feet of the huge creature that is unsuspectingly spouting on the surface of a quiet swell. The hunter hurls his harpoon with all his strength, while his men, ready for every danger, bend their energies to prevent the rope from tangling. The deadly weapon is driven deeply into the whale's body, and as quick as an eye-movement the harpooner draws out the harpoon stalk. The barbed points hold fast, and instantly the buoys and rope attached are thrown into the sea. The plunging of the wounded beast begins.

Quickly the whale goes down, drawing with him the lanyard rope of the harpoon to which are attached the sealskin buoys. These go skimming along over the water like so many tops, while the canoes follow as rapidly as they can. Again and again the whale comes to the surface, and each time he is harpooned with deadly effect. The fight may continue for hours, or it may be ended in a brief time. The monster may smash a canoe in frenzied fury, and it may also break the rope and escape. As a rule, however, its speed finally slackens, and the hunters, armed with their spears and lances, then finish their work at close quarters.

As soon as it is dead, the crew or crews attach a huge cedar-root rope cable to it and commence towing it ashore. As they thus tow, they sing day and night to keep the evil spirit, Ko-kwo-til, from alighting on it or taking possession of it, for "should it get on it, it would make it lean." They also sing songs to Se-kah-til, the mother earth, to aid them in bringing it ashore.

The whale is landed as high up on the beach as possible. When the tide recedes, all who are entitled to a share swarm around the carcass with long, thick-bladed butcher knives and begin stripping off the blubber in blocks about two feet square. The saddle is considered sacred and is always the property of the hunter who first drove his harpoon into the whale, provided that the blow proved fatal. The other parts are divided and distributed according to an established rule, so that each individual knows just how much whale blubber or meat he is to receive. The cutting up of the whale is a merry and joyous occasion, for at such times the Indians invariably seem good-tempered. If some one gets more than he can use, the surplus is given to some less-favored friend, but it is assumed that there will be a return gift either of cash or something of equivalent value. The more unfortunate ones get a share of the meat by helping themselves.

After the skin is removed, the blubber is cut into strips and boiled that the oil may be extracted, large iron pots now being used for the purpose. The oil is very carefully skimmed off with clamshells or thin saucers. The blubber is then hung up in the smoke of the fish house to dry. Before being eaten, it is sometimes cooked for twenty minutes or more, but it is not unusual to eat it cold with dried halibut.

The extracted oil is used in eating potatoes, camas, dried clams, and boiled or dried fish, which are dipped into it. As receptacles for this oil the Indians use the stomach of the sea lion or the seal and whale's bladder and intestines, which have previously been inflated and dried for the purpose. The surplus oil is sold to or traded with other tribes, or is sold to logging camps or to traders for use as logging-skid grease and in general lubrication.

The skin of the whale is also considered very palatable and is usually given to the children. In fact, there is hardly any part of the animal that has not its uses for the coast natives.

The saddle is put on a pole supported at each end by a forked post, on which are hung the harpoons and lines used in the capture of the whale. It is also customary to stick eagle feathers in a row along its crest and in a bunch at each end of the pole. The saddle is then covered or sprinkled over with down. A vessel is placed underneath it to catch the dripping oil. Thereupon a "potlatch" (give-away feast dance) in honor of the whale's saddle is held, with the compliments of the harpooner who killed the whale. At this feast the participants always relate the story of the whale hunt and never fail to congratulate the host on his ability. Some one makes a speech, telling of the ancestral trait of the family or clan of the harpooner, of his past achievements, and the honor that others will bestow upon him. The ceremony is closed by a "vote of thanks," after which the guests carry home with them whatever is left of the saddle.



## AGRICULTURE

At the time of European contact agriculture was practiced among tribes widespread throughout much of the areas we now know as the United States and Mexico. Agriculture, and particularly the domestication of maize, originated in Mesoamerica and was diffused throughout areas of North America over a period of several thousand years. This history, which has been scientifically established with some confidence, should not in any way stand in tension with the many Native American accounts of the origin of corn and other plants. The genre of the origin story permits the peoples whose lives literally depend upon the presence of the crops to describe and to express how important these plants are to them. To describe the origin of food plants in stories is to bestow a spiritual dimension upon them, it is to consider their importance in terms global and fundamental in significance. Therefore, such stories as the origin of plants are of prime importance to us in an effort to appreciate the nature and character of the religions of Native Americans.

The several selections that follow describe the origin of corn. Perhaps surprising is that while the origin of corn, and other food crops, is commonly associated with a female figure, this figure is not the benevolent all-giving mother figure that we might expect. Rather, this figure is often a complex magical figure that others may associate with evil and witchcraft. Here, as we have found elsewhere, actions that would normally be unacceptable are bound with the establishment of the nature of culture and human existence.

The following two stories from tribes in the southeastern U.S. show something of the enormous variations that may occur in stories of the origin of corn. The Cherokee selection notably combines the origin of hunting and corn cultivation.

### *THE ORIGIN OF CORN (Natchez)*[7]

Corn-woman lived at a certain place in company with twin girls. When the corn was all gone she went into the corn house, taking two baskets, and came out with the baskets full. They lived on the hominy which she made from this.

One time the girls looked into this corn house and saw nothing there. They said to each other, "Where does she get it? Next time she goes in there we will creep up and watch her."

When the corn was all gone she started to go in and they saw her. So they crept after her and when she entered and closed the door they peeped through a crack. They saw her set down the basket, stand astride of it and rub and shake herself, and there was a noise, tságak, as if something fell off. In this way she filled one basket with corn. Then she stood over the other, rubbed herself and shook, the noise tsắgak was heard and that basket was full of beans. After that the girls ran away.

"Let us not eat it," they said. "She defecates and then feeds us with the excrement." So when the hominy was cooked they did not eat it, and from that she knew they had seen her. "Since you think it is filthy, you will have to help yourselves from now on. Kill me and burn my body. When summer comes things will spring up on the place where it was burned and you must cultivate them, and when they are matured they will be your food."

They killed Corn-woman and burned her body and when summer came corn, beans, and pumpkins sprang up. They kept cultivating these and every day, when they stopped, stuck their hoes up in the ground and went away. But on their return more ground would be hoed and the hoes would be sticking up in different places.

They said, "Let us creep up and find out who is hoeing for us," and they did so. When they looked they saw that the hoes were doing it of themselves and they laughed. Immediately the hoes fell down and did not work for them any more. They did not know that it was just those two hoes which were helping them and they themselves spoiled it.

## *KANA'TĬ AND SELU: THE ORIGIN OF GAME AND CORN (Cherokee)*[8]

When I was a boy this is what the old men told me they had heard when they were boys.

Long years ago, soon after the world was made, a hunter and his wife lived at Pilot knob with their only child, a little boy. The father's name was Kana'tĭ (The Lucky Hunter), and his wife was called Selu (Corn). No matter when Kana'tĭ went into the wood, he never failed to bring back a load of game, which his wife would cut up and prepare, washing off the blood from the meat in the river near the house. The little boy used to play down by the river every day, and one morning the old people thought they heard laughing and talking in the bushes as though there were two children there. When the boy came home at night his parents asked him who had been playing with him all day. "He comes out of the water," said the boy, "and he calls himself my elder brother. He says his mother was cruel to him and threw him into the river." Then they knew that the strange boy had sprung from the blood of the game which Selu had washed off at the river's edge.

Every day when the little boy went out to play the other would join him, but as he always went back again into the water the old people never had a chance to see him. At last one evening Kana'tĭ said to his son, "Tomorrow, when the other boy comes to play, get him to wrestle with you, and when you have your arms around him hold on to him and call for us." The boy promised to do as he was told, so the next day as soon as his playmate appeared he challenged him to a wrestling match. The other agreed at once, but as soon as they had their arms around each other, Kana'tĭ's boy began to scream for his father. The old folks at once came running down, and as soon as the Wild Boy saw them he struggled to free himself and cried out, "Let me go; you threw me away!" but his brother held on until the parents reached the spot, when they seized the Wild Boy and took him home with them. They kept him in the house until they had tamed him, but he was always wild and artful in his disposition, and was the leader of his brother in every mischief. It was not long until the old people discovered that he had magic powers, and they called him I'năge-utăsûñ'hĭ (He-who-grew-up-wild).

Whenever Kana'tĭ went into the mountains he always brought back a fat buck or doe, or maybe a couple of turkeys. One day the Wild Boy said to his brother, "I wonder where our father gets all that game; let's follow him next time and find out." A few days afterward Kana'tĭ took a bow and some feathers in his hand and started off toward the west. The boys waited a little while and then went after him, keeping out of sight until they saw him go into a swamp where there were a great many of the small reeds that hunters use to make arrowshafts. Then the Wild Boy changed himself into a puff of bird's down, which the wind took up and carried until it alighted upon Kana'tĭ's shoulder just as he entered the swamp, but Kana'tĭ knew nothing about it. The old man cut reeds, fitted the feathers to them and made some arrows, and the Wild Boy—in his other shape—thought, "I wonder what those things are for?" When Kana'tĭ had his arrows finished he came out of the swamp and went on again. The wind blew the down from his shoulder, and it fell in the woods, when the Wild Boy took his right shape again and went back and told his brother what he had seen. Keeping out of sight of their father, they followed him up the mountain until he stopped at a certain place and lifted a large rock. At once there ran out a buck, which Kana'tĭ shot, and then lifting it upon his back he started for home again. "Oho!" exclaimed the boys, "he keeps all the deer shut up in that hole, and whenever he wants meat he just lets one out and kills it with those things he made in the swamp." They hurried and reached home before their father, who had the heavy deer to carry, and he never knew that they had followed.

A few days later the boys went back to the swamp, cut some reeds, and made seven arrows, and then started up the mountain to where their father kept the game. When they got to the place, they raised the rock and a deer came running out. Just as they drew back to shoot it, another came out, and then another and another, until the boys got confused and forgot what they were about. In those days all the deer had their tails hanging down like other animals, but as a buck was running past the Wild Boy struck its tail with his arrow so that it pointed upward. The boys thought this good sport, and when the next one ran past the Wild Boy struck its tail so that it stood straight up, and his brother struck the next one so hard with his arrow that the deer's tail was almost curled over his back. The deer carries his tail this way ever since. The deer came running past until the last one had come out of the hole and escaped into the forest. Then came droves of raccoons, rabbits, and all the other four-footed animals—all but the bear, because there was no bear then. Last came great flocks of turkeys, pigeons, and partridges that darkened the air like a cloud and made such a noise with their wings that Kana'tĭ, sitting at home, heard the sound like distant thunder on the mountains and said to himself, "My bad boys have got into trouble; I must go and see what they are doing."

So he went up the mountain, and when he came to the place where he kept the game he found the two boys standing by the rock, and all the birds and animals were gone. Kana'tĭ was furious, but without saying a word he went down into the cave and kicked the covers off four jars in one corner, when out swarmed bedbugs, fleas, lice, and gnats, and got all over the boys. They screamed with pain and fright and tried to beat off the insects, but the thousands of vermin crawled over them and bit and stung them until both dropped down nearly dead. Kana'tĭ stood looking on until he thought they had been punished enough, when he knocked off the vermin and made the boys a talk. "Now, you rascals," said he, "you have always had plenty to eat and never had to work for it. Whenever you were hungry all I had to do was to come up here and get a deer or a turkey and bring it home for your mother to cook; but now you have let out all the animals, and after this when you want a deer to eat you will have to hunt all over the woods for it, and then maybe not find one. Go home now to your mother, while I see if I can find something to eat for supper."

When the boys got home again they were very tired and hungry and asked their mother for something to eat. "There is no meat," said Selu, "but wait a little while and I'll get you something." So she took a basket and started out to the storehouse. This storehouse was built upon poles high up from the ground, to keep it out of the reach of animals, and there was a ladder to climb up by, and one door, but no other opening. Every day when Selu got ready to cook the dinner she would go out to the storehouse with a basket and bring it back full of corn and beans. The boys had never been inside the storehouse, so wondered where all the corn and beans could come from, as the house was not a very large one; so as soon as Selu went out of the door the Wild Boy said to his brother, "Let's go and see what she does." They ran around and climbed up at the back of the storehouse and pulled out a piece of clay from between the logs, so they could look in. There they saw Selu standing in the middle of the room with the basket in front of her on the floor. Leaning over the basket, she rubbed her stomach—*so*—and the basket was half full of corn. Then she rubbed under her armpits—*so*—and the basket was full to the top with beans. The boys looked at each other and said, "This will never do; our mother is a witch. If we eat any of that it will poison us. We must kill her."

When the boys came back into the house, she knew their thoughts before they spoke. "So you are going to kill me?" said Selu. "Yes," said the boys, "you are a witch." "Well," said their mother, "when you have killed me, clear a large piece of ground in front of the house and drag my body seven times around the circle. Then drag me seven times over the ground inside the circle, and stay up all night and watch, and in the morning you will have plenty of corn." The boys killed her with their clubs, and cut off her head and put it up on the roof of the house with her face turned to the west, and told her to look for her husband. Then they set to work to clear the ground in front of the house, but instead of clearing the whole piece they cleared only seven little spots. This is why corn now grows only in a few places instead of over the whole world. They dragged the body of Selu around the circle, and wherever her blood fell on the ground the corn sprang up. But instead of dragging her body seven times across the ground they dragged it over only twice, which is the reason the Indians still work their crop but twice. The two brothers sat up and watched their corn all night, and in the morning it was full grown and ripe.

When Kana'tĭ came home at last, he looked around, but could not see Selu anywhere, and asked the boys where was their mother. "She was a witch, and we killed her," said the boys; "there is her head up there on top of the house." When he saw his wife's head on the roof, he was very angry, and said, "I won't stay with you any longer; I am going to the Wolf people." So he started off, but before he had gone far the Wild Boy changed himself again to a tuft of down, which fell on Kana'tĭ's shoulder. When Kana'tĭ reached the settlement of the Wolf people, they were holding a council in the townhouse. He went in and sat down with the tuft of bird's down on his shoulder, but he never noticed it. When the Wolf chief asked him his business, he said: "I have two bad boys at home, and I want you to go in seven days from now and play ball against them." Although Kana'tĭ spoke as though he wanted them to play a game of ball, the Wolves knew that he meant for them to go and kill the two boys. They promised to go. Then the bird's down blew off from Kana'tĭ's shoulder, and the smoke carried it up through the hole in the roof of the townhouse. When it came down on the ground outside, the Wild Boy took his right shape again and went home and told his brother all that he had heard in the townhouse. But when Kana'tĭ left the Wolf people, he did not return home, but went on farther.

The boys then began to get ready for the Wolves, and the Wild Boy—the magician—told his brother what to do. They ran around the house in a wide circle until they had made a trail all around it excepting on the side from which the Wolves would come, where they left a small open space. Then they made four large bundles of arrows and placed them at four different points on the outside of the circle, after which they hid themselves in the woods and waited for the Wolves. In a day or two a whole party of Wolves came and surrounded the house to kill the boys. The Wolves did not notice the trail around the house, because they came in where the boys had left the opening, but the moment they went inside the circle the trail changed to a high brush fence and shut them in. Then the boys on the outside took their arrows and began shooting them down, and as the Wolves could not jump over the fence they were all killed, excepting a few that escaped through the opening into a great swamp close by. The boys ran around the swamp, and a circle of fire sprang up in their tracks and set fire to the grass and bushes and burned up nearly all the other Wolves. Only two or three got away, and from these have come all the wolves that are now in the world.

Soon afterward some strangers from a distance, who had heard that the brothers had a wonderful grain from which they made bread, came to ask for some, for none but Selu and her family had ever known corn before. The boys gave them seven grains of corn, which they told them to plant the next night on their way home, sitting up all night to watch the corn, which would have seven ripe ears in the morning. These they were to plant the next night and watch in the same way, and so on every night until they reached home, when they would have corn enough to supply the whole people. The strangers lived seven days' journey away. They took the seven grains and watched all through the darkness until morning, when they saw seven tall stalks, each stalk bearing a ripened ear. They gathered the ears and went on their way. The next night they planted all their corn, and guarded it as before until daybreak, when they found an abundant increase. But the way was long and the sun was hot, and the people grew tired. On the last night before reaching home they fell asleep, and in the morning the corn they had planted had not even sprouted. They brought with them to their settlement what corn they had left and planted it, and with care and attention were able to raise a crop. But ever since the corn must be watched and tended through half the year, which before would grow and ripen in a night.

As Kana'tĭ did not return, the boys at last concluded to go and find him. The Wild Boy took a gaming wheel and rolled it toward the Darkening land. In a little while the wheel came rolling back, and the boys knew their father was not there. He rolled it to the south and to the north, and each time the wheel came back to him, and they knew their father was not there. Then he rolled it toward the Sunland, and it did not return. "Our father is there," said the Wild Boy, "let us go and find him." So the two brothers set off toward the east, and after traveling a long time they came upon Kana'tĭ walking along with a little dog by his side. "You bad boys," said their father, "have you come here?" "Yes," they answered, "we always accomplish what we start out to do—we are men." "This dog overtook me four days ago," then said Kana'tĭ, but the boys knew that the dog was the wheel which they had sent after him to find him. "Well," said Kana'tĭ, "as you have found me, we may as well travel together, but I shall take the lead."

Soon they came to a swamp, and Kana'tĭ told them there was something dangerous there and they must keep away from it. He went on ahead, but as soon as he was out of sight the Wild Boy said to his brother, "Come and let us see what is in the swamp." They went in together, and in the middle of the swamp they found a large panther asleep. The Wild Boy got out an arrow and shot the panther in the side of the head. The panther turned his head and the other boy shot him on that side. He turned his head away again and the two brothers shot together—*tust, tust, tust!* But the panther was not hurt by the arrows and paid no more attention to the boys. They came out of the swamp and soon overtook Kana'tĭ, waiting for them. "Did you find it?" asked Kana'tĭ. "Yes," said the boys, "we found it, but it never hurt us. We are men." Kana'tĭ was surprised, but said nothing, and they went on again.

After a while he turned to them and said, "Now you must be careful. We are coming to a tribe called the Anăda'dûñtăskĭ ("Roasters," i.e., cannibals), and if they get you they will put you into a pot and feast on you." Then he went on ahead. Soon the boys came to a tree which had been struck by lightning, and the Wild Boy directed his brother to gather some of the splinters from the tree and told him what to do with them. In a little while they came to the settlement of the cannibals, who, as soon as they saw the boys, came running out, crying, "Good, here are two nice fat strangers. Now we'll have a grand feast!" They caught the boys and dragged them into the townhouse, and sent word to all the people of the settlement to come to the feast. They made up a great fire, put water into a large pot and set it to boiling, and then seized the Wild Boy and put him down into it. His brother was not in the least frightened and made no attempt to escape, but quietly knelt down and began putting the splinters into the fire, as if to make it burn better. When the cannibals thought the meat was about ready they lifted the pot from the fire, and that instant a blinding light filled the townhouse, and the lightning began to dart from one side to the other, striking down the cannibals until not one of them was left alive. Then the lightning went up through the smokehole, and the next moment there were the two boys standing outside the townhouse as though nothing had happened. They went on and soon met Kana'tĭ, who seemed much surprised to see them, and said, "What! are you here again?" "O, yes, we never give up. We are great men!" "What did the cannibals do to you?" "We met them and they brought us to their townhouse, but they never hurt us." Kana'tĭ said nothing more, and they went on.

He soon got out of sight of the boys, but they kept on until they came to the end of the world, where the sun comes out. The sky was just coming down when they got there, but they waited until it went up again, and then they went through and climbed up on the other side. There they found Kana'tĭ and Selu sitting together. The old folk received them kindly and were glad to see them, telling them they might stay there a while, but then they must go to live where the sun goes down. The boys stayed with their parents seven days and then went on toward the Darkening land, where they are now. We call them Anisga'ya Tsunsdi' (The Little Men), and when they talk to each other we hear low rolling thunder in the west.

After Kana'tĭ's boys had let the deer out from the cave where their father used to keep them, the hunters tramped about in the woods for a long time without finding any game, so that the people were very hungry. At last they heard that the Thunder Boys were now living in the far west, beyond the sun door, and that if they were sent for they could bring back the game. So they sent messengers for them, and the boys came and sat down in the middle of the townhouse and began to sing.

At the first song there was a roaring sound like a strong wind in the northwest, and it grew louder and nearer as the boys sang on, until at the seventh song a whole herd of deer, led by a large buck, came out from the woods. The boys had told the people to be ready with their bows and arrows, and when the song was ended and all the deer were close around the townhouse, the hunters shot into them and killed as many as they needed before the herd could get back into the timber.

Then the Thunder Boys went back to the Darkening land, but before they left they taught the people the seven songs with which to call up the deer. It all happened so long ago that the songs are now forgotten—all but two, which the hunters still sing whenever they go after deer.

In the region of the eastern United States, one of the most important ceremonial occasions coincided with the ripening of the corn. The eating of green corn was commonly forbidden until the conclusion of the green corn ceremonies. Since the ripening of corn meant that life was assured for another year, the green corn ceremonies commonly had the character and effect of a festival of the new year.

In the plains areas where tribes depend not only upon seasonal agriculture but also upon hunting (and in the last century especially upon buffalo), the stories of the origin of corn and buffalo are combined. These major sources of sustenance are commonly paired in the religious symbolism of major ceremonial events like the Sun Dance. The following Cheyenne story is one of the many such stories to be found among plains tribes.

## *THE ORIGIN OF CORN AND BUFFALO (Cheyenne)*[9]

The people were having a "medicine" hunt; they knew nothing then about the buffalo. Before making a "medicine" hunt, the medicine-men all came together and pledged themselves to make a hunt; they appointed a man to be leader and also his wife, so that, when they caught animals they would get the females as well as the males. After these had pledged themselves, they sent out runners to see what they could find.

This time they chose two men to go out to look for ducks, geese, and other birds. This was when the Cheyenne were far on the other side of the Missouri River where there are many lakes. The men came back and reported that a certain lake was covered with water-fowl of all kinds; so the whole camp moved over to it, the dogs hauling the travois. The lake was not large, and the men, women, children, and dogs surrounded it, and made a great slaughter of birds, for they had called on the spiritual powers to aid them so that the birds should not fly away.

When they moved again, they sent two more runners ahead to see what they could find. These two went toward a high grassy table-land and climbed up on it. They reached it towards sunset, and, as they stood there, they saw the grass moving and found quantities of skunks all around, so they went back to the camp and told what they had seen. Next morning everybody started for the table-land. They all got around it early in the morning and killed great numbers of skunks; everybody was loaded down with them. The next day they again sent two men to the same place, and many more skunks were seen, so that on this day more were killed than the day before. They sent them again the next day, and when they had finished killing they could hardly carry away the meat. Again a fourth time the two men reported skunks there, and many were caught and killed.

The next day they camped near a little knoll, where a spring came out of the rock. This spring is called "Old Woman's Water" (Mā'-tā-mā Hĕh'k-ā-īt). They camped near this spring with the opening of the camp towards it. There was a fine place for the camp in the plain there. There was a little brush near the spring. Nothing happened that night.

In the morning two sets of hoops and sticks were taken to the centre of the camp, and they rolled them there and gambled on the game. Two games were going on. They selected the head of the hunting party as one of the men to keep the count. While they were gambling, a man came from the right side of the camp to the centre, where they were playing. He was naked except for his breech-cloth, and was painted yellow all over and striped down with the fingers; on his breast was a round circle, in red, and on the back a half moon of the same color. His face under his eyes was painted black, and there was a red stripe around his wrists and ankles; he had a yellow down feather on his scalp-lock and wore his robe hair side out. He stood for a time and watched them playing. While he stood there, a man came from the left side of the camp, whose paint and dress were just the same as his. While they were rolling the wheel, the man who had come from the right said to the players, "My friends; stop for a moment." He walked toward the other and asked him to come towards him, so they met in the centre of the camp and stopped a short distance apart. They stood facing each other, and the first one said to the other, "Why do you imitate me? This is spiritual paint." The second said, "Mine also is spiritual paint." The game had stopped and all the players were listening.

The first man said, "Who gave you your spiritual paint, and where did you get it?" The other replied, "Who gave you yours?" The first man pointed to the spring and said, "My paint came from there" (meaning that at the spring he was instructed to paint himself in that way). The other said, "Mine also came from the spring." Then the first man said, "Let us do something for the hunters, the old men, old women, young women, girls and boys." And the second said, "Yes, let us do so." By this time every one in the camp was listening. So the first man said again, "Soldiers of all societies, every one of you shall feel happy this day," and the other said, "Yes, you shall all feel happy this very day." The first speaker walked toward the spring, and the other followed close behind him. When he came to the spring, he covered his head with his robe and plunged under the water into the opening out of which the spring came. His friend followed him closely and did the same thing. All the people in the camp watched them and saw them go in.

The first man came up under the spring, and there under the knoll sat a very old woman. As he stepped in, she said to him, "Come in, my grandchild." She took him in her arms; held him for a few minutes and made him sit down at her left side. As the other man came in, she said again, "Come in, my grandchild." She took him in her arms, held him for a minute, and set him on her right side. Then she said to both of them, "Why have you not come sooner? why have you gone hungry so long? now that you have come here, I must do something for your people." She had near her two old-fashioned earthen jars. She brought them out and set them down before her and also brought out two earthen dishes; one was filled with buffalo meat, and one with corn. She said, "Come, my children; eat the meat first." They ate it very fast, for it was very good; but, when they had eaten all they could, the dish was still full; it was the same way with the corn. They could not empty the dishes; they were full when the men stopped. They were both satisfied, but the dishes did not show that they had been touched.

The old woman untied the feathers they had on their heads, and threw them in the fire. She painted each man with red paint; striped him, and repainted his wrists and ankles, and the sun and moon, yellow; then she stretched her hand out over the fire and brought out two down feathers painted red and tied them to their scalp-locks. After that, she pointed to her left and said, "Look that way." They looked and could see the earth covered with buffalo. The dust was flying up in clouds where the bulls were fighting. Then she said, "Look this way" (pointing partly behind her), and they saw immense cornfields. She said, "Look that way" (pointing to the right), and they saw the prairie covered with horses. The stallions were fighting and there was much movement. She said, "Look that way again," and they saw Indians fighting. They looked closely, and among the fighters recognized themselves, painted just as they were then. She said, "You will always be victorious in your fights; you will have good fortune, and make many captives. When you go away from here, go to the centre of your village; call for two big bowls and have them wiped out clean. Say to your people, women and children and all the bands of the societies, 'We have come out to make you happy; we have brought out something wonderful to give you. Tell your people that when the sun goes down I will send out buffalo.'" To each of the young men she gave some corn tied up in sacks and told them to divide this seed among the people. She told them to take some of the meat from the dish with one hand and some corn with the other, and sent them away. So they passed out of her lodge and came out of the water of the spring.

All the people of the village were sitting in a circle watching the spring. The two young men walked on together to the centre of the village, where the one who had first appeared said, "Old men, old women, young men, young girls, I have brought out something that is wonderful. Soldiers, I have brought out something wonderful for you. When the sun goes down, the buffalo will come out." The other young man repeated these words. The first man stood ahead, and the other right behind him. The first man said, "I want two wooden bowls, but they must be clean." A young man ran to the right and another to the left to get the bowls. They set one down on each side of him, and with his right hand he put the meat in the right-hand bowl, and with his left hand he put the corn into the left-hand bowl. The bowls became half full. The other man did the same, and the bowls were filled.

Just before leaving the old woman, she had said, "The medicine hunter is to eat first," so the medicine hunter performed the ceremony of nĭv-stăn-ĭ-vō'—making a sacrifice of a piece of the meat at the four points of the compass—and the first man said to him, "Eat all you can."

The old woman had told them that the oldest men and women were to eat first. They all ate, first of the meat and then of the corn; then the young men, young women, and the children ate, but the pile in each dish remained nearly the same. After that the people in the camp ate all they could, and after all had eaten there was but little left. At the last came two orphans, a boy and a girl; they both ate, and when they had finished the meat was all gone and also the corn. It was just as the young men had said, every one was happy, for now they had plenty to eat.

As the sun went down, all the village began to look toward the spring. After a time, as they watched, they saw a four-year-old bull leap out. He ran a little distance and began to paw the ground, and then turned about and ran back and plunged into the spring. After he had gone back, a great herd of buffalo came pouring out of the spring and all night long they could hear them. No one went to sleep that night, for the buffalo made too much noise. Next morning at sunrise the earth, as far as they could see, was covered with buffalo. That day the medicine hunters went out and brought in all the meat they could eat.

The village camped there all winter and never lacked food. Toward spring they sent out two young men to look for moist ground to plant the seed in, for the old woman had told them that it must be planted in a damp place. They divided the corn seed; every one got some, for there was enough for all. They made big caches in the earth to hold the meat they had dried, and then went to the place the young men had found and planted the seed. They made holes with sticks and put the seed in the ground. Sometimes when they were planting the corn they would go back to get their dried meat, for the buffalo had moved to another place. Once, when they returned with their dried meat, they found that some of the seed had been stolen, and they thought that it was the Pawnees or the Arickarees—and that that was the way these tribes got their corn.

We will conclude this section with a description of the planting rites of the Hopi, a Pueblo tribe in the southwest. Pueblo tribes have extensive and amazingly complex religious beliefs, practices, and symbols that are inseparable from agriculture, especially corn. To know about corn is nearly synonymous with knowing about Hopi religion, yet we must not forget that even these agriculturalists hold hunting to be important. Something of the richness and complexity of the religious aspects of agriculture are revealed in the following description of some Hopi ritual practices associated with agricultural activities. While these may seem complex, involving numerous figures, extensive ritual, complex relationships between life and death, material and spiritual, and even hunting and agriculture, these practices are far from the order of complexity and involvement of the kachina performances so common at Hopi throughout the spring and summer.

## *HOPI RITUAL IN AGRICULTURE by Ernest Beaglehole*[10]

In the agricultural cycle, direct ritual begins with the winter solstice ceremonies when seed corn is left on the kiva [a partially subterranean ceremonial chamber] altar overnight and then returned to the store house "to help the crops." Sand or adobe mud from the altar is sprinkled over the seed corn to protect it from damage. Prayer sticks and corn meal effigies of peaches, melons and other crops are buried in field and orchard to promote increase and secure the fertility of the crops. Later on at planting time and especially if an individual has large fields to plant with corn, katsina or Masau [a figure here associated with germination, but in other contexts associated with death] will be invited to participate in a working party. Second Mesa practice in this context may be described in some detail for comparative village study of the custom.

Katsina planting is arranged by one man, or perhaps two men acting jointly. The arranger notifies the chiefs of his wish to have katsina plant for him in the preceding February when katsina dances for the coming season are arranged. The planting date is called out four days ahead, and on the set day, katsina, almost invariably Navaho katsina, ᴅasə'f kapzi·'na, though one informant though that any katsina might be danced, go out in the morning with the working party, each katsina providing himself with a small handful of mixed seeds, seeds of various colored corns, cotton, melon, sunflower, gourd and beans all mixed together. While the leader of the working party plants the prayer stick in the field, katsina remain at the side and smoke for rain. After this is finished each katsina plants a few holes with mixed seeds, starting in the middle of the field "because this part belongs to the katsina." The katsina then retire again to smoke and the working party finishes planting the field. At lunch time and in the late afternoon men and katsina race together to help the corn grow. After all the work is finished the group of katsina dances on the edge of the field. All go back to the village and the katsina dance again in the village plaza. Next day a regular all-day katsina dance is held in the village. The group of dancers is fed on both days by the household of the arrangers. One informant thought that katsina often danced in the fields without masks for the reason that "once they danced this way and they brought good luck to the fields and plenty of corn, but another time when katsina took masks with them, they brought bad luck to the field and a whirlwind cut all the young shoots so that hardly any corn grew." The katsina party is termed kaᴅzi·' nam ī·'yis wisa, "katsina field working."

Any man who has fields to plant or harvest may arrange for Masau to be present. The occasion is usually the holding of a so·'ḥkⁱau working party and when the latter is discussed with the village chiefs, the chief of the ma·swi'mpḳya, society of Masau, is asked to provide a man to act as Masau. The working party is called out four days ahead, and during these four days Masau goes into seclusion, sleeping by day in a darkened room, eating no salt or meat but only the corn food wī·'ᴅaḳa, "so as to become skinny and a fast runner." Each night he goes out after midnight running an anti-clockwise circuit which becomes smaller on succeeding occasions so that on the last night the circuit is round the villages on the mesa ledge. He places prayer sticks and meal on the various Masau shrines about the village and places prayer sticks also in the principal grave yards. The running is to help the corn to grow, the decreasing circuits to bring the rain clouds nearer.

This midnight running is considered hazardous in the extreme. One informant related:

*A man who acted as Masau told me he was frightened all the time he ran. Once he went into a cave where children are buried to put prayer sticks on a shrine. It was very dark and he could not see. When he turned to leave he could not find the entrance and there was no light, not even star light. His nerve gave way, he wailed and screamed in his fear, and when he finally got out he fell on the ground bathed in sweat and almost unconscious.*

Another informant said:

*It is dangerous to go out at night like this. One man, just initiated, went out on the first night. He became so crazy with fear that he tried to kill himself by throwing himself over the mesa edge onto the rocks below. Masau, the spirit, saved him from certain death, however, and he lived to go out again. When a man runs at night and sees something moving in front of him, he must go up to the thing whether it turns out to be bush, tree, or stone, and rub some of the stuff of which the thing is made over his body. This will make him brave and strong and no longer afraid.*

On the third day a rabbit hunt is held. The hunt chief is a member of the ma·swi'mpkya and all men in the village participate. Each man presents the first rabbit he kills to the house where Masau is in seclusion, but keeps the rest of his kill for himself. The women in Masau's house skin the rabbits and save the skin, blood and meat. Next day, the working party goes out to the fields early. About noon Masau and another society man go to a cave in the rocks above le·mī·'va spring and here Masau dresses. "No one else would come round at this time since he who trespassed would have to take Masau's place and dress like him." Masau's body is painted red with rabbit blood. He wears bead necklace, earrings, a loin cloth, a woman's dress, and different colored cobs of corn hang from his waist. His face is streaked with black pigment and a corn husk is put round each eye and over his mouth. He wears a rabbit skin mask, the fur inside and the outside skin soaked in rabbit blood.

About the middle of the afternoon Masau goes out to the fields. As the working party returns he hides in the washes, jumps out suddenly, and chases the people to frighten them. Alternately he may go straight to the field being planted, chase the workers and then plant a few holes with mixed colored seed corn. Masau carries with him a small cylinder-shaped sack filled with cotton or other soft substance; he strikes people with this sack (ma$^{u}$wi·'ḳi) and they fall down as if dead. "All this running about is good for the crops."

The party later returns to the village, Masau also. While the workers eat at the arranger's house, Masau makes an anti-clockwise circuit of the village four times. The people finish eating and come to the dance court to see Masau meet there some twelve "Hair" katsina, called for this occasion ma·s ḳaᴅzi·'nam, "Masau katsina." The katsina dance and Masau goes off to eat. After the dancers have left, Masau returns to the dance court. Any men who wish dress up in costume, in katsina or cowboy clothes for instance, and come to the court one man at a time. As each appears, Masau chases him with clownish antics and finally hits him with his cylindrical sack. The man falls as if dead and Masau strips him of his clothes, putting them on himself but in the wrong manner, ties the sash on the left side instead of on the right, puts moccasins on the wrong feet and so on. This comedy is enacted with each man until no more come forward.

It may now be well after sunset. Men bring a bundle of juniper bark to the court. One lights a piece of this and advances with it towards Masau, who, being afraid of light and fire, falls as if dead. The men carry Masau to the mesa edge and roll him over, but he jumps up and chases the men back to the court. This is done four times but on the last time Masau walks back slowly and stands in the court while men and women give him prayer feathers and meal with prayers for long life, rain, good crops and many children. Masau takes these feathers to his shrine ma·'sGi near Corn Rock and deposits them there. He leaves his special costume in a cave close to the shrine.

Masau may also appear at harvesting time when a so·'hḳ'au' party is gathering corn. He comes down from his cave and crawls under a pile of corn, coming out suddenly from this hiding place to frighten and chase the workers. On return to the village, Masau katsina do not dance, but the clowning is as before.

Katsina cannot appear to participate in harvesting, but at Second Mesa, a man who has large quantities of corn may arrange with the la·'Gon chief for the women of this society to work and dance for his field on the day after the public la·'Gon dance. The regular so·'hk'au' party is held. The la·'Gon women help the men harvest the corn and when all is finished the women dance once in the fields. All go back to the village, eat at the house of the arranger and then the women dance again in the village plaza.

Besides the racing in connection with planting activities, semi-ritual movement of various kinds is also believed to have beneficial effect on the crops. This is one reason, the esoteric one, for the program of games and races that takes place in early spring, when kick-ball race games (na na·'munwa) and shinny games (naho'Da·'Datci) are frequently played "just for fun." In shinny, kiva competes against kiva, clan against clan and occasionally katsina against men and boys. The First Mesa custom of playing a four-day shinny game with a buckskin ball filled with seed is known but not practiced at Second Mesa. Further examples of movement with direct magical import, typical of many similar customs, occur after the spring kiva katsina dances when prayer feathers are taken to the principal springs by fast runner that rain will come, and corn will grow very quickly. At the summer solstice again, prayer feathers are taken before sunrise to a special shrine by a boy who awaits the sunrise and then slowly returns to the village picking flowers on his way, that the sun may advance slowly in the sky. On the last day of the Snake ceremonies and for the four following days, it is the custom for the youths to race about the village with foodstuffs in their hands. They are pursued by women and maids who attempt to take away the goods that the youths are carrying. This custom of running and pursuit (wī'ī·'Diwa'') is believed to have beneficial effects on crops and rain, the fields belonging to the household of the girl strong and fleet enough to secure many articles, being particularly favored with good crops. According to Stephen, a similar ritual-diversion occurs during the January moon when women and maids struggle with katsina in the kivas for the possession of food and other objects. Second Mesa informants however, saw no connection between the two patterns.

## NOTES

1. Franz Boas, *The Central Eskimo* (Washington, D. C.: Bureau of American Ethnology, Annual Report no. 6, 1888), pp. 583–85.
2. For important accounts of hunting cultures that give careful attention to the religious dimensions, see Frank G. Speck, *Naskapi: The Savage Hunters of the Labrador Peninsula* (Norman: University of Oklahoma Press, 1935 and 1977) and Adrian Tanner, *Bringing Home Animals: Religious Ideology and Mode of Production of the Mistassini Cree Hunters* (New York: St. Martin's Press, 1979). For an important interpretive essay on hunting ritual,

see Jonathan Z. Smith, "The Bare Facts of Ritual," *History of Religions* 20 (1980):112–27.

3. James Paytiamo, *Flaming Arrow's People* (New York: Duffield and Green, 1932), pp. 69–82. Reprinted by permission of Dodd, Mead & Company, Inc.
4. Alanson P. Skinner, "Menomini Social Life and Ceremonial Bundles," *Anthropological Papers American Museum of Natural History* 13 (1913):147–49. Reprinted by permission of The American Museum of Natural History.
5. James A. Teit, "Tahtlan Tales," *Journal of American Folklore* 32 (1919):203–4. Reprinted by permission of the American Folklore Society. For other versions of the story, see Franz Boas, *Comparative Study of Tsimashian Mythology* (Washington, D.C.: Bureau of American Ethnology, Annual Report 31, 1916), pp. 653–56.
6. Albert B. Reagan, "Whaling of the Olympic Peninsula Indians of Washington," *Natural History* 25 (1925):25–32. Copyright The American Museum of Natural History, 1925. Reprinted by permission of The American Museum of Natural History.
7. John R. Swanton, *Myths of the Southeastern Indians* (Washington, D.C.: Bureau of American Ethnology, Bulletin 88, 1929), p. 230. Reprinted by permission of the Smithsonian Institution.
8. James Mooney, *Myths of the Cherokee* (Washington, D.C.: Bureau of American Ethnology, Annual Report 19, 1900), pp. 242–248. Another version of this story appears in James Mooney, "Myths of the Cherokees," *Journal of American Folklore* 1 (1888):97–108.
9. George B. Grinnell, "Some Early Cheyenne Tales," *Journal of American Folklore* 10 (1907):169–94. Reprinted by permission of the American Folklore Society.
10. Ernest Beaglehole, "Hopi Economic Life," *Yale University Publications in Anthropology* 15 (1937):45–48. Notes omitted. Reprinted by permission of Yale University Publications in Anthropology.

# CHAPTER 7

# *The Indian and New Religions*

## INTRODUCTION

We have strongly maintained that throughout much of the history of Native American religions, tribal boundaries were also the boundaries of traditions and religious world views. We have insisted that differences among tribal traditions are significant and that we must strive to consider the religions of Native Americans in light of particular tribal traditions. We have adopted the term "Native American" to refer collectively to the peoples indigenous to the Americas. Indeed, we have had to adopt, or invent, a term for this collective since one did not exist among the peoples themselves. Yet in the period since the beginning of European presence in America, the various tribes began to recognize that they shared a common identity, even if it was often one which stood somewhat apart from their tribal identities. The recognition of this common identity has often correlated with the intensity of the pressure that European-Americans have placed upon Native Americans and with the extent of the threat to, and loss of, tribal traditions. The term "Indian" was slowly appropriated by Native Americans to give label to their shared identity.

In this chapter we will present selections that reflect the religious dimensions of the rising new "Indian" identity and some of the formal religious movements which have accompanied and instituted it.

## A HISTORY OF PROPHECY AND THE RISE OF INDIAN IDENTITY

Doubtless prophecy has been present in Native American religions for a very long time. Throughout the history of religions, prophets commonly arise to give expression to needs felt by their communities and to initiate a course of action leading to a new future. While there is scant evidence of prophets in North America in the era before the sixteenth century, there is abundant documentation of many prophetic figures since that time. This history of prophecy is intimately connected with the pressures of acculturation and loss of culture. In his important study of the history of Delaware prophecy, A.F.C. Wallace has shown that there is a strong correlation between the extent of contact with European-American culture and the incidence of prophets.[1]

In reading the following accounts it is important to consider the response to European-American presence, the acceptance (or rejection) of European-American ways, the militant dimension, the millennial expectations, the tendency toward establishing a confederacy of tribes, the recognition of a common Indian identity, and the extent to which these responses take on a religious character or precipitate a religious movement. We should be attentive to the ways and the extent that both tribal traditions and Christianity inform these prophetic movements and the attitudes the movements hold toward tribal traditions and Christianity.

Perhaps the greatest of Delaware prophets was Neolin, commonly known as "the Delaware Prophet," who, in 1762, traveled among the tribes in the area of Cayahaga near Lake Erie proclaiming the message given him in an event of revelation. The Delaware Prophet was most concerned about the loss of land to European-Americans, the progressive assumption of European-American ways by the Indians, the Indian acceptance of alcohol, and the loss of native traditions. Notably, the sign of the Delaware Prophet's authority was a map which he used to illustrate the Indian way and their unfortunate loss of land. This map was called "the great Book or Writing." It is not uncommon in prophetic movements that are, in part, a response to colonialism with its accompanying missionary effort to teach the Bible, that some "document" is the basis for prophetic authority. The message of the Delaware Prophet is clearly nativistic, that is, it beseeches the elimination of the ways of the European-Americans and a return to native traditions and ways. However, we must not overlook the fact that this prophetic movement served to establish an alliance among tribes with the common concern being the retention of lands and life ways in opposition to European-American pressures. Indeed, based on the Delaware Prophet's message, Pontiac, the great Algonkian chief of the Ottawas, formed a confederacy of all of the northwestern tribes to oppose the further progress of the European-Americans.

Some hold the view that the Seneca prophet, Handsome Lake, must have had contact with the Delaware Prophet, or been aware of his prophetic preaching. This may well have been the case, but the similarity of their messages need not require contact, for they speak to the conditions suffered by Native Americans and these were similar wherever European-Americans pressed for the acquisition of native lands and made strong efforts to "civilize" and Christianize "the Indians"—loss of land, loss of tradition, loss of life ways, acquisition of "white ways," degradation because of the use of alcohol, a breakdown in social relationships. Handsome Lake suffered from all of these prior to his revelations. The first revelation took place on June 15, 1799. This and several subsequent revelations contained the basis for the establishment of *Gaiwiio*, or the Good Word, the religion of Handsome Lake.

The religion of Handsome Lake has had a complex history, yet remains a vital force among the Seneca. Handsome Lake's revelation, as recounted by Edward Cornplanter in the following selection, emphasizes the recovery and revival of some aspects of the older tribal tradition. It is the basis for purging the community of both Native American and European-American elements that are deterrents to the survival and health of the community. Yet the new religion of Handsome Lake provided a base for accommodating and even accepting certain outside influences. It offered an effective basis for a major cultural reformation. The selection describes the situation of Handsome Lake's vision. It is followed by a formal recounting of more than one hundred messages that constitute "The Code of Handsome Lake," the basic teachings of the religion.

## *THE REVELATION OF HANDSOME LAKE recounted by Edward Cornplanter*[2]

### *Now This Is Gaiwiio*

The beginning was in Yai''kni [May], early in the moon, in the year 1800.

It commences now.

*A Time of Trouble.* The place is* Ohi'io [on the Allegany river], in Diono'sade'gĭ [Cornplanter village].

Now it is the harvest time, so he† said.

Now a party of people move. They go down in canoes the Allegany river. They plan to hunt throughout the autumn and the winter seasons.

Now they land at Ganowoñ'go$^{n}$ [Warren, Pa.] and set up camp.

The weather changes and they move again. They go farther down the river. The ice melts opening up the stream and so they go still farther down. They land at Diondēgă [Pittsburgh]. It is a little village of white people [literally, "our younger brethren"‡]. Here they barter their skins, dried meat and fresh game for strong drink. They put a barrel of it in their canoes. Now all the canoes are lashed together like a raft.

Now all the men become filled with strong drink (gonigä'nongi). They yell and sing like demented people. Those who are in the middle canoes do this.§

Now they are homeward bound.

Now when they come to where they had left their wives and children these embark to return home. They go up Cornplanter creek, Awe'gäo$^{n}$.

Now that the party is home the men revel in strong drink and are very quarrelsome. Because of this the families become frightened and move away for safety. So from many places in the bushlands camp fires send up their smoke.

Now the drunken men run yelling through the village and there is no one there

*The present tense is always used by Chief Cornplanter.

†The narrator, Handsome Lake.

‡The Seneca term is Honio''o$^{n}$', meaning "our younger brother."

§The intoxicated men were put in the middle canoes to prevent their jumping into the water. The more sober men paddled from the outer canoes. This debauchery was common among the Six Nations at the beginning of the 19th century.

except the drunken men. Now they are beastlike and run about without clothing and all have weapons to injure those whom they meet.

Now there are no doors left in the houses for they have all been kicked off. So, also, there are no fires in the village and have not been for many days. Now the men full of strong drink have trodden in the fireplaces. They alone track there and there are no fires and their footprints are in all the fireplaces.

Now the dogs yelp and cry in all the houses for they are hungry.

So this is what happens.

*The Sick Man.* And now furthermore a man becomes sick. Some strong power holds him.

Now as he lies in sickness he meditates and longs that he might rise again and walk upon the earth. So he implores the Great Ruler to give him strength that he may walk upon this earth again. And then he thinks how evil and loathsome he is before the Great Ruler. He thinks how he has been evil ever since he had strength in this world and done evil ever since he had been able to work. But notwithstanding, he asks that he may again walk.

So now this is what he sang: O'gi'we,* Ye'ondă'thă,† and Gone'owo$^{n}$.‡ Now while he sings he has strong drink with him.

Now it comes to his mind that perchance evil has arisen because of strong drink and he resolves to use it nevermore. Now he continually thinks of this every day and every hour. Yea, he continually thinks of this. Then a time comes and he craves drink again for he thinks that he can not recover his strength without it.

Now two ways he thinks: what once he did and whether he will ever recover.

*The Two Ways He Thinks.* Now he thinks of the things he sees in the daylight.

The sunlight comes in and he sees it and he says, "The Creator made this sunshine." So he thinks. Now when he thinks of the sunshine and of the Creator who made it he feels a new hope within him and he feels that he may again be on his feet in this world.

Now he had previously given up hope of life but now he begs to see the light of another day. He thinks thus for night is coming. So now he makes an invocation that he may be able to endure the night.

Now he lives through the night and sees another day. So then he prays that he may see the night and it is so. Because of these things he now believes that the Great Ruler has heard him and he gives him thanks.

Now the sick man's bed is beside the fire. At night he looks up through the chimney hole and sees the stars and he thanks the Great Ruler that he can see them for he knows that he, the Creator, has made them.

Now it comes to him that because of these new thoughts he may obtain help to arise from his bed and walk again in this world. Then again he despairs that he will ever see the new day because of his great weakness. Then again he has confidence that he will see the new day, and so he lives and sees it.

For everything he sees he is thankful. He thinks of the Creator and thanks him for the things he sees. Now he hears the birds singing and he thanks the Great Ruler for their music.

So then he thinks that a thankful heart will help him.

Now this man has been sick four years but he feels that he will now recover.

And the name of the sick man is Ganio'dai'io'§ a council chief [Hoya'ne].

---

*The Death chant.

†The Women's song.

‡The Harvest song.

§Handsome Lake, one of the fifty hereditary sachems, or lords. Hoya'ne means, *perfect one* or *noble*, and is translated *lord* by the Canadian Six Nations.

*The Strange Death of the Sick Man.* Now at this time the daughter of the sick man and her husband are sitting outside the house in the shed and the sick man is within alone. The door is ajar. Now the daughter and her husband are cleaning beans for the planting. Suddenly they hear the sick man exclaim, "Niio'!"* Then they hear him rising in his bed and they think how he is but yellow skin and dried bones from four years of sickness in bed. Now they hear him walking over the floor toward the door. Then the daughter looks up and sees her father coming out of doors. He totters and she rises quickly to catch him but he falls dying. Now they lift him up and carry him back within the house and dress him for burial.

Now he is dead.

*The People Gather About the Dead Man.* Then the daughter says to her husband, "Run quickly and notify his nephew, Tää'wõnyăs,† that he who has lain so many years in bed has gone. Bid him come immediately."

So the husband runs to carry the message to Tää'wõnyăs. And Tää'wõnyăs says, "Truly so. Now hasten to Gaiänt'wakă,‡ the brother of the dead man and say that he who lay sick for so many years is dead. So now go and say this."

So the husband goes alone to where Gaiänt'wakă lives and when he has spoken the wife says, "Gaiänt'wakă is at the island planting." So he goes there and says, "Gaiänt'wakă your brother is dead. He who was sick for so many years is dead. Go at once to his bed."

Then Gaiänt'wakă answers, "Truly, but first I must finish covering this small patch of seed. Then when I hoe it over I will come."

Now he who notifies is Hătgwi'yot, the husband of the daughter of Ganio'ai'io'. So now he returns home.

Now everyone hearing of the death of the sick man goes to where he lies.

Now first comes Tää'wõnyăs. He touches the dead man on every part of his body. Now he feels a warm spot on his chest and then Tää'wõnyăs says, "Hold back your sadness, friends," for he had discovered the warm spot and because of this he tells the people that perhaps the dead man may revive. Now many people are weeping and the speaker sits down by his head.

Now after some time Gaiänt'wakă comes in and feels over the body of the dead and he too discovers the warm spot but says nothing but sits silently down at the feet of the dead man.

And for many hours no one speaks.

Now it is the early morning and the dew is drying. This is a time of trouble for he lies dead.

Now continually Tää'wõnyăs feels over the body of the dead man. He notices that the warm spot is spreading. Now the time is noon and he feels the warm blood pulsing in his veins. Now his breath comes and now he opens his eyes.

*The Dead Man Revives.* Now Tää'wõnyăs is speaking. "Are you well? What think you? (Isege$^{n}$' onĕnt'gayei' hĕnesni'goĕ')?"

Now the people notice that the man is moving his lips as if speaking but no words come. Now this is near the noon hour. Now all are silent while Tää'wõnyăs asks again, "My uncle, are you feeling well? (onigĕnt'gaiye')."

Then comes the answer, "Yes I believe myself well." So these are the first words Ganio'dai'io' spoke ("Iwi'' nai' o'nĕ't'gai'ye hĕ'' nekni'goĕ$^{n}$)."

Now then he speaks again saying, "Never have I seen such wondrous visions! Now at first I heard some one speaking. Some one spoke and said, 'Come out awhile' and said this three times. Now since I saw no one speaking I thought that in my sickness I myself was speaking but I thought again and found that it was

*Meaning, *So be it.*
†Meaning, Needle or Awl Breaker, one of the fifty sachems.
‡Meaning, Planter, commonly called Cornplanter, the half-brother of Handsome Lake.

not my voice. So I called out boldly, 'Niio'!' and arose and went out and there standing in the clear swept space I saw three men clothed in fine clean raiment. Their cheeks were painted red and it seemed that they had been painted the day before. Only a few feathers were in their bonnets. All three were alike and all seemed middle aged. Never before have I seen such handsome commanding men and they had in one hand bows and arrows as canes. Now in their other hands were huckleberry bushes and the berries were of every color.

"Then said the beings, addressing me, 'He who created the world at the beginning employed us to come to earth. Our visit now is not the only one we have made. He commanded us saying "Go once more down upon the earth and [this time] visit him who thinks of me. He is grateful for my creations, moreover he wishes to rise from sickness and walk [in health] upon the earth. Go you and help him to recover."' Then said the messengers, 'Take these berries and eat of every color. They will give you strength and your people with us will help you rise.' So I took and ate the berries. Then said the beings, 'On the morrow we will have it that a fire will be in the bushes and a medicine steeped to give you strength. We will appoint Odjis'kwăthĕ$^{n}$* and Gayänt'gogwŭs,† a man and his wife, to make the medicine. Now they are the best of all the medicine people. Early in the morning we will see them and at that time you will have the medicine for your use and before noon the unused medicine will be cast away because you will have recovered. Now moreover before noon many people will gather at the council house. These people will be your relatives and will see you. They will have gathered the early strawberries‡ and made a strawberry feast, and moreover will have strawberry wine sweetened with sugar. Then will all drink the juice of the berry and thank the Creator for your recovery and moreover they severally will call upon you by your name as a relative according as you are.'

"Now when the day came I went as appointed and all the people saw me coming and it was as predicted."

*The Message of the Four Beings.* "Now the messengers spoke to me and said that they would now tell me how things ought to be upon the earth. They said: 'Do not allow any one to say that you have had great fortune in being able to rise again. The favor of the four beings is not alone for you and the Creator is willing to help all mankind.'

"Now on that same day the Great Feather§ and the Harvest dances were to be celebrated and at this time the beings told me that my relatives would restore me. 'Your feelings and spirits are low,' they said, 'and must be aroused. Then will you obtain power to recover.' Verily the servants of the Creator (Hadio$^{n}$yă''geono$^{n}$) said this. Now moreover they commanded that henceforth dances of this same kind should be held and thanksgiving offered whenever the strawberries were ripe. Furthermore they said that the juice of the berry must be drunk by the children and the aged and all the people. Truly all must drink of the berry juice, for they said that the sweet water of the berries was a medicine and that the early strawberries were a great medicine. So they bade me tell this story to my people when I move upon the earth again. Now they said, 'We shall continually reveal things unto you. We, the servants of him who made us, say that as he employed us to come unto you to reveal his will, so you must carry it to your people. Now we are they whom he created when he made the world and our duty is to watch

---

*Dry Pudding.

†Dipped Tobacco.

‡The earliest of the wild strawberries are thought to be of great medicinal value and are eagerly eaten as soon as ripe. So sacred a plant is the strawberry that it is thought to grow along the "heaven road." A person recovering from a severe illness says, "I almost ate strawberries."

§The Osto'wä'gō'wā, the chief religious dance.

over and care for mankind. Now there are four of us but the fourth is not here present. When we called you by name and you heard, he returned to tell the news. This will bring joy into the heaven-world of our Creator. So it is that the fourth is not with us but you shall see him at another time and when that time is at hand you shall know. Now furthermore we must remind you of the evil things that you have done and you must repent of all things that you believe to have been evil. You think that you have done wrong because of O'gi'wē, Ye'ondă'thă and Gone'owo$^{n}$ and because you partook of strong drink. Verily you must do as you think for whatsoever you think is evil is evil.'"

*Ganiodaiio Commanded to Proclaim the Gaiwiio [Good News].* "'And now behold! Look through the valley between two hills. Look between the sunrise and the noon!'

"So I looked, and in the valley there was a deeper hollow from which smoke was arising and steam as if a hot place were beneath.

"Then spoke the messengers saying, 'What do you see?'

"I answered, 'I see a place in the valley from which smoke is arising and it is also steaming as a hot place were beneath.'

"Then said the beings, 'Truly you have spoken. It is the truth. In that place a man is buried. He lies between the two hills in the hollow in the valley and a great message is buried with him. Once we commanded that man to proclaim that message to the world but he refused to obey. So now he will never rise from that spot for he refused to obey. So now to you, therefore, we say, proclaim the message that we give you and tell it truly before all people.'

"'Now the first thing has been finished and it remains for us to uncover all wickedness before you.' So they said."

One of the figures who has most stimulated the sympathies and imaginations of Native Americans and European-Americans alike is the Shawnee named Tecumseh. He was champion of the Indian cause, an eloquent spokesman for "the Indians," one with courage to confront "white" oppressors with their insatiable needs for lands and their efforts to destroy the very existence of Native Americans. Tecumseh has lived in the memories of Americans as a heroic figure. His biography has been written a number of times. He has even been the inspiration for popular drama. Tecumseh was a prophetic figure, but he worked in alliance with his brother, Tenskwatawa, The Open Door, who was first and more deeply engaged in prophecy. The messages and religion of Tenskwatawa were the basis for action by his brother, Tecumseh, who traveled among the tribes in an effort to establish a strong confederacy of tribes with which to repell the demands of European-Americans. Throughout the first decade of the nineteenth century, these Shawnee brothers had much effect on the tribes in the region and were a constant thorn in the side of General William H. Harrison, then governor of the Indiana territory.

Something of Tenskwatawa's and Tecumseh's approach may be seen in the following selections. One is a speech delivered to Gen. Harrison by "the Prophet" in July, 1808. We may see that it appears accommodative of European-American presence while steadfastly rejecting certain of the things they introduced, such as alcohol. Their approach rests upon the assumption that Native Americans will be permitted to retain their lands, yet that they must establish a new way of life so that they may survive. Notably, the religion of the Prophet is the basis for that new way of life. This religion is based upon a new consciousness of a common "Indian" identity. He says, "Those

Indians were once different peoples; they are now but one." The second selection is the recollection of Thomas Forsyth of some of the principles of this prophetic religion. This movement was brought to an abrupt halt when Tecumseh was killed at the Battle of Thames in 1813.

## *THE SHAWNEE PROPHET'S SPEECH TO GENERAL HARRISON (1808)*[3]

"Father:—It is three years since I first began with that system of religion which I now practice. The white people and some of the Indians were against me; but I had no other intention but to introduce among the Indians, those good principles of religion which the white people profess. I was spoken badly of by the white people, who reproached me with misleading the Indians; but I defy them to say that I did any thing amiss.

"Father, I was told that you intended to hang me. When I heard this, I intended to remember it, and tell my father, when I went to see him, and relate to him the truth.

"I heard, when I settled on the Wabash, that my father, the governor, had declared that all the land between Vincennes and fort Wayne, was the property of the Seventeen Fires. I also heard that you wanted to know, my father, whether I was God or man; and that you said if I was the former, I should not steal horses. I heard this from Mr. Wells, but I believed it originated with himself.

"The Great Spirit told me to tell the Indians that he had made them, and made the world that he had placed them on it to do good, and not evil.

"I told all the red skins, that the way they were in was not good, and that they ought to abandon it.

"That we ought to consider ourselves as one man; but we ought to live agreeably to our several customs, the red people after their mode, and the white people after theirs; particularly, that they should not drink whiskey; that it was not made for them, but the white people, who alone knew how to use it; and that it is the cause of all the mischiefs which the Indians suffer; and that they must always follow the directions of the Great Spirit, and we must listen to him, as it was he that made us: determine to listen to nothing that is bad: do not take up the tomahawk, should it be offered by the British, or by the long knives: do not meddle with any thing that does not belong to you, but mind your own business, and cultivate the ground, that your women and your children may have enough to live on.

"I now inform you, that it is our intention to live in peace with our father and his people forever.

"My father, I have informed you what we mean to do, and I call the Great Spirit to witness the truth of my declaration. The religion which I have established for the last three years, has been attended to by the different tribes of Indians in this part of the world. Those Indians were once different people; they are now but one: they are all determined to practice what I have communicated to them, that has come immediately from the Great Spirit through me.

"Brother, I speak to you as a warrior. You are one. But let us lay aside this character, and attend to the care of our children, that they may live in comfort and peace. We desire that you will join us for the preservation of both red and white people. Formerly, when we lived in ignorance, we were foolish; but now, since we listen to the voice of the Great Spirit, we are happy.

"I have listened to what you have said to us. You have promised to assist us: I now request you, in behalf of all the red people, to use your exertions to prevent the sale of liquor to us. We are all well pleased to hear you say that you will endeavor to promote our happiness. We give you every assurance that we will follow the dictates of the Great Spirit.

"We are all well pleased with the attention that you have showed us; also with the good intentions of our father, the President. If you give us a few articles, such as needles, flints, hoes, powder, &c., we will take the animals that afford us meat, with powder and ball."

## *SOME TENETS OF THE RELIGION OF THE SHAWNEE PROPHET*[4]

The Prophet with all his brothers are pure Indians of the Shawnee nation, and when a boy, was a perfect vagabond and as he grew up he would not hunt and become a great drunkard. While he lived near Greenville in the State of Ohio, where spirituous liquor are plenty he was continually intoxicated; having observed some preachers who lived in the vicinity of Greenville a preaching or rather the motions, etc., in preaching (as he cannot understand a word of English) it had such an effect on him, that one night he dremt that the Great Spirit found fault with his way of living, that he must leave of[f] drinking, and lead a new life, and also instruct all the red people the proper way of living. He immediately refrained from drinking any kind of spirituous liquor, and recommended it strongly to all the Indians far and near to follow his example, and laid down certain laws that was to guide the red people in future. I shall here give you as many of those laws or regulations as I can now remember, but I know I have forgot many.

1st Spirituous liquor was not to be tasted by any Indians on any account whatever.

2nd No Indian was to take more than one wife in future, but those who now had two or three or more wives might keep them, but it would please the Great Spirit if they had only one wife.

3d No Indian was to be running after the women; if a man was single let him take a wife.

4th If any married woman was to behave ill by not paying proper attention to her work, etc., the husband had a right to punish her with a rod, and as soon as the punishment was over, both husband and wife, was to look each other in the face and laugh, and to bear no ill will to each other for what had passed.

5th All Indian women who were living with whitemen was to be brought home to their friends and relations, and their children to be left with their fathers, so that the nations might become genuine Indians.

6th All medicine bags, and all kinds of medicine dances and songs were to exist no more; the medicine bags were to be destroyed in *presens* of the whole of the people collected for that purpose, and at the destroying of such medicine, etc., every one was to make open confession to the Great Spirit in a loud voice of all the bad deeds that he or she had committed during their lifetime, and beg for forgiveness as the Great Spirit was too good to refuse.

7th No Indian was to sell any of their provision to any white people, they might give a little as a present, as they were sure of getting in return the full value in something else.

8th No Indian was to eat any victuals that was cooked by a White person, or to eat any provisions raised by White people, as bread, beef, pork, fowls, etc.

9th No Indian must offer skins or furs or any thing else for sale, but ask to exchange them for such articles that they may want.

10th Every Indian was to consider the French, English, and Spaniards, as their fathers or friends, and to give them their hand, but they were not to know the Americans on any account, but to keep them at a distance.

11th All kind of white people's dress, such as hats, coats, etc., were to be given to the first whiteman they met as also all dogs not of their own breed, and all cats were to be given back to white people.

12th The Indians were to endeavour to do without buying any merchandise as much as possible, by which means the game would become plenty, and then by means of bows and arrows, they could hunt and kill game as in former days, and live independent of all white people.

13th All Indians who refused to follow these regulations were to be considered as bad people and not worthy to live, and must be put to death. (A Kickapoo Indian was actually burned in the spring of the year 1809 at the old Kickapoo Town for refusing to give up his medicine bag, and another old man and old woman was very near sharing the same fate at the same time and place.)

14th The Indians in their prayers prayed to the earth, to be fruitful, also to the fish to be plenty, to the fire and sun, etc., and a certain dance was introduced simply for amusement, those prayers were repeated morning and evening, and they were taught that a diviation from these duties would offend the Great Spirit. There were many more regulations but I now have forgot them, but those above mentioned are the principal ones.

One of the most often quoted of Native American statements is that of Smohalla, a Wanapum who lived at Priest Rapids on the Columbia River. He maintained a movement of resistance to the transformations that swept over the northwest area in the mid-nineteenth century. In little more than a quarter of a century, the native people were forced to give up much of their lands, to adopt new lifeways including agriculture and mining, and to become Christian. The Nez Perce tribe has been a major example; their history is well documented, and the dramatic plight of Chief Joseph has become well known. Smohalla and his followers maintained a resistance into the 1880s based in a religious movement known as "the Dreamers." They were such a small group by this time that they offered little threat to European-American settlers, but Major J. W. MacMurray was sent to confer with Smohalla and his followers in the mid-1880s to settle their dissatisfaction. We may gain much from MacMurray's report to the Albany Institute in January 1886. It reflects the character of Smohalla's religion and the extent to which it was influenced by and designed to respond to the crisis situation brought on by the European-American presence.

## *THE "DREAMERS" OF THE COLUMBIA RIVER VALLEY by Maj. J. W. MacMurray*[5]

General Miles sent me to look over the situation in all its aspects, and instructed me to exercise the utmost patience with the Indians humoring their desire to explain their view, which I afterward found extended to the discussion of the philosophy of the universe, from the creation to futurity; and they were anxious to impress General Miles, through me, with the purity of their intentions, and the theological authority for their opinions. A number had, as I have intimated, taken homesteads. There were many more who would be glad to do so, fearing they might be late in the race with the incoming whites, but who dreaded the vengeance of their "mother, the earth, from whence all things come, and where all must go."

I was invited to visit every village of Indians, and on my arrival found all the people, from the oldest to the youngest, assembled, and solemnly performing their religious service; the shrill voices of the women making a weird chanting, while the drums beat in unison.

Occasional silences were broken, by men's voices orating, by ringing of hand bells followed by the drums, and again the weird chanting. At Celilo, Tune water, Umatilla, Yakima Gap and other places, I had seen some disciple of this faith lead his home people in their peculiar services which were not always identical in form; but I saw its greatest development at the fountain head, Priest Rapids, on the main Columbia river, the home of Smohalla, the "Prophet" and High Priest of the Dreamer theology. I found that he was the brake and the wheel of progress of his people, as to retain his influence he advised them to resist any of the advances of civilization, as improper for a true Indian, and the violation of the faith of their ancestors. . . .

[In Smohalla's village we] were met by a procession headed by Smohalla in person, all attired in gorgeous array and mounted on their best chargers. We wended our way through sage brush and sand dunes to the village street, not a soul being visible; but from the mat-roofed and walled salmon houses there came forth the most indescribable sound of bell-ringing, drum-beating, and cat-surpassing screeches. I noticed that the street was neatly swept and well sprinkled, an unusual thing in any Indian village. This, Smohalla said, was in my honor, and to show that his people had cleanly tastes. Our procession passed on beyond the village to a new canvass tent which had a brush shade to keep off the sun, and was lined and carpeted with new and very pretty matting. This, Smohalla said, had been prepared especially for me and was to be my house as long as I should stay with him. To cap the climax, he had constructed a bench for me, having sent to Ainsworth on the Northern Pacific railroad, more than ninety miles distant for the nails.

Fresh salmon, caught in a peculiar trap among the rocks and broiled on a plank, were regularly furnished my party, and with hard-tack and coffee of our own supplying, we got enough to eat and drink. Our own blankets furnished sleeping conveniences. The river was within two yards of our tent door, and was an ample lavatory.

At daybreak the next morning the sound of drums was again heard, and for days it continued. I do not remember that there was any intermission, except for a few minutes at a time.

I was invited to be present, and took great interest in the ceremonies, which I shall endeavor to describe.

There was a small open space to the north of the larger house, which was Smohalla's residence and the village assembly-room as well. The space was inclosed by a light fence, made of boards which had drifted down the river from far to the north,—British Columbia, possibly. The fence was whitewashed, because military posts often have whitewashed fences. In the center space was a flagstaff bearing a rectangular flag, suggesting a target. In the center was a round, red patch; the field was yellow, representing grass (which is of a yellow hue in that region), and a green border indicated the boundary of the world (the hills being moist and green near their tops); at the top of the flag was a small extension of blue color, with a white star in the center.

Smohalla explained.

"This is my flag and it represents the world. God told me to look after my people—all are my people. There are four ways in the world—north and south and east and west. I have been all those ways. This is the center, I live here; the red spot is my heart; everybody can see it. The yellow grass grows everywhere around this place. The green mountains are far away all around the world! There is only water beyond, salt water. The blue (referring to the blue cloth strip) is the sky, and the star is the north star. That star never changes; it is always in the same place. I keep my heart on that star; I never change."

There are frequent services, a sort of processional around the outside of the fence, the prophet, and a small boy with a bell, entering the inclosure, where, after hoisting the flag, he pronounces a sort of lecture or sermon. Captains or class leaders give instructions to the people, who are arranged in the order of their stature, the men and women in different classes marching in single file to the sound of drums. There seems to be a regular system of signals, at command of the prophet, by the boy with the bell, upon which the people chant loud or low, quick or slow, or remain silent. These out-door services occurred several times each day.

Smohalla invited me to participate in what he considered a grand ceremonial service within the larger house. Singing and drumming had been going on for some time when I arrived; the air was resonant with the voices of some hundreds of Indians, male and female, and the banging of drums. The room was about seventy-five feet long by twenty-five feet wide, and was somber in color and light. Smoke curled from a fire on the floor at the back end of the room, and the ceiling of the rear part was hung with hundreds of salmon, split and drying in the smoke. Some smoke pervaded the atmosphere generally. The scene was a strange one. On either side of the room was a row of twelve women, erect, arms crossed, hands extended, with tips of fingers at the shoulders. They kept time to the drums and their own voices, by balancing on the balls of their feet, tapping with their heels on the floor, while they chanted with varying pitch and time.

Those on the right hand were dressed in garments of red color with an attempt at uniformity. Those on the left wore costumes of white buckskin, with red and blue trimmings. All wore such finery as silver plates, the size of blacking-box lids, or such other form of glittering ornaments as they possessed. A canvass covered the floor, and on it knelt, in lines of seven, the men and boys. Each seven had similar colored shirts as a rule, and the largest were in front, the mass descending to the distant rear.

Children and ancient hags, filled in any spare space. In front on a mattress knelt Smohalla his left hand covering his heart, and at his right was the boy bell-ringer, in similar posture. Smohalla wore a white garment, which he was pleased to call a priest's gown, but it was simply a shirt.

I with my two assistants, were seated on a mattress about ten feet in front of the prophet; which fortunately placed us near the door, and incidentally near fresh air.

There were two other witnesses, two Indians from distant villages, who sat at one side, with Smohalla's son looking on.

In person, Smohalla is peculiar. Short, thick-set, bald-headed and almost hunch-backed, he is not prepossessing at first sight; but he has an almost Websterian head, with a deep brow, over bright intelligent eyes.

He is a finished orator; his manner mostly of the bland, insinuating, persuasive style, but when aroused, he is full of fire, and seems to handle invectives, effectively. The whole of his audience to a man (or woman) seemed spell-bound under his magic manner, and it never lost interest to me, though in a language comprehended by few white men and translated to me at second or third hand.

His immediate followers are his abject slaves; in villages quite distant the people believe in his inspiration; and this inventor of a new faith (or rather remodeller of several old ones) has upturned the religious convictions of tribes of Indians quite remote, and even of such intelligence as the Nez Perces. Much of this influence is due to knowledge gained from white men, but mainly to his native intelligence and qualities as an orator and natural leader of men.

When a boy, he lived at the Cœur d'Alene Indian mission, where he was familiar with the Catholic service, and learned a little French. He was engaged in several wars, and was growing in influence and popularity, unusual for an Indian of his "social class," when chief Moses attacked and nearly killed him.

Indeed he was left for dead, but managed to crawl away and commenced a long journey which carried him among many tribes, to many cities, even into Mexico, whence he worked his way north through Utah and Idaho. At the end of several years, owing to the removal of Moses to a distance, he returned to his own people, announcing that he had been dead and in heaven, and had now returned by God's command to guide his people. He admitted to me that he had been in Utah and had seen Mormon priests in trances, getting commands direct from heaven.

This plausible, tongued orator blended what he could remember of the forms of military parade, the Catholic mass and processionals, with many of the Mormon practices such as revelations and tithings, and since then, his influence has been assured. It was fully believed that he had been resurrected.

The fact that he had prophesied eclipses to his people, by the aid of a medical almanac, and the explanation of some land surveyors was proof of celestial authority also.

At this meeting or service I was asked to explain the Indian Homestead law, and how white men divided land. This I did, illustrating with a checker board, saying, that the black squares in all the surrounding country belonged to the railroad, and that the white squares, except the school sections, were available for homesteads by either white, or black or red-men. That the vertical lines were run toward the north star, and that cross lines were run from the direction of sunrise to that of the sunset, and thus divided the land into square pieces, so that each man could find his own, and thereby prevent all disputes. I urged them to apply for land, to settle upon it, and so avoid trouble with the white settlers who were seeking homes for their families.

Smohalla replied saying he knew all this, and much more, and he did not like this new law; it was against nature. I will tell you about it. Once the world was all water, and God lived alone; he was lonesome, he had no place to put his foot; so he scratched the sand up from the bottom, and made the land and he made rocks, and he made trees, and he made a man, and the man was winged and could go anywhere. The man was lonesome, and God made a woman. They ate fish from the water, and God made the deer and other animals,and he sent the man to hunt, and told the woman to cook the meat and to dress the skins. Many more men and women grew up, and they lived on the banks of the great river whose waters were full of salmon. The mountains contained much game, and there were buffalo on the plains. There were so many people that the stronger ones sometimes oppressed the weak and drove them from the best fisheries, which they claimed as their own. They fought, and nearly all were killed, and their bones are to be seen in the sand hills yet. God was very angry at this, and he took away their wings and commanded that the lands and fisheries should be common to all who lived upon them. That they were never to be marked off or divided, but that the people should enjoy the fruits that God planted in the land and the animals that lived upon it, and the fishes in the water. God said he was the father, and the earth was the mother of mankind; that nature was the law; that the animals and fish and plants obeyed nature, and that man only was sinful. This is the old law.

I know all kinds of men. *First there were my people* (the Indians) God made them first. Then he made a *Frenchman* (referring to the Canadian Voyageurs of the Hudson Bay Company), and then he made a *priest* (priests were with these expeditions of the Hudson Bay Company). A long time after that came "*Boston man*" (Americans came in 1796 into the river in the ship Columbia from Boston). And then "*King George men*" (English soldiers). Bye and bye came "black man" (negroes), and last he made a *Chinaman* with a tail. He is of no account, and he has to work all the time.

All these are new people; only the Indians are of the old stock. After awhile, when God is ready, he will drive away all the people except the people who have obeyed his laws.

Those who cut up the lands or sign papers for lands will be defrauded of their rights, and will be punished by God's anger.

Moses was bad. God did not love him. He sold his people's houses and the graves of their dead. It is a bad word that comes from Washington. It is not a good law that would take my people away from me to make them sin against the laws of God. You ask me to plough the ground! Shall I take a knife and tear my mother's bosom? Then when I die she will not take me to her bosom to rest.

You ask me to dig for stone! Shall I dig under her skin for her bones? Then when I die I can not enter her body to be born again.

You ask me to cut grass and make hay and sell it, and be rich like white men, but how dare I cut off my mother's hair?

It is a bad law and my people can not obey it. I want my people to stay with me here. All the dead men will come to life again; their spirits will come to their bodies again. We must wait here, in the homes of our fathers, and be ready to meet them in the bosom of our mother.

Prophetic movements of a millenarian character arose often in the northwest region of the United States after the middle of the nineteenth century. The Ghost Dance of 1870, among others, is often considered to be part of the history of movements that led to the most extensive and important of millenarian movements, the Ghost Dance of 1890. This movement arose upon the prophecy of Wovoka, a Piaute who lived at Walker Lake. It spread among tribes of the northwest, the northern plains, and eventually reached the southwest and southern plains. For the Sioux the movement came to a sudden and tragic end with the massacre at Wounded Knee at the end of December, 1890. We see many of the same issues—loss of land; the destructive force of alcohol; destruction due to radical change in way of life, religion, and values—as in the earlier prophetic movements. The following selections reflect various aspects of the Ghost Dance movement experience.

As the news of the revelation of Wovoka began to spread among the tribes, many tribes sent delegations to him to receive his message first hand. In August, 1891, the Cheyenne and Arapaho sent a delegation to him. The Cheyenne, Black Short Nose, dictated the message as he heard it to his daughter who rendered it into more fluent English.

### *WOVOKA'S GHOST DANCE MESSAGE (Cheyenne version), by Black Short Nose*[6]

When you get home you have to make dance. You must dance four nights and one day time. You will take bath in the morning before you go to yours homes, for every body, and give you all the same as this. Jackson Wilson likes you all, he is glad to get good many things. His heart satting fully of gladness, after you get home, I will give you a good cloud and give you chance to make you feel good. I give you a good spirit, and give you all good paint, I want you people to come here again, want them in three months any tribs of you from there. There will be a good deal snow this year. Some time rains, in fall this year some rain, never give you any thing like that, grandfather, said, when they were die never cry, no hurt any body, do any harm for it, not to fight. Be a good behave always. It will give a satisfaction in your life. This young man is a good father and mother. Do not tell the white people about this, Juses is on the ground, he just like cloud. Every body is a live again. I don't know when he will be here, may be will be this fall or in spring. When it happen it may be this. There will be no sickness and return to young again. Do not refuse to work for white man or do not make any trouble with them until you leave them. When the earth shakes do not be afraid it will not hurt you. I want you to make dance for six weeks. Eat and wash good clean yourselves [The rest of the letter had been erased].

### *Free Rendering*

When you get home you must make a dance to continue five days. Dance four successive nights, and the last night keep up the dance until the morning of the fifth day, when all must bathe in the river and then disperse to their homes. You must all do in the same way.

I, Jack Wilson, love you all, and my heart is full of gladness for the gifts you have brought me. When you get home I shall give you a good cloud [rain?] which will make you feel good. I give you a good spirit and give you all good paint. I want you to come again in three months, some from each tribe there [the Indian Territory].

There will be a good deal of snow this year and some rain. In the fall there will be such a rain as I have never given you before.

Grandfather [a universal title of reverence among Indians and here meaning the messiah] says, when your friends die you must not cry. You must not hurt anybody or do harm to anyone. You must not fight. Do right always. It will give you satisfaction in life. This young man has a good father and mother. [Possibly this refers to Casper Edson, the young Arapaho who wrote down this message of Wovoka for the delegation].

Do not tell the white people about this. Jesus is now upon the earth. He appears like a cloud. The dead are all alive again. I do not know when they will be here; maybe this fall or in the spring. When the time comes there will be no more sickness and everyone will be young again.

Do not refuse to work for the whites and do not make any trouble with them until you leave them. When the earth shakes [at the coming of the new world] do not be afraid. It will not hurt you.

I want you to dance every six weeks. Make a feast at the dance and have food that everybody may eat. Then bathe in the water. That is all. You will receive good words again from me some time. Do not tell lies.

Although this document captures the fundamental Ghost Dance message, the broader historical and cultural situation, the Native American view of European-Americans, and the aura in which Wovoka appeared as "the Christ" or "the Son of God" is reflected in fuller accounts of those who went to see Wovoka. The following selection is the account of George Sword, an Oglala Sioux. He tells of the 1890 journey of Good Thunder, Cloud Horse, Yellow Knife, and Short Bull to see Wovoka. The account also describes how the prophetic messages were received and acted upon by the Oglala people.

## *THE SIOUX AND THE GHOST DANCE* by *George Sword*[7]

"From the country where the Arapaho and Shoshoni we start in the direction of northwest in train for five nights and arrived at the foot of the Rocky mountains. Here we saw him and also several tribes of Indians. The people said that the messiah will come at a place in the woods where the place was prepare for him. When we went to the place a smoke descended from heaven to the place where he was to come. When the smoke disappeared, there was a man of about forty, which was the Son of God. The man said:

"'My grandchildren: I am glad you have come far away to see your relatives. This are your people who have come back from your country.' When he said he want us to go with him, we looked and we saw a land created across the ocean on which all the nations of Indians were coming home, but, as the messiah looked at the land which was created and reached across the ocean, again disappeared, saying that it was not time for that to take place. The messiah then gave to Good Thunder some paints—Indian paint and a white paint—a green grass [sagebrush twigs?]; and said, 'My grandchildren, when you get home, go to farming and send all your children to school. And on way home if you kill any buffalo cut the head, the tail, and the four feet and leave them, and that buffalo will come to live again. When the soldiers of the white people chief want to arrest me, I shall stretch out my arms, which will knock them to nothingness, or, if not that, the earth will open and swallow them in. My father commanded me to visit the Indians on a purpose. I have came to the white people first, but they not good. They killed me, and you can see the marks of my wounds on my feet, my hands, and on my back. My father has given you life—your old life—and you have come to see your friends, but you will not take me home with you at this time. I want you to tell when you get home your people to follow my examples. Any one Indian does not obey me and tries to be on white's side will be covered over by a new land that is to come over this old one. You will, all the people, use the paints and grass I give you. In the spring when the green grass comes, your people who have gone before you will come back, and you shall see your friends then, for you have come to my call.'"

The people from every tipi send for us to visit them. They are people who died many years ago. Chasing Hawk, who died not long ago, was there, and we went to his tipi. He was living with his wife, who was killed in war long ago. They live in a buffalo skin tipi—a very large one—and he wanted all his friends to go there to live. A son of Good Thunder who died in war long ago was one who also took us to his tipi so his father saw him. When coming we come to a herd of buffaloes. We killed one and took everything except the four feet, head, and tail, and when we came a little ways from it there was the buffaloes come to life again and went off. This was one of the messiah's words came to truth. The messiah said, "I will short your journey when you feel tired of the long ways, if you call upon me." This we did when we were tired. The night came upon us, we stopped at a place, and we called upon the messiah to help us, because we were tired of long journey. We went to sleep and in the morning we found ourselves at a great distance from where we stopped.

The people came back here and they got the people loyal to the government, and those not favor of the whites held a council. The agent's soldiers were sent after them and brought Good Thunder and two others to the agency and they were confined to the prison. They were asked by the agent and Captain Sword whether they saw the Son of God and whether they hold councils over their return from visit, but Good Thunder refused to say "yes." They were confined in the prison for two days, and upon their promising not to hold councils about their visit they were released. They went back to the people and told them about their trouble with the agent. Then they disperse without a council.

In the following spring the people at Pine Ridge agency began to gather at the White Clay creek for councils. Just at this time Kicking Bear, from Cheyenne River agency, went on a visit to the Arapaho and said that the Arapaho there have ghost dancing. He said that people partaking in dance would get crazy and die, then the messiah is seen and all the ghosts. When they die they see strange things, they see their relatives who died long before. They saw these things when they died in ghost dance and came to life again. The person dancing becomes dizzy and finally drop dead, and the first thing they saw is an eagle comes to them and carried them to where the messiah is with his ghosts. The man said this:

The persons in the ghost dancing are all joined hands. A man stands and then a woman, so in that way forming a very large circle. They dance around in the circle in a continuous time until some of them become so tired and overtired that they became crazy and finally drop as though dead, with foams in mouth all wet by perspiration. All the men and women made holy shirts and dresses they wear in dance. The persons dropped in dance would all lie in great dust the dancing make. They paint the white muslins they made holy shirts and dresses out of with blue across the back, and alongside of this is a line of yellow paint. They also paint in the front part of the shirts and dresses. A picture of an eagle is made on the back of all the shirts and dresses. On the shoulders and on the sleeves they tied eagle feathers. They said that the bullets will not go through these shirts and dresses, so they all have these dresses for war. Their enemies weapon will not go through these dresses. The ghost dancers all have to wear eagle feather on head. With this feather any man would be made crazy if fan with this feather. In the ghost dance no person is allow to wear anything made of any metal, except the guns made of metal is carry by some of the dancers. When they come from ghosts or after recovery from craziness, they brought meat from the ghosts or from the supposed messiah. They also brought water, fire, and wind with which to kill all the whites or Indians who will help the chief of the whites. They made sweat house and made holes in the middle of the sweat house where they say the water will come out of these holes. Before they begin to dance they all raise their hands toward the northwest and cry in supplication to the messiah and then begin the dance with the song, "*Ale misunkala ceya omani-ye*," etc.

The performance of the Ghost Dance was one of the prophetic conditions. Those who danced would be saved from the coming catastrophic events that would cleanse the earth of the European-Americans and their influences. Those dancing would be rejoined with their dead relatives; indeed, the visionary experience which often accompanied dancing most often involved a reunion with a deceased relative.

The following selection is a description of the dance as it was observed by a teacher, Mrs. Z. A. Parker, on the Pine Ridge Reservation in 1890. It also describes the ghost shirts and dresses worn by some dancers.

## *THE PINE RIDGE GHOST DANCE (Sioux)*[8]

We drove to this spot about 10.30 oclock on a delightful October day. We came upon tents scattered here and there in low, sheltered places long before reaching the dance ground. Presently we saw over three hundred tents placed in a circle, with a large pine tree in the center, which was covered with strips of cloth of various colors, eagle feathers, stuffed birds, claws, and horns—all offerings to the

Great Spirit. The ceremonies had just begun. In the center, around the tree, were gathered their medicine-men; also those who had been so fortunate as to have had visions and in them had seen and talked with friends who had died. A company of fifteen had started a chant and were marching abreast, others coming in behind as they marched. After marching around the circle of tents they turned to the center, where many had gathered and were seated on the ground.

I think they wore the ghost shirt or ghost dress for the first time that day. I noticed that these were all new and were worn by about seventy men and forty women. The wife of a man called Return-from-scout had seen in a vision that her friends all wore a similar robe, and on reviving from her trance she called the women together and they made a great number of the sacred garments. They were of white cotton cloth. The women's dress was cut like their ordinary dress, a loose robe with wide, flowing sleeves, painted blue in the neck, in the shape of a three-cornered handkerchief, with moon, stars, birds, etc., interspersed with real feathers, painted on the waist and sleeves. While dancing they wound their shawls about their waists, letting them fall to within 3 inches of the ground, the fringe at the bottom. In the hair, near the crown, a feather was tied. I noticed an absence of any manner of bead ornaments, and, as I knew their vanity and fondness for them, wondered why it was. Upon making inquiries I found they discarded everything they could which was made by white men.

The ghost shirt for the men was made of the same material—shirts and leggings painted in red. Some of the leggings were painted in stripes running up and down, others running around. The shirt was painted blue around the neck, and the whole garment was fantastically sprinkled with figures of birds, bows and arrows, sun, moon, and stars, and everything they saw in nature. Down the outside of the sleeve were rows of feathers tied by the quill ends and left to fly in the breeze, and also a row around the neck and up and down the outside of the leggings. I noticed that a number had stuffed birds, squirrel heads, etc, tied in their long hair. The faces of all were painted red with a black half-moon on the forehead or on one cheek.

As the crowd gathered about the tree the high priest, or master of ceremonies, began his address, giving them directions as to the chant and other matters. After he had spoken for about fifteen minutes they arose and formed in a circle. As nearly as I could count, there were between three and four hundred persons. One stood directly behind another, each with his hands on his neighbor's shoulders. After walking about a few times chanting, "Father, I come," they stopped marching, but remained in the circle, and set up the most fearful, heart-piercing wails I ever heard—crying, moaning, groaning, and shrieking out their grief, and naming over their departed friends and relatives, at the same time taking up handfuls of dust at their feet, washing their hands in it, and throwing it over their heads. Finally, they raised their eyes to heaven, their hands clasped high above their heads, and stood straight and perfectly still, invoking the power of the Great Spirit to allow them to see and talk with their people who had died. This ceremony lasted about fifteen minutes, when they all sat down where they were and listened to another address, which I did not understand, but which I afterwards learned were words of encouragement and assurance of the coming messiah.

When they arose again, they enlarged the circle by facing toward the center, taking hold of hands, and moving around in the manner of school children in their play of "needle's eye." And now the most intense excitement began. They would go as fast as they could, their hands moving from side to side, their bodies swaying, their arms, with hands gripped tightly in their neighbors', swinging back and forth with all their might. If one, more weak and frail, came near falling, he would be jerked up and into position until tired nature gave way. The ground had been worked and worn by many feet, until the fine, flour-like dust lay light and loose to the depth of two or three inches. The wind, which had increased, would sometimes take it up, enveloping the dancers and hiding them from view. In the ring were men, women, and children; the strong and the robust, the weak consumptive, and those near to death's door. They believed those who were sick would be cured by joining in the dancing and losing consciousness. From the beginning they chanted to a monotonous tune, the words—

Father, I come;
Mother, I come;
Brother, I come;
Father, give us back our arrows.

All of which they would repeat over and over again until first one and then another would break from the ring and stagger away and fall down. One woman fell a few feet from me. She came toward us, her hair flying over her face, which was purple, looking as if the blood would burst through; her hands and arms moving wildly; every breath a pant and a groan; and she fell on her back, and went down like a log. I stepped up to her as she lay there motionless, but with every muscle twitching and quivering. She seemed to be perfectly unconscious. Some of the men and a few of the women would run, stepping high and pawing the air in a frightful manner. Some told me afterwards that they had a sensation as if the ground were rising toward them and would strike them in the face. Others would drop where they stood. One woman fell directly into the ring, and her husband stepped out and stood over her to prevent them from trampling upon her. No one ever disturbed those who fell or took any notice of them except to keep the crowd away.

They kept up dancing until fully 100 persons were lying unconscious. Then they stopped and seated themselves in a circle, and as each one recovered from his trance he was brought to the center of the ring to relate his experience. Each told his story to the medicine-man and he shouted it to the crowd. Not one in ten claimed that he saw anything. I asked one Indian—a tall, strong fellow, straight as an arrow—what his experience was. He said he saw an eagle coming toward him. It flew round and round, drawing nearer and nearer until he put out his hand to take it, when it was gone. I asked him what he thought of it. "Big lie," he replied. I found by talking to them that not one in twenty believed it. After resting for a time they would go through the same performance, perhaps three times a day. They practiced fasting, and every morning those who joined in the dance were obliged to immerse themselves in the creek.

## PEYOTE RELIGION, OR THE NATIVE AMERICAN CHURCH

Among tribes in North America Peyote religion is rooted in the mid-to-late nineteenth century and linked with the rapid changes being endured by tribes throughout the United States. Peyote, an edible cactus capable of producing hallucenogenic effects if taken in sufficient quantities, grows in southern Texas and Mexico. Doubtless used by tribes in Mexico for visionary and religious purposes for centuries, peyote became the focus for a new form of religion which began to spread among tribes throughout the plains in the late nineteenth century.

Peyote religion has not been a millenarian or prophetic movement, although there are often visionary experiences. It has not necessarily rejected the ways and religious influences of European-Americans. But it is a strong "Indian" religion that supports community and encourages strict moral and behavioral patterns. It has been particularly effective in combatting alcoholism. Peyote religion became incorporated as various branches of the Native American Church beginning in 1918 in Oklahoma, in an effort to retain the legal rite to use peyote for religious purposes.

The growth of the peyote religious movement has continued throughout the twentieth century, so that today it is one of the most widespread and well-established religions among Native Americans. Its strength rests in its ability to address contemporary "Indian" problems by supporting "Indian" identity, by serving social and moral needs, and by doing so without completely rejecting the cultural and economic forms introduced by European-Americans.

There are variations in the ritual practices of peyote religion from community to community and from tribe to tribe. Peyote leaders like John Wilson and John Rave traveled from tribe to tribe teaching their own forms of the religion. Still, the practice of peyote ritual is remarkably homogeneous throughout the plains area and beyond.

The following selection is a description of a late nineteenth century Arapaho peyote ritual. Its basic form and elements remain much the same in present day peyote ceremony. In the account, A. L. Kroeber uses the terms "mescal" and "peyote" apparently interchangeably to refer to the peyote cactus (*Lophophora williamsii*). This is an erroneous identity that unfortunately continues to appear in writings on peyote religion.

## *ARAPAHO PEYOTE CEREMONY* ***described by Alfred L. Kroeber***[9]

Toward evening the man who is to conduct the ceremony selects a suitable place for a tent. He stands facing westward of where the centre of the tent will be. Raising his right hand, he prays. The grass is scraped from the ground, being cut first from west to east, and then from north to south. The tent is then put up, facing, as usual, the east. The wood that is to be burned during the night is stacked inside the tent to the south of the door. Small sticks of a wood that will burn without sparks are used. The leader of the ceremony takes a blanket, and, gathering red or reddish-brown earth or sand, brings it into the tent, or perhaps sends some one to do this. This reddish earth is put in a semicircle around the fireplace in the middle of the lodge, the centre of the crescent being toward the back of the tent, opposite the door. The diameter of the semicircle is perhaps four or five feet. Sage is pulled out, and laid on the ground around the inside of the tent, to be sat upon. The men sitting on this can stretch forward and reach the semicircle of soil. Sometimes the participants bathe just before making the ceremony. In the water they make one plunge against and one with the current of the stream. On coming out of the water, they may rub themselves with sage. The clothing and head are sometimes rubbed with teaxuwine$^{n}$ or waxuwahan, scented plants that are chewed.

The mescal-plants, hahaayā$^{n}$x, which are wooden-looking disks an inch or more across, tufted with dull white, are soaked in water. When the dry plants are very hard, the soaking renders them sufficiently soft to be chewed, but with some difficulty. Before the tent is entered for the ceremony, the plants are taken from the water, which has become brownish, and are laid in a cloth. The dirty and very bitter liquid remaining is passed around to the participants, each of whom takes two sips of it, though this is not obligatory.

The drum consists of an ordinary small earthenware pot over which is stretched a piece of buckskin, or sometimes canvas, which is kept wet through the night by a little water inside of the jar. The skin is stretched by a rope. This rope, however, does not pass through holes in the skin, but is wound around seven glass marbles which have been rolled up in the skin. This device prevents the stretching of the skin, or the tearing out of perforations in it when the string is tightened. The seven glass marbles also play a part in the symbolical rites the next morning. The drum is made on the evening of the ceremony, and hours are sometimes consumed in adjusting it. When at last the right degree of tension is secured, together with the proper saturation of the skin, the effect is a tone moderately loud and deep, and very resonant. The drum is usually beaten very rapidly so that the reverberations from the separate blows fuse.

Inside the drum are a small quantity of ashes and three small billets of pinewood. . . .

The rattle which is held by each man as he sings is a small gourd stuck on a stick, and containing ordinary small glass beads. As compared with the clattering sound produced by the gravel contained in some Indian rattles, the noise of these peyote implements is a swish rather than a rattle.

Pocket-knives and other sharp instruments must be left outside the tent in which the ceremony is conducted. Not even forks may be used with the food eaten in the tent, or at the mid-day meal on the following day out of doors. The symbolism of this observance seems to be the idea that the ceremony is an occasion of peace and good-feeling, which must not be disturbed. For the same reason, perhaps, all food eaten in connection with the ceremony must be cooked entirely without salt. This ceremonial idea is, however, found in many regions without being based on any specific reason.

The participants in the ceremony gather outdoors; and the leader of the ceremony, the one in whose tent it is held, selects a fire-tender, called hictänä$^{n}$tcä ("fire chief"), silently pointing to him with an eagle wing-feather. This feather the fire-tender uses as a fan for the fire during the ceremony. The place of the fire-tender is just inside of the door, to its left or north. The fire chief goes first, and starts the fire inside the tent. When this begins to be illuminated, the other worshippers gather their blankets about them, and in single file walk to the tent. The fire chief kneels or stands on the prairie, outside the door, with his head bowed, facing the tent, or, according to one account obtained, in the opposite direction. The conductor of the ceremony, who has led the row of men, stands, and prays in a low voice, and then enters. He is followed by the others singly. The fire chief goes last, and closes the door of the tent. The worshippers then sit down, the director of the ceremony always at the middle of the back of the tent.

Usually corn-husk cigarettes are first smoked, and are lighted with a stick taken from the fire by the fire-tender. The leader of the ceremony then produces from a small beaded purse or pouch a mescal-plant, which he keeps permanently, often carrying it on his person. The plant selected is usually large, round, and even. He carefully smoothes a little space at the middle point of the crescent of reddish earth before him. Breaking eight short stems of sage, he lays them on this spot in the form of two superimposed crosses, the ends of the stems pointing in the cardinal directions and between. On this sage his mescal-plant is then laid (usually a head feather plume, which may have been worn in the hair on entering the tent, is stuck in the ground so that its tip nods over the plant); then, starting from the plant, the leader makes a crease along the top of the crescent of earth, first to the right, then to the left. This is continued at its two ends by the worshippers sitting on each side of the leader, and their neighbors carry it farther until the end of the crescent is reached. This crease or line is made by pressing the thumb into the loose earth. It represents the path by which the thoughts of the worshippers travel to the mescal-plant.

After this altar, as it might be called, has been completed, the peyote is eaten. The director gives to each of the participants four of the plants, which he takes out of the cloth or handkerchief. They are exceedingly bitter, and still quite hard.

They are ground between the teeth, one at a time, until they crumble; and the chewing is continued until they are fine. The mass is then pressed by the tongue into a round ball, which, being soft, is easily swallowed. Most of the furry tufts on the face of the plant are spit out during the chewing. In a tent full of worshippers, a constant sputtering breaks the silence for a few minutes. After these first four plants have been eaten, more can be called for in the course of the night, whenever any one wishes them. Four are generally eaten at a time. The average number taken varies considerably, but seems to be about twelve. Sometimes more than thirty are eaten.

Sometimes, just before receiving the plants, the worshippers chew sage, and rub themselves with it. The director passes the cloth of soaked plants four times over cedar incense. He takes one himself, and gives one to the man on his left, who will drum for him. After they have eaten these, the director gives each of the participants four plants, first stretching his hand toward the east.

After the first four plants have been disposed of by all, the leader takes up his rattle and begins to sing. Sometimes he rests his left hand upon a staff, holding in this hand an eagle-feather fan. Such a fan is quite commonly used in the ceremony. The man at his left drums for him. Just before the singing, the drum, rattle, fan, and staff have been passed four times over cedar incense. The leader passes the rattle to his left-hand neighbor, and drums. After four songs, the third worshipper takes the rattle. It goes about the tent from left to right, from right to left, as the worshippers sit, making circuit after circuit, each man singing four songs. Except in the case of the singing of the leader, the man on the singer's right always drums for him. About midnight, on the completion of a round of singing, the woman present, who is usually the wife of the leader of the ceremony, leaves the tent. She soon returns with a jar of water, which is placed before her husband. He then, at least on some occasions, takes an eagle bone whistle with which he imitates the cry of an eagle as it gradually descends from a great height to the ground in search of water. The gradual approach of the bird from a distance is very vividly indicated, ending with a climax of shrill cries. The end of the whistle is then dipped into the water. After this the leader drinks from the jar. The water is then passed about the tent from left to right in regular ceremonial order, and every one drinks four swallows. The effects of the peyote make the participants very thirsty, but this occasion is the only interruption in the ceremonies of the night. From this time on until sunrise, the singing and the drumming go on continuously.

Sometimes, it is said, the leader goes out of the tent before the water is brought in at midnight, the worshippers remaining in the tent, and praying. Facing the east, he prays to the morning star; then, facing west, he prays to the peyote, which is in the tent, west of him. On his return, cedar is put on the fire as incense, to carry the prayers up. The fire-tender scrapes the ashes into a crescentic shape, inside the crescent of earth, and then stands and dances. His dancing consists of a shaking. The leader of the ceremony sings and rattles; the man at his left drums; and a third participant, it is said, blows the whistle, imitating a bird. At the end of four songs, the fire-tender, still carrying his eagle wing-feather, goes out. He returns with the water, which he sets before the director.

During the night, the songs usually refer to the peyote itself, to the birds regarded as its messengers, and to the long duration of the night. In the morning, as the tent begins to become diffused with light, the songs refer to the morning star and the end which it brings to the ceremony. At sunrise the woman leaves the tent, and after a short time re-appears with four dishes of food and drink, which she places in a row on the ground, between the fire and the door. On one occasion, the woman on this re-appearance wore a symbolically painted buckskin dress. Soon after her entrance, the last round of singing is completed, the rattle is laid aside, and the fire is allowed to burn out. The drum is then loosened and taken apart; and each portion of it is passed around the ring of participants. A little of the water still remaining in the jar is drunk by each worshipper. Every man, in turn, wrings the wet skin, and, as the rope with which it was stretched is passed to him, he throws a loop of it over his foot, and tugs at it. This is a symbol of the roping of horses. The seven glass marbles are pressed by each man against his chest, his shoulders, and other parts of his body, in order to ward off disease. One man has been seen to roll all seven out of his palm into his mouth, and then drop them back one by one. The leader's fetish, which has lain all night at the back of the crescent of earth, is passed by each man to his neighbor, and is held and looked at for a short time. When it has made the circuit and returns to the leader, he puts it back carefully into his pouch. He distributes to the participants the bits of sage-stems on which the plant has rested. The worshippers then wash the paint from their faces, and comb their hair; water, a towel, a mirror, and a comb also making the round of the tent. Then at last the drinking-water is passed around the circle, and is followed by the dishes of food, one after the other. After the food has gone around several times, and none of the dishes are any longer touched by any one, the worshippers rise, stretch themselves, shake their blankets (which have usually lain behind them during the night), and, one behind the other, leave the tent in the same order in which they entered it the night before.

It is perhaps eight in the morning when the tent is left. For the rest of the day the worshippers lie on blankets in a pleasant spot under trees, under a shade, or in the house. From time to time one of them sings, shaking the rattle softly. The drum is no longer used. Occasionally more than one man will sing different songs at the same time. The effect of the drug is still very strong. The physiological discomforts have usually worn off, and the pleasurable effects are at their height. It appears that new songs, inspired perhaps by the visions of the night, are often composed during this day. At noon a meal is again served, most of the food at which is sweet. At this meal only one spoon is allowed in the company, and food requiring the use of this is therefore passed around from one participant to the other. At dark the worshippers saddle their horses and ride home, or go to bed if they live at the leader's house.

## PERSISTENCE AND CHANGE

It is perhaps tempting to think that Native Americans are either undergoing the final stages of acculturation or the final stages of degradation, but this would be to fall to the same mistaken idea that has been proposed for a century. Clearly while new religious forms like Peyote religion are gaining strength and while more and more Native Americans are finding Christianity to be meaningful to them, there is an equally strong resurgence of the old tribal ways and values although often in somewhat modified forms. The history and nature of this persistence of tribal and native values among plains peoples is the subject of the following essay by Joseph Epes Brown. It provides a fitting conclusion to this chapter and to the anthology.

### *THE PERSISTENCE OF ESSENTIAL VALUES AMONG NORTH AMERICAN PLAINS INDIANS by Joseph Epes Brown*[10]

#### *Introduction*

The focus for this examination of the complex question of the persistence of essential traditional values among American Indian groups will be upon the Indians of the great plains of North America. This selection in a sense is arbitrary, for similar studies could well be extended to almost any of the American Indian groups scattered in reserves throughout the United States, many of whom still retain, underneath the more evident surface changes and adaptations, a world view and life-ways still deeply rooted in ancient values. Since my closest personal contacts, however, have been the Plains tribes such as the Sioux, Cheyenne, Crow, Blackfoot, Arapaho, and Shoshone, I have chosen to look to these cultures for evidences of persistence in essential traditional values.

The use of the term "essential values" in the context of this paper refers to transcendent metaphysical principles which have been central to the spiritual ways of the Plains Indian, and which, it is insisted by this writer at least, constitute for these original Americans a valid dialect of what has been called the *Religio Perennis*. The uniqueness, or possibly strangeness, to us of the Indian's ritual forms or symbolical language should never blind us to this universal quality of the underlying values themselves. Due to this nature of the values we are here concerned with, there is not called in question the survival of the values themselves, for being ultimately timeless and eternal they can never in themselves be qualified by the vicissitudes of the socio-cultural environment. The question being accounted for, rather, is the degree to which forced changes issuing from an alien and generally profane culture will allow these values to continue to be operative within a changing cultural matrix and thus within the human substance of the individual himself.

This report will present first a description of selected core indigenous values of the Plains Indian as they are conveyed through their ritual supports, and thus as they contribute to methods of spiritual realization. This necessarily synthetic treatment should provide a reference base for the second part of the report which will deal with several dimensions in the dynamics of contact, as the indigenous culture confronts the pervasive and disruptive influences issuing from a materially dominant Anglo-American culture. The report will conclude with a brief statement concerning essential values which have remained viable to this day despite the often excessive breakdown of many traditional life-ways. It will be noted, in fact, that certain rites and ceremonies among some groups have not only persisted, but are actually, through a number of complex factors, now undergoing a period of vigorous revival.

## *Values*

Among the many sacred ceremonies of the Plains Indian I have selected three major rituals within each of which, and in their totality, there is provided all necessary dimensions of a true way of spiritual realization for the individual and for the social group as a whole. These rites are those of purification, the annual tribal Sun Dance, and the individual spiritual retreat.

The rites of purification, considered to be essential preparation for any important or sacred undertaking, are centered in a simple dome-shaped lodge made of intertwined willows and covered over tightly with bison robes. In the circular form of the lodge, and in the materials used in its construction, the Indian sees a symbolical representation of the world in its totality. Indeed, it has been expressed that the lodge is the very body of the Great Spirit. Inside this lodge of the world the participants submit themselves to intensely hot steam produced when water is sprinkled on rocks which had previously been heated in a special sacred fire always located to the east of the lodge. As the men pray and chant, the steam, actually conceived as the visible image of the Great Spirit, acts as in an alchemical work to dissolve both physical and psychic "coagulations" so that a spiritual transmutation may take place. The four elements, with the invisible spiritual Presence—or "fifth element"—contribute their respective powers to this purifying process so that man may become virtually who he is through first dissolving the illusory sense of separateness, then becoming reintegrated, or harmoniously unified, within the totality of the universe. In finally going forth from the dark lodge, leaving behind all physical impurities and spiritual errors, the men are reborn into the wisdom of the light of day. All the aspects of the world have been witnesses to this cycle of corruption, death, wholeness, and rebirth; indeed, the cosmic powers have all contributed to the process.

In the rites of the Sun Dance there is a shift in perspective and function. These dramatic and powerful rites, normally of four days duration, are generally performed only once annually, and should be participated in, directly or indirectly, by the entire tribal group. A major overt goal of this prayer dance is the regeneration or renewal not only of the individual directly participating in the rites, but also of the tribe and ultimately of the entire universe. The ritual dances take place within a large circular pole lodge, at the centre of which is a tall cottonwood tree representing the axis of the universe, the vertical link joining heaven and earth, and thus the path of contact with the solar power, the sun, symbol of the Supreme Principle or Great Spirit. Supported day and night by the powerful rhythm of a huge drum energetically beaten by many men, and by songs which are both heroic and nostalgic, the dancers hold eagle plumes and continually orient themselves either towards the sacred central tree, or towards one of the four directions of space. Blowing upon whistles made from the wing bone of the eagle, the men dance individually with simple and dignified steps towards the central tree from which they receive supernatural power, and then dance backwards to the periphery of the circle without shifting their gaze from the centre. The sacred forms and ritual actions are virile, dignified, and direct, and though the rites usually take place only once a year the power of the sacred centre, now realized within themselves, remains with each individual and contributes to the unity of the people.

The third quality of spiritual way is the solitary retreat known as the "lamenting", or the vision quest. In this quest the individual, naked and alone, and in constant prayer, endures a total fast for a specified number of days at a lonely place, usually a mountain top. In utter humility of body and mind, often emphasized by the offering of pieces of his flesh, or the joint of a finger, the man stands before the forms and forces of nature seeking the blessing of sacred power which should come to him through a dream, or preferably a vision, of some aspect of nature, possibly an animal, who offers guidance for the future direction of the man's life. These natural forms or forces, conceived as messengers or Agents, constitute for the Indian a well understood "iconography" in which forms, with their accompanying powers, are ranked according to their ability to express most directly the ultimate Power, or essence, of the Great Spirit. Essential to this metaphysic of nature is the Indian's belief that in silence, found within the solitude of Nature, there is ultimately heard the very voice of the Great Spirit. This quest for supernatural power, coming symbolically from the "outside," but in reality being awakened from within, has always been essential to the spiritual life of Plains Indian men and women, and its influence upon the quality of their lives should never be underestimated.

Mention must be made, finally, of that important ritual implement, the sacred tobacco pipe which is central to all the rites which have here been described. In carrying this portable altar the Indian has at all times access to an effective synthetic support for spiritual realization. The rites of the pipe express sacrifice and purification, they affirm the integration of the individual within the macrocosm, and they lead finally to the realization of unity, prefigured by the totality of the grains of tobacco becoming one with the fire of the Great Spirit.

Pervading these spiritual ways of purification, of the Sun Dance, the retreat, and the use of the sacred pipe, there may be discerned a pattern for which parallels may be found in virtually all legitimate methods of realization within the world's great religions. This universal pattern affirms the sequence first of purification, followed by an expansive process in the realization of totality, or the state of human perfection, leading finally to the ultimate possibility of contact and identity with the one transcendent Supreme Principle.

## *Contact: Dynamics of the Acculturation Process*

It is necessary now to pose the very difficult question which for decades has plagued those with a serious concern for the future of the American Indian: Is it possible today for small minority groups within the United States, or anywhere for that matter, to retain the integrity of cultural patterns and spiritual ways similar to those just described; ways which are rooted in traditions of primordial origin, and which had their essential supports in a world of nature still virgin and unscarred by the hand of any man?

All the forces of historical contact between the American Indian and the materially dominant White-American civilization seem to be totally against the possibility of any traditional continuity for the Indian. The power of alien forces and the inevitable disruption of life-ways which have ensued must not be minimized. It should be recalled that the people's subsistence base, the bison, was brought to near extinction through commercial exploitation combined with an avowed policy of extermination by the United States Army. Freedom of movement was restricted through force to reservations often arbitraily chosen. Governing techniques based on the accumulated wisdom of the elders were replaced by an imposed bureaucratic system which could never, even if it wished, understand the real problems of the people under its charge. In accord with White-American concept of ownership, the random distribution of parcels of land on the basis of individual family units shattered the cohesive unity of the Indian's own larger consanguinial groupings, and the prohibition of plural marriages disrupted the immediate family units. School systems were imposed which had as their avowed goals the suppression and eventual elimination of traditional values in order to hasten forcefully the process of total assimilation. This is a policy, with all too few exceptions, which is still basic to the reservation school system of today. Ill-conceived government attempts at economic rehabilitation again and again ended in total failure largely due to the fact that agriculture, then identified by the whiteman with civilization, was a practice contradictory to all Indian values which held the earth as sacred and inviolate and not to be torn up with a plough. Among the most difficult trials, however, were the hostile attitudes towards the Indian's religious practices. Sacrificial elements of the Sun Dance were prohibited, as were the rites held for the departing souls of the dead, and it is well known how participation in the much misunderstood Ghost Dance ended with the infamous massacre of Wounded Knee.

What is seen in the assemblage of these series of traumatic shocks received by the Indian is obviously not just the inevitable result of straightforward military defeats, as devastating as these were, but rather we have the tragic drama of two cultures in conflict, each representing to the other diametrically opposed values on every possible level and in all domains. Such conflict between cultures was undoubtedly intensified by the fact that those segments of White-American society with which the Indian had the most contact were, with few exceptions, probably the least enlightened carriers of the more positive facets of "civilization." With the exception of some Christian missionaries of "good heart" the Indian found no segment of American society with which he could identify himself.

After more than a century of this quality of bitter confrontation with accompanying disruptions in the social, economic, political, and religious life, it is difficult to understand how the people have survived at all. Yet the Plains Indians, as well as other groups, have survived with such tenacity and even vitality that certain rites and ceremonies are today actually undergoing renewed affirmation. Much to the surprise of the social scientists, and the Bureau of Indian Affairs itself, the "vanishing American" has somehow not vanished at all. It had been incorrectly assumed, among other factors, that just as so many European immigrants had readily assimilated into the great American "melting pot," so too would the Indian. There was obviously the failure here to take into account the tremendous differences between the European and the American Indian. The result of this new awareness, on the part of the anthropologists at least, has led to a growing number of hypotheses to explain this phenomena of the tenacity of traditional values and cultures.

One such hypothesis has been the isolation of the reservations. This is undoubtedly a factor of importance, yet it must be recalled that with certain groups, the Mohawk for example who work in high steel in New York City, close and frequent contact has not resulted in total abandonment of ancient values. The sustaining power of culture-bearing indigenous languages has with validity been pointed to in the literature; certainly this is a factor which has been well understood by the reservation school systems which to this day often forbid children, under threat of punishment, to speak their own native language.

It has been suggested, with reason, that policies of forced or "directed" acculturation to which all Indian groups have been subjected, may lead to violent reactions which reject change and reaffirm traditionalism. A converse possibility which has been neglected by the specialists has been the role of the half-informed, usually sentimental, "Indian lovers," the "do gooders," who would preserve certain of the "more noble" Indian values, albeit they should be incorporated with those "logical" modern innovations in such things as housing and hygiene. Paradoxically, such seemingly sympathetic approaches to Indian traditions may be far more corrosive to traditional values than the uncompromising ethnocentric attitudes of those agents of civilization who insist on total assimilation achieved through force if necessary.

Among the vast array of forces which may work for the persistence of traditional values is the often neglected psychological factor of the inherent stability of the basic personality structure which acts as a selective screen in processes of change. A dimension central to this complex question, but which is inaccessible to the quantitative experiential tools of either cultural anthropology or psychology, is the qualitative power of metaphysical, or cosmological, principles and the degree to which these become virtual or effective within the individual substance through participation in traditional rites and spiritual methods. Related to this entire question of the quality of personality is the fact that where Indians are still able to live within a world of as yet unspoiled Nature, potentially they have access to a vast array of transcendent values. It is essential to add, however, that for this potential source to become virtual for the Indian he must still possess, to a certain degree at least, the Indian's traditional metaphysic of nature. Where this metaphysic is still understood, and can be directly related to the supporting forms of the natural world, here the Indian has perhaps his strongest ally for the persistence of essential values; it is also in this metaphysic of nature that we find the Indian's most valuable message for the contemporary world.

A final factor relating to the persistence of values must be mentioned since it is crucial today to a multitude of problems deriving from attitudes in America towards minority groups of various ethnic backgrounds. White-American racial attitudes have historically so tended to devaluate physical types of other cultural traditions that these peoples generally have been relegated to positions of inferior status in the larger society. With the possibility of social or cultural mobility thus being denied, many of these groups have tended to seek retention of cohesion and identity through reaffirmation of their own traditional values. The resulting low index of intermarriage between these minority groups and the dominant majority has in addition tended to slow acculturation. This is a situation, incidentally, which has not occurred in Mexico where positive valuation has been given to the Indian heritage. Among the ramifications of negative racist attitudes is the fact that many Indians who do attempt to assimilate into segments of White-American culture tend to undergo a cycle of progressive disenchantment, a process often hastened by the slum conditions of cities, or by participation in foreign wars. When such persons then attempt to reintegrate back into their own traditional patterns they often serve as powerful agents for the preservation of traditional values.

This review of factors contributing to the holding power of indigenous values under conditions of extreme stress, is obviously very incomplete. Yet the sampling may be useful to an understanding of the final concern of this report which will be a brief assessment of the viability of rites and their values on the plains Indian reservations today.

## *Contemporary Assessment*

Reactions of the diverse plains Indian groups to several centuries of directed contact with White-Americans has resulted in such a broad spectrum of adjustments, conservative reactions, or total changes, that it is obviously impossible to make valid generalizations in terms of the contemporary persistence of values. Ranged on this spectrum of multiple possibilities are examples, across groups as well as within particular groups, of near total retention of traditional values at the one end of the scale to near total assimilation at the other end. The vast majority of groups or individuals, however, probably lie in the midrange and generally represent a more or less synthetic reassemblage of Indian and White-American values, always with the retention, however, of a remarkable degree of traditional Indianness.

If the range of possibilities on this spectrum are to be evaluated in terms of the major concern of this study, it should be pointed out that available data indicates that concordant with a high degree of traditional persistence there is generally a quality of culture that has cohesiveness, direction, and affords personal dignity. Assimilation, on the other hand, can be a double-edged term since it often represents acculturation into the lowest and least enlightened segments of White-American society, and this can be the first step leading to such extreme limits of cultural disintegration that we have the dangerous phenomena of a decultured people living precariously in a vacuum wherein they are unable to identify either with Indianness or with any of the White-American values.

In viewing the degrees of cultural wreckage strewn today across the prairies, a most impressive and hopeful phenomena is found in the fact that so many of the core indigenous values, with their supporting rites, are generally persisting among most plains groups. In spite of the virtual disappearance of a host of minor rites, still being practiced are the rites of purification, the Sun Dance, the spiritual retreat, and the rites of the sacred pipe. Sacred arrows, the original sacred pipe, and sacred bundles in general, are still being kept with reverence and respect, even though some of the spiritual meanings of these forms may have been lost. One of the most notable aspects of these examples of traditional tenacity is the fact that those who today affirm these forms and values are not necessarily just the "long hairs," the old men, but rather there is a growing interest and participation on the part of the younger generations.

An outstanding example of the contemporary process of reaffirmation is the increasing participation throughout the plains generally in the Sun Dance. Among the complex factors contributing to this revitalization, which cannot be explained here in detail, is the example and stimulus afforded by a dynamic series of interpersonal and intercultural relationships between the Crow Indians of Montana and the Shoshone of Wyoming. The renewing interest among the younger generations may be partly explained by the fact that the youth have not been able to find channels in the whiteman's society for the expression of specific needs, personal qualities, or virtues, which had always been central, and which still are relevant, to the indigenous cultures. Public display of personal courage, sacrifice, and generosity, for example, are key Indian themes dramatically affirmed in the context of the Sun Dance.

Although the three or four day total fast required in the Sun Dance is still observed, the self-torture features have not been publically participated in since the government prohibitions of 1890. Such tortures, however, are still engaged in secretly by certain individuals. Also little known to outside groups is the fact that the spiritual retreat is frequently used today not only by the old, but also by younger men. It is evident, although it has not been specifically mentioned, that crucial to the spiritual ways which have been mentioned is the presence of the shaman or "medicine man." Judging partly from the present frequency and popularity of "yuwipi" rites, which allow for the ritual demonstration of shamanistic powers, it is evident that shamanism still plays a meaningful role among the people, and that it continues to have mechanisms for the transmission of power. The high personal quality and magnetism of many of these men is a very strong contributing factor to the holding power of traditional values.

The true nature of a growing number of Pan-Indian movements, or what I call the "pow-wow syndrome," still remains questionable, for the stimulus behind many of these movements represents reactions to White-American attitudes towards ethnic minorities. In being rejected the Indian affirms his Indianness, yet in doing this he often seeks to identify with the whiteman's image of what an Indian is—or should be. The result is a complex of heterogeneous forms and practices which have popular appeal and commercial advantage, but which risk sacrificing true spiritual content. The phenomenal growth of the new Black Elk Sweat Lodge Organization, with membership cards and all, is undoubtedly a good example of this double-edged phenomena of Pan-Indianism.

In concluding, there are a few basic questions which must at least be referred to, for the issues are vital both to the continuing viability of essential values within Indian cultures, and also to the ultimate quality of the larger American culture itself:

Will educational policy, which for so long has been dictated to the Indian, honour and support indigenous values and life-ways so that the young may grow with a rightful pride in their own heritage? Or, must the schools continue in their efforts towards total assimilation, thus denying to the Indian his birthright, and robbing the larger American culture of the possibility of a spiritual enrichment which present crises indicate is so desperately needed?

May not Indian lands be allowed to remain inviolate, so that a unique religious heritage may continue to retain its supports in a world of sacred natural forms? Or, must policies for rapid termination of protective mechanisms continue so that remaining Indian-held lands will melt away under the pressures of often unscrupulous commercial interests?

But above all, and crucial to these and many other questions: Cannot it be affirmed that all peoples, regardless of skin colour, of ethnic background, or of religious affiliation, are rightful members of one family of man? Should not differences of appearance, of culture, or of religion, be affirmed as valid and even necessary expressions of a greater Reality, so that they may contribute to a richer world? Any alternative cannot but lead to drab mediocrity and ultimate chaos.

Whatever the outcome, we might well heed the words attributed to a great Indian after whom one of our cities was named, Seattle.

*We are two distinct races with separate origins and separate destinies. To us the ashes of our ancestors are sacred and their resting place is hallowed ground. You wander far from the graves of your ancestors and seemingly without regret . . .*

*But why should I mourn at the untimely fate of my people? Tribe follows tribe and nation follows nation, and regret is useless. . .*

*But when the last Red man shall have become a myth among the White man . . . when your children's children think themselves alone in the field . . . or in the silence of the pathless woods, they will not be alone . . . your lands will throng with the returning hosts that once filled them and still love this beautiful land. The White man will never be alone.*

*Let him be just and deal kindly with my people, for the dead are not powerless. Dead—I say? There is no death. Only a change of worlds.**

## NOTES

1. A.F.C. Wallace, "New Religions Among the Delaware Indians, 1680–1900," *Southwestern Journal of Anthropology* 12,1 (1956):1–22.
2. Arthur C. Parker, "The Code of Handsome Lake, the Seneca Prophet," *New York State Museum*, Bulletin 163 (Albany: University of the State of New York, 1912), pp. 20–26. Reprinted by permission of the New York State Museum. The code is found on pp. 27–80.
3. Benjamin Drake, *Life of Tecumseh and his Brother the Prophet* (Cincinnati: H.S. & J. Applegate & Co., 1852), pp. 107–9. Originally published 1841. Currently published in New York: Arno Press, 1969
4. Emma Blair, ed.: *The Indian Tribes of the Upper Missouri Valley and Region of the Great Lakes* (Cleveland: Arthur H. Clark, 1912), vol. II, pp. 274–78. Notes omitted. Reprinted by permission of the publishers, The Arthur H. Clark Company.
5. J. W. MacMurray, "The 'Dreamers' of the Columbia River Valley in Washington Territory," *Transactions of the Albany Institute* XI (Albany, 1887), selections from pp. 241–48.
6. Mooney, *The Ghost-Dance Religion and the Sioux Outbreak of 1890* (Washington, D.C.: Fourteenth Annual Report (part 2) of the Bureau of Ethnology to the Smithsonian Institution, 1896), p. 781.
7. Ibid., pp. 797–98.
8. Ibid., pp. 916–917, see footnotes in Mooney for references to several other publications of this account.
9. Alfred L. Kroeber, "The Arapaho," *American Museum of Natural History Bulletin*, vol. XVIII (1907):399–405.
10. Joseph Epes Brown, "The Persistence of Essential Values among North American Plains Indians," *Studies in Comparative Religion* 3:4 (Autumn 1969): 216–225. The article is from a paper presented to the International Congress of the Istituto Accademico di Roma, October, 1968. Reprinted by permission of Joseph Epes Brown.

---

*From: Frank Waters, "Two Views of Nature: White and Indian." *The South Dakota Review*, May 1964, pp. 28, 29.

# *Audio-Visual Aids*

The wonderfully sensual character of Native American religions and the absence of sacred writings and philosophical treatises seem to demand an extensive use of audio-visual materials to support the teaching of this area. Furthermore, there is no scarcity of audio-visual materials. Still, there are cautions that must be taken. Such factors as overdone explanations and staged performances tend to characterize so much of these materials that their use often proves embarrassing. Even the mechanical and electronic devices that must be manipulated seem often in tension with the nature of the material, as do the order and structure of a classroom. We should never underestimate the capacity of the imagination when fed by rich verbal description and perhaps a few carefully selected and used audio-visual materials. To assist in finding and using some of these materials, the following suggestions are offered.

FILMS I know of no single film that can be used uncritically and without comment. Most films, and there are hundreds of them, present a radically biased view of Native Americans, usually in the direction of romanticizing and primitivizing them. This can be accomplished not only by the heavy hand of a script, but also by the selection of setting, music, and subtle cinematic techniques. Even these films may be of use, however, in the study of the way images of Native Americans are manipulated by this powerful medium.

Most college and university film libraries contain numerous films on Native Americans and their religions. For film lists on Native Americans see Roger C. Owen, *et al.*, *The American Indians* (New York: Macmillan, 1967) which lists some 300 films, pp. 718–44; *Films About Indians of the Americas*, Bureau of Indian Affairs, Washington, D. C.; Carla M. Blakey, "The American Indian in Films," *Film News* 27/5 (1970); Peggy V. Beck and A. L. Walters, "Film and Filmstrip Guide," *The Sacred: Ways of Knowledge, Sources of Life*

(Tsaile, AZ: Navajo Community College Press, 1977), pp. 356–60; and Virgil J. Vogel, "Selected Audio-Visual Aids," *This Country Was Ours: A Documentary History of the American Indian* (New York: Harper & Row, 1972), pp. 350–59.

SOUND RECORDINGS In some ways sound recordings may be used more easily than visuals. Perhaps this is because they support the visualization process and help to create mood more effectively than they transmit information on religious beliefs and practices. There is an abundance of excellent music and dance recordings available. See Bernard Klein and Daniel Icolari, *Reference Encyclopedia of the American Indian* (New York: B. Klein, 1967), pp. 168–72 for a list of sources. The principal sources are: Canyon Records, 4143 N. 16th Street, Phoenix, AZ 85016; Folkway Records, 43 West 61st Street, New York, NY 10023; and Recording Laboratory, Music Division, Library of Congress, Washington, DC 20540.

MAPS Maps are often helpful in teaching Native American religions, but there are confounding difficulties. Since land has been a major issue in the history of Native American–European American contact, the locations of Native Americans have changed constantly throughout these several centuries. Therefore, the limitation common to all maps, that they show locations as of a given moment, is an acute one relative to Native Americans. Virgil Vogel, *This Country Was Ours*, lists a number of helpful maps and charts, pp. 357–59. I find most helpful, "The North American Indians, 1950 Distribution of Descendants of the Aboriginal Population of Alaska, Canada, and the United States," prepared under the direction of Sol Tax, Department of Anthropology, University of Chicago, 1126 E. 59th St., Chicago, IL 60637, published in 1960; "Native Tribes of North America," University of California Map Series, no. 13, map 1a, from A. L. Kroeber, "Culture and Natural Areas of Native North America 1939" to accompany *University of California Publications in American Archaeology and Ethnology*, vol. 38, 1939; and the many maps in Harold Driver, *Indians of North America*, 2nd rev. ed. (Chicago: University of Chicago Press, 1969).

FIELDTRIPS Few communities in the United States and Canada are isolated from one or another kind of resource valuable to the study of Native American religions. There are many excellent museums, libraries, and historical societies that exhibit Native American materials. Consult the current *Directory, Historical Societies and Agencies in the United States and Canada* (Nashville, TN: American Association for State and Local History) and the current *Museums Directory of the United States and Canada* (Washington, DC: American Association of Museums and the Smithsonian Institution).

Many Native American communities welcome visitors, often even on religious occasions. Visits to Native American communities are often the most valuable experiences for students, but the utmost care must be taken to assure that you are not infringing on privacy or overextending Native American courtesy. Generally, the rule is that no photography, sketching, and notetaking should done and especially not without permission. I also believe it inadvisable to take large groups to most Native American communities and ceremonial or festival events. A large group is not only more difficult to control, it can easily become the most obvious and dominant presence at the event, ruining it for all. For some sensible advice as well as detailed information on visiting Native American communities and museums see, Jamake Highwater, *Fodor's Indian America* (New York: David McKay, 1975). For a calendar of annual events of the tribes in the American Southwest, see Bertha P. Dutton, *Indians of the American Southwest* (Englewood Cliffs, NJ: Prentice-Hall, 1975), pp. 265–69.

# Index